Java Design

Building Better Apps and Applets

Selected Titles from the

YOURDON PRESS COMPUTING SERIES

Ed Yourdon, *Advisor*

ANDREWS AND LEVENTHAL Fusion: Integrating IE, CASE, and JAD
ANDREWS AND STALICK Business Reengineering: The Survival Guide
AUGUST Joint Application Design
BODDIE The Information Asset: Rational DP Funding and Other Radical Notions
BOULDIN Agents of Change: Managing the Introduction of Automated Tools
COAD AND MAYFIELD Java Design: Building Better Apps and Applets
COAD AND NICOLA Object-Oriented Programming
COAD AND YOURDON Object-Oriented Analysis, 2/E
COAD AND YOURDON Object-Oriented Design
COAD WITH NORTH AND MAYFIELD Object Models, Strategies, Patterns, and Applications, 2/E
CONNELL AND SHAFER Object-Oriented Rapid Prototyping
CONNELL AND SHAFER Structured Rapid Prototyping
CONSTANTINE Constantine on Peopleware
CONSTANTINE AND YOURDON Structure Design
DEGRACE AND STAHL Wicked Problems, Righteous Solutions
DEMARCO Controlling Software Projects
DEMARCO Structured Analysis and System Specification
EMBERLY, KURTZ, AND WOODFIELD Object-Oriented Systems Analysis
GARMUS AND HERRON Measuring the Software Process: A Practical Guide to Functional Measurements
GLASS Software Conflict: Essays on the Art and Science of Software Engineering
GROCHOW Information Overload: Creating Value with the New Information Systems Technology
JONES Assessment and Control of Software Risks
KING Project Management Made Simple
LARSON Interactive Software: Tools for Building Interactive User Interfaces
McMENAMIN AND PALMER Essential System Design
MOSLEY The Handbook of MIS Application Software Testing
PAGE-JONES Practical Guide to Structured Systems Design, 2/E
PINSON Designing Screen Interfaces in C
PUTNAM AND MEYERS Measures for Excellence: Reliable Software on Time within Budget
RODGERS ORACLE®: A Database Developer's Guide
RODGERS UNIX®: Database Management Systems
SHLAER AND MELLOR Object Lifecycles: Modeling thc World in Statcs
SHLAER AND MELLOR Object-Oriented Systems Analysis: Modeling the World in Data
STARR How to Build Shlaer-Mellor Object Models
THOMSETT Third Wave Project Management
WANG (cd.) Information Tcchnology in Action
WARD System Development Without Pain
WARD AND MELLOR Structured Development for Real-Time Systems
YOURDON Decline and Fall of the American Programmer
YOURDON Managing the Structured Techniques, 4/E
YOURDON Managing the System Life-Cycle, 2/E
YOURDON Modern Structured Analysis
YOURDON Object-Oriented Systems Design
YOURDON Rise and Resurrection of the American Programmer
YOURDON Structured Walkthroughs, 4/E
YOURDON Techniques of Program Structure and Design
YOURDON AND ARGILA Case Studies in Object-Oriented Analysis and Design
YOURDON, WHITEHEAD, THOMANN, OPPEL, AND NEVERMAN Mainstream Objects: An Analysis and Design Approach for Business
YOURDON INC. YOURDON™ Systems Method: Model-Driven Systems Development

Java Design

Building Better Apps and Applets

Enjoy!

Peter Coad

Mark Mayfield

To join a Prentice Hall PTR Internet mailing list, point to:
http://www.prenhall.com/register

YOURDON PRESS
PRENTICE HALL BUILDING
Upper Saddle River, NJ 07458
http://www.prenhall.com

Library of Congress Cataloging-in-Publication Data
Coad, Peter.
Java design: building better apps and applets / Peter Coad, Mark Mayfield.
p. cm.
Include bibliographical references and index.
ISBN 0-13-271149-4 (pbk.)
1. Java (Computer program language) I. Mayfield, Mark.
II. Title.
QA76.73.J38C65 1996
005.13'3–dc21 96-47956
CIP

Editorial Production: *Precision Graphic Services, Inc.*
Acquisitions Editor: *Paul W. Becker*
Manufacturing Manager: *Alexis R. Heydt*
Marketing Manager: *Dan Rush*
Cover Design Director: *Jerry Votta*
Cover Design: *Debbie Baker*

Published by Prentice Hall PTR
Prentice-Hall, Inc.
A Simon & Schuster Company
Upper Saddle River, NJ 07458

The publisher offers discounts on this book when ordered in bulk quantities. For more information, contact:

Corporate Sales Department
Prentice Hall PTR
1 Lake Street
Upper Saddle River, NJ 07458
Phone: 800-382-3419
FAX: 201-236-7141
E-mail: corpsales@prenhall.com

Printed in the United States of America
10 9 8 7 6 5 4 3

ISBN 0-13-271149-4

Prentice-Hall International (UK) Limited, *London*
Prentice-Hall of Australia Pty. Limited, *Sydney*
Prentice-Hall Canada, Inc., *Toronto*
Prentice-Hall Hispanoamericana S.A., *Mexico*
Prentice-Hall of India Private Limited, *New Delhi*
Prentice-Hall of Japan, Inc., *Tokyo*
Simon & Schuster Asia Pte. Ltd., *Singapore*
Editora Prentice-Hall do Brasil, Ltda., *Rio de Janeiro*

From Peter Coad

To David Thomas Coad
My very loving son.

From Mark Mayfield

To Casey Lee Mayfield
My inquisitive one.

Contents

Chapter 3

Design with Interfaces 83

Chapter 4

Design with Threads 131

Chapter 5

Design with Notification 175

Acknowledgments

Special thanks to our friends and colleagues who inspire, encourage, and expect the best from us. We especially appreciate their advice, feedback, and support during the development of this book:

Frank Baker
Andy Carmichael
Dietrich Charisius
David E. DeLano
Peter Durcansky
Michael Gerasimov
Ray Haygood
J.D. Hildebrand
Tatsuya Hirooka
Fyodor Isakov
Kazuyuki Ishibashi
Shingo Kamiya
Dmitri Krasnov
Jill Nicola
Nikolai Puntikov
Hanspeter Siegrist
Erik Stein
Frank Sterkmann
Mats Weidmar

with very special thanks to Jon Kern.

Java Design

Building Better Apps and Applets

Why Java Design?

Building materials profoundly affect design techniques.

Home construction materials affect home design. Fabrics affect clothing design. And yes, programming construction materials (languages) affect software design.

In every field of human endeavor, new construction materials are followed by new design methods; hence, "design with Java."

From a designer's perspective, it's worth taking a closer look at Java. What new building materials will it give us? How will these materials affect the way we think about, discuss, trade off, and improve our designs?

Java was designed to *prevent* common mistakes in object-oriented design and programming, especially C++ design and programming.

Java design is profound. It has forever changed how we think about object models and scenarios. It makes object models and scenario views pluggable—unplug an object from one class; plug in an object from another class; and continue on your way, as long as both classes implement the needed interface. This is very significant indeed.

Design

Chapter 1 delivers a practical "how-to" guide for effective design. It introduces a business example and a real-time example that wind their way through the entire book.

Design by Example

- Identify purpose and features
- Select classes
- Sketch a user interface
- Work out dynamics with scenarios
- Build an object model

If you are well-versed in object-oriented design, you may choose to scan Chapter 1 and then proceed with Chapter 2.

Java-Inspired Design

Chapter 2 establishes that composition is the norm, inheritance is the exception; composition is more flexible, inheritance is more rigid; composition is more encapsulated; inheritance is only somewhat encapsulated. It points out a fivefold checklist for deciding when it's a good idea to use inheritance, and (more often) when it's a good idea to avoid it.

Design with Composition, Rather than Inheritance

- Composition: the norm
- Inheritance: the exception (and its risks)

Inheritance vs. interfaces

Five "must satisfy" criteria

Chapter 3 presents the most significant aspects of Java-inspired design: freedom from object connections that are hardwired to just one class of objects and freedom from scenario interactions that are hardwired to just one class of objects. For systems in which flexibility, extensibility, and pluggability are key issues, Java-style interfaces are a must. Indeed, the larger the system and the longer the potential life span of a system the more significant interface-centric scenario development becomes.

Design with Interfaces

Factor out repeaters

Factor out to a proxy

Factor out for analogous apps

Factor out for future expansion

Chapter 4 brings out when to use concurrency and how to use it safely. Most designs must account for multiple streams of program execution; this chapter shows how to do that safely. Threads give you a system-level, simple way to provide concurrent execution paths that can be prioritized to handle your main tasks and your lower priority auxiliary tasks.

Design with Threads

How; why; when to avoid; how long

Sync: what's guaranteed, what's not

Shared value (and keeping out of trouble)

Shared resource (and keeping out of trouble)

Multiple clients, multiple threads within an object

Multiple thread objects, multiple threads within an object

Interface adapters

Chapter 5 examines how one object notifies others about a significant change. Passive notification is simple yet resource intensive. Timer-based notification is a useful pattern, yet active notification is the most interesting choice. This is an essential ingredient for problem-domain object reuse; it's an essential ingredient for designing loosely-coupled subsystems. Java's own active notification mechanism (observable-observer) is defective; this chapter goes beyond its weaknesses, showing you how to really get the job done.

Design with Notification

- Three kinds: passive, time-based, active
- Going beyond observable-observer
- Observable components (composition and interfaces to the rescue)
- Repeaters
- Threaded-observable components

Three appendices follow Chapter 5: Design Strategies, Notation Summary, and Java Visibility.

A Design Book

We love Java programming. It's contagious, way cool, and lots of fun.

But that is not the subject of this book.

This book is about design. Indeed, it is about better design strategies that were inspired by the intrinsic language features found in Java.

These strategies may be applied in any design, even if the target language is not Java.

Java snippets, short and to-the-point examples and excerpts, appear throughout this book. They include lots of comments, so you can read along and understand the design issue, even without prior experience with Java.

Eventually, you might want to read a programming book on Java. We own a stack of them! Our personal favorites to date are

> Cornell, Gary, and Horstmann, Cay: *Core Java*.
> Prentice Hall, 1996.
> This programming book has a good blend of illustrations and source code. It includes quite a bit of material on threads too.
>
> Flanagan, David: *Java in a Nutshell*. O'Reilly
> & Associates, 1996.
> This programming book is source-code intensive with few illustrations. It includes lots and lots of well-documented Java source code.

The Companion CD-ROM

The Companion CD-ROM includes:

- Complete Java source code for this book, ready-to-use in your own apps
- Playground®, a design whiteboard that will help you get the most out of this book (shareware, free for personal study and classroom use)
- Strategies and Patterns Handbook: Hypertext Edition, a comprehensive collection of 177 strategies and 31 object-model patterns (a handy guide that will help you design better apps)

How to Get Updates

We'll post the most recent versions of the CD-ROM goodies at Object International's web site (www.oi.com). Check there for updates.

While visiting at that site, consider subscribing to the free newsletters and discussion groups—tools that can help you get the most out of this book.

Feedback and Hands-On Workshops

Please feel free to send in feedback; it is much appreciated. In addition, if you are interested in custom-in-house or CD-ROM workshops, please visit our web sites for more information.

Peter Coad
coad@oi.com www.oi.com

Mark Mayfield
mlm@jencon.com www.jencon.com

Chapter 1

Design by Example

This chapter teaches design activities by example.

The following design activities can be done in any order; for this chapter, we've chosen this sequence:

- Identify features
- Select classes
- Sketch a user interface (UI)
- Work out dynamics with scenarios
- Build an object model

If you already practice object-oriented design, you might want to just scan this first chapter and then proceed to the Java-inspired chapters that follow:

- Design with composition, rather than inheritance
- Design with interfaces

- Design with threads
- Design with notification

Let's begin.

1.1 Five Major Activities

This design approach consists of five major activities.

Please note that these are *activities*, not *steps*. If it weren't so impractical, we'd write all five sections in parallel columns, jumping back and forth from one section to the next to illustrate the independent nature of the activities.

In practice, we gain a lot of synergy by working back and forth between these activities. You see, each activity helps us discover new content for the other activities. Here's how.

The *Identify System Purpose and Features* activity helps us discover classes, understand UI needs, identify which scenarios are the ones to pay attention to, and grapple with what to include or not include within an object model.

The *Select Classes* activity helps us challenge the breadth of purpose and features, establish UI content, and provide the building blocks for scenario views and an object model.

The *Sketch a UI* activity helps us discover new purpose and features, find additional classes, identify some of the most significant scenarios, and work out the UI influences within an object model.

The *Work Out Dynamics with Scenarios* activity helps us discover variations on purpose and features, find additional classes, add detail (e.g., action buttons) to the UI sketches, and add substance—specifically, "must have" methods—to an object model.

And yes, the *Build an Object Model* activity helps us discover additional purpose and features, apply patterns, add more classes and interrelationships, refine UI design hierarchy, and discover new scenarios.

The point? It's far better to apply these strategies synergistically, rather than sequentially. This way, each facet gets better and better with each activity.

1.2 Example, Example, Example

The best way we know how to teach is by example, by example, by example. It seems, however, that we are in good company:

> *Example* is the school of mankind, and they will learn at no other.
>
> —Edmund Burke

> *Example* is not the main thing in influencing others, it is the only thing.
>
> —Albert Schweitzer

> *Example* isn't another way to teach, it is the only way to teach.
>
> —Albert Einstein

This book teaches by example, pointing out strategies and other important lessons along the way.

Actually, two examples are woven throughout the very fabric of this book: a business example and a real-time example. These provide complementary problem domains that touch on very different design issues.

If you are a business app developer, please study both examples. Carefully consider the business example. Then read the real-time example to gain added insights on concurrency and notification.

If you are a real-time system developer, please study both examples. Read the business example first; that is where you'll find detailed "how to" strategies and discussions. Then study the real-time example, gaining additional insights into real-time issues along the way.

Let the games begin.

1.3 Charlie's Charters

The business example that runs throughout this book is called, "Charlie's Charters" (Figure 1-1).

Charlie's Charters is a small regional carrier with small-aircraft service to nearby destinations. Charlie's Charters needs an application for scheduling flights and making reservations.

1.3.1 Identify System Purpose and Features

1.3.1.1 Identify system purpose

Begin by identifying the purpose of the system. What's this new application all about—its essence, its critical success factor, its unique selling proposition?

Identify Purpose Strategy: *State the purpose of the system in 25 words or less.*

We talk things over with the manager of Charlie's Charters and establish this purpose: to describe flights, to schedule flights, and to make reservations.

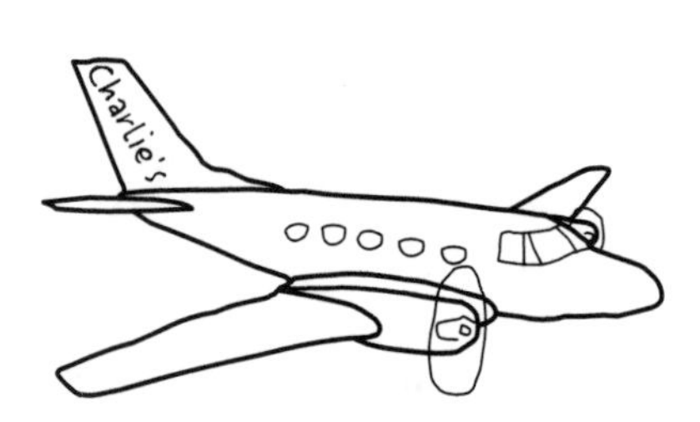

Figure 1-1. Charlie's Charters.

Sometimes it's hard to come up with a concise system purpose statement. When that happens, shift gears and develop a features list first; then prioritize those features, and incorporate the most important ones into an official-sounding system purpose statement. This works quite well too.

1.3.1.2 Identify Features

What are the features for this system? Hmmm. Developers can get really (really) carried away, identifying feature after feature after feature.

How can we get to a meaningful features list?

Look for features that produce a desired outcome. The best features satisfy a "want" for the consumer who will be served by the system or a "want" for whomever is paying for the system.

Your customer will vote with his wallet. You need to deliver features that satisfy the "wants" of those two audiences. Adding extra bells and whistles, features that don't satisfy a "want," waste time, budget, talent, *and* profits.

Identify Features Strategy: *List the features for setting up and conducting the business and assessing business results.*

Let's apply this strategy to the Charlie's Charters application.

Setting up

1. Enter (add, change, delete) airports.
2. Enter flight descriptions.
3. Enter scheduled flights.

Conducting the business

4. Enter passengers.
5. Enter a reservation.

Assess business results

6. Does a scheduled flight have any room left? (Something that must be assessed whenever a reservation is added.)

Together, we've defined system purpose and identified key features—a good start.

Over time, we'll discover additional features and add them to the list. This comes from added understanding about what the customer and purchaser want. As we build an application, we'll understand more about what features are really wanted and what features you could add to bring additional competitive advantage to the customer and to the purchaser. This is not feature creep! We can add features to your features list at any time. Yet until we commit to doing them, until you add a milestone for that feature in the project schedule, they are just proposed features, not committed-to features—a big difference.

With additional committed-to features, you might need to adjust the purpose statement, too. Change is inevitable. Early software development methods fought change ("the requirements are fixed and cannot be changed on this project"—a fantasy that is no longer possible in today's fast-paced world). Effective object-oriented design embraces continual change. In building an object model, use problem domain (PD) classes both to partition the data and to partition the functionality. We can add new attributes (data), new methods (functions), and even new classes without changing the overall shape of the model.

We've identified system purpose and features. What's next?

1.3.2 Select Classes

1.3.2.1 Object, Class

An *object* is a person, place, or thing. Yes, it's a noun. In software, it's a small piece of running software with its own values and its own behavior.

For example, a scheduled flight object might have its own value (date = July 26) and its own behavior ("add reservation").

A *class* is a description that applies to each of some number of similar objects. In software, it's where you write application code, establishing

- the interface for each object in that class (its method signatures)
- the internals for each object in that class

  what each object knows (its attributes)

  who each object knows (its object connections)

  what each object does (its methods).

It might also describe

- the interface for the class itself (method signatures that apply across all of the objects in that class)
- the internals for the class itself

  what the class itself knows (its class attributes)

  what each class does (its class methods).

A class also describes

how this class relates to others (its superclasses).

For example, a "scheduled flight" class might describe

- an attribute called "date"
- an object connection to a "flight description" (a catalog entry, containing standard details about that flight)
- a method called "has room"

  so each scheduled flight object can respond to the inquiry, "Do you have room for another passenger on this flight?"

1.3.2.2 Select Classes

Here, we want to select some initial classes. This means we will look at persons, places, and things (objects) and form classes (descriptions).

Person, place, or thing? Let's expand that list a bit, to cover the kinds of objects that we'll find again and again when building object models. Here is the strategy:

Select Classes Strategy: *Feature by feature, look for: role-player, role, transaction (moment or interval), place, container, or catalog-like description. For real-time systems, also look for data acquisition and control devices.*

Apply this strategy to the Charlie's Charters application (Figures 1-2 and 1-3):

1. Enter (add, change, delete) airports.

   place: airport

2. Enter flight descriptions.

   catalog-like description: flight description (flight number, arrival time, departure time, and the like)

3. Enter scheduled flights.

   transaction (moment or interval): scheduled flight

   place: airport

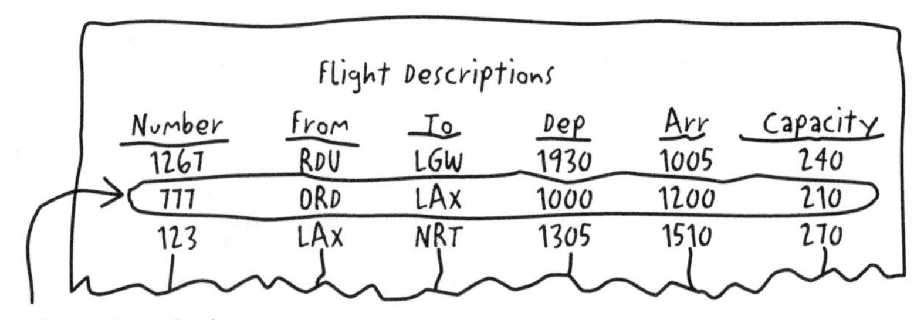

Figure 1-2. A flight description.

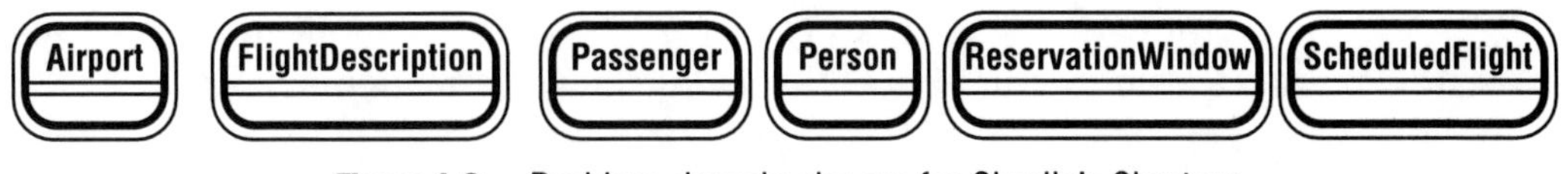

Figure 1-3. Problem-domain classes for Charlie's Charters.

4. Enter a passenger.

   role-player: person

   role: passenger

5. Enter a reservation.

   role-player: person

   role: passenger

   catalog-like description: flight description

   transaction (moment or interval): reservation, scheduled flight

6. Does a scheduled flight have room? (needed when adding a reservation).

   transaction (moment or interval): scheduled flight

So far, so good. The classes we've selected are shown in Figure 1-3.

1.3.3 Sketch a UI

We've established system purpose and features and identified initial classes. Now it's time to sketch out a user interface (UI), the windows and reports for delivering those features.

First, list the key ingredients, the content we need. Then sketch a mock-up.

1.3.3.1 List Key Ingredients

UI Content Strategy: *Feature by feature, establish content: selections, lists, entry fields, display fields, actions, assessments.*

Apply this strategy to the Charlie's Charters application. For each feature, we'll think of the supporting information needed:

1. Enter airports.

   primary selection and list: airport; airport list

2. Enter flight descriptions.

   primary selection and list: flight description; flight-description list

   secondary selections and lists: from, to; from list, to list

   entry fields: flight number, departure time, arrival time

   actions: add a scheduled flight

3. Enter scheduled flights.

   primary selection and list: scheduled flight; scheduled-flight list

   secondary selection and list: flight description; flight-description list

   entry fields: date

   actions: has room?, add a reservation

4. Enter passengers.

   primary selection and list: passenger; passenger list

   entry fields: name, address, type (regular, gold, platinum)

   display fields: number

5. Enter a reservation.

   primary selection and list: passenger; passenger list

   secondary selection and list: flight description; flight-description list

   tertiary selection and list: scheduled flight; scheduled-flight list

   display fields: date and time made, expiration date and time

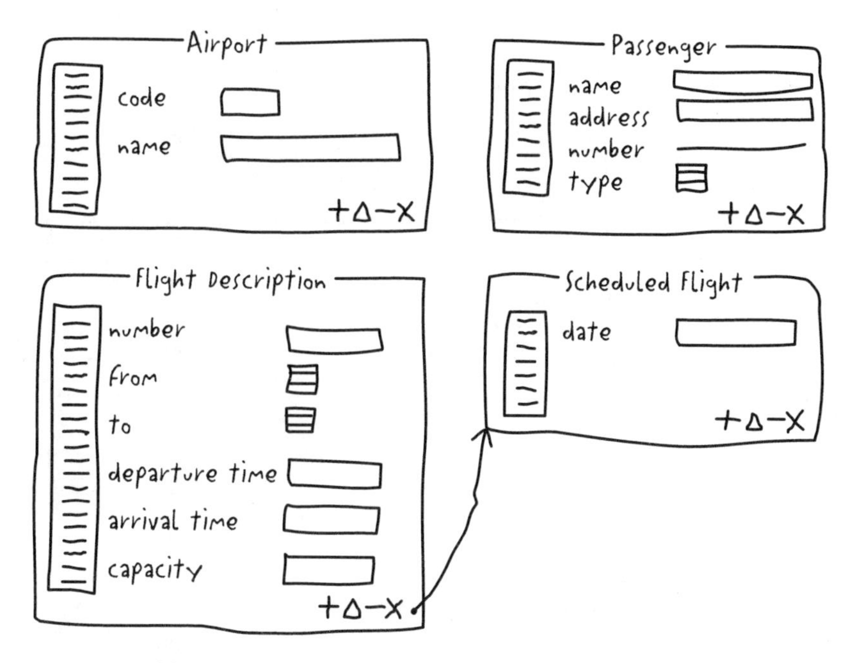

Figure 1-4. Mock-ups for entering airports, flight descriptions, scheduled flights, and passengers.

1.3.3.2 Sketch a Mock-Up

Figure 1-4 depicts a sketch for entering airports, flight descriptions, scheduled flights, and passengers.

Figure 1-5 is a sketch for entering a reservation.

Based upon the UI sketches in Figures 1-4 and 1-5, add these initial UI classes to the object model (Figure 1-6).

1.3.4 Work Out Dynamics with Scenarios

1.3.4.1 Scenario Views for Setting Up

Work out the scenario views for setting up, to get things ready to go for making reservations.

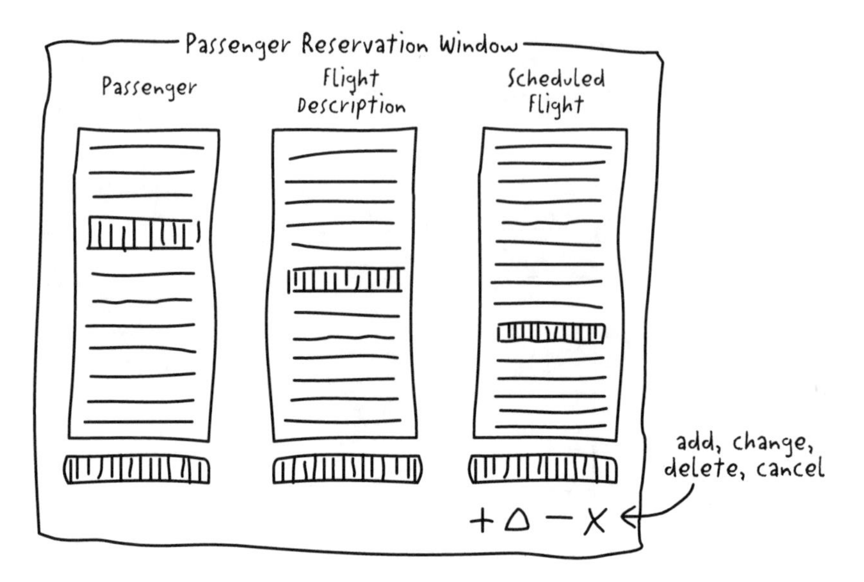

Figure 1-5. Mock-up for entering a reservation.

Figure 1-6. UI classes for Charlie's Charters.

Normally, we won't work out most "setting up" scenarios because they are fairly boring. Once we've worked out several of them, the pattern is pretty clear and consistent:

- a UI object
- one or two PD objects
- and some simple messaging:

  create and initialize an object

  possibly send it to another object, to connect the two to each other

In fact, the only reason we are including the "setting up" scenarios here is for instruction. These are simple scenarios, good for first describing what scenarios are all about. These scenarios often occur so it's good for you to know what they look like in case someone wants to see a simple example. These are also boring scenarios—once you see them, we hope you'll feel comfortable about skipping them altogether, spending more time on scenarios that will help you discover additional methods, classes, attributes, and features.

1.3.4.1.1 Enter airports

The "enter airport" scenario describes the time-ordered sequence of object interactions for building an airport window, followed by entering (adding, changing, or deleting) an airport.

It has four parts: build (the window), add an airport, change an airport, and delete an airport (Figure 1-7).

AirportUI		Airport
build invokeAdd invokeChange invokeDelete		getList get new add set delete remove

Name:

Add airport.

AirportUI		Airport	Comments:
build			
	--c·▶	getList	(; list)
	--n·▶	get	(; values) //get values for display
invokeAdd			
	--c·▶	new	(code, name ; airport)
		c->add	(airport ;) //add to list
invokeChange			
	---▶	set	(values ;)
invokeDelete			
	---▶	delete	
		c->remove	(airport ;) //remove from list

Figure 1-7. Build an airport window, then enter (add, change, and delete) an airport.

What about persistent storage? If we are working with an object DBMS, then the scenario view is fine as it is (the object DBMS provides the needed infrastructure for loading, searching, and saving airport objects). If we are working with a relational DBMS, then the scenario view needs an additional class called AirportDM that is responsible for interacting with one or more tables in the database to provide the persistence mechanism. Working with relational databases is outside the scope of this book (if you are interested in this specific aspect of design, see [Coad97] and [CoadLetter]).

1.3.4.1.2 An aside: scenario-view notation

Here are some details about scenario view notation (see Figure 1-7).

The inner rounded rectangle represents a class. The outer rounded rectangle represents one or more objects in that class. In a scenario view, the outer rounded rectangle is pulled downward, so one can see a specific time-ordered sequence of object interactions.

Now take a look at the lower section. The horizontal lines separate the steps within a time-ordered sequence of object interactions. The bold horizontal lines separate little scenarios (a convenience, to get the most out of each scenario view). The arrows are messages, showing that an object in one column is messaging an object in another column. The arrows may be annotated with a little "c" (meaning it is a message that is being sent to the class itself) or with a little "n" (meaning it is sent to some number of objects in that class).

The comments section lists parameters in this format: (inputs ; output); it also includes whatever descriptive text might be needed for guiding a reader through a scenario view.

1.3.4.1.3 Enter flight descriptions; enter passengers

In fact, we don't show these scenario views here. Why? The shape would be exactly the same as in Figure 1-7; only the class names and parameters would change.

Enter flight descriptions. The class names are FlightDescriptionUI and FlightDescription. The "new" method creates an object and initializes it. That method's input parameters are number, from, to, departureTime, arrivalTime, capacity; the method returns a flight description.

We could add an AircraftDescription class, with attributes such as model number, cruising range, and capacity. For now, though, let's consider capacity as the capacity for a scheduled flight. That's enough, at this point.

Enter passengers. The class names are PassengerUI and Passenger. The parameters are: (name, address ; passenger).

Once you've done one of the "setting up" scenario views, you really don't get too excited about doing them again and again.

There is a variation on this theme, however, with a bit more to it. Take a look at it next.

1.3.4.1.4 Enter scheduled flights

When entering a scheduled flight, one must select a corresponding flight description.

This same scenario view shape applies whenever we need to enter an object (in this case, a scheduled flight) and select a related object (in this case, a flight description, standard catalog information for that flight).

Again, the pattern is

- a UI object
- one or two PD objects
- and some simple messaging:

  create and initialize an object

  possibly send it to another object, to connect the two to each other.

Figure 1-8 illustrates this kind of "setting up" scenario view.

Interesting, yet it's still not a scenario view we'd want to write down again and again.

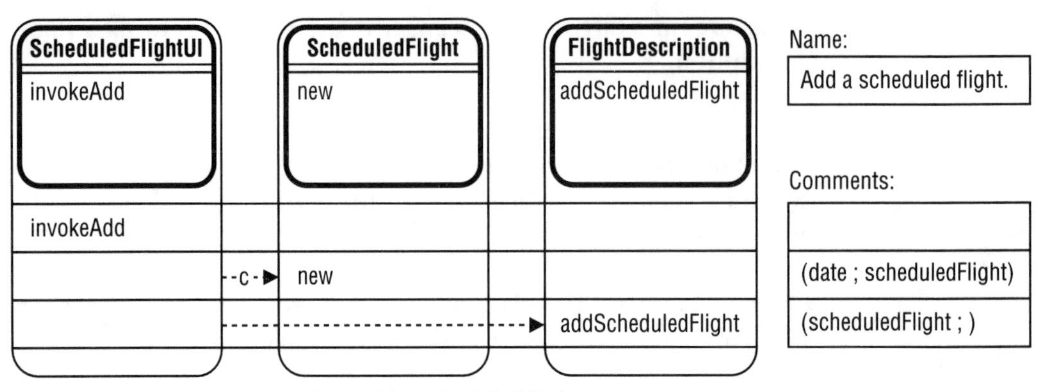

Figure 1-8. Add a scheduled flight.

We cannot document every scenario for an application. So we must focus on the ones that will give us the most added value, the most insights. Where do we find them? Read on.

1.3.4.2 Scenario Views for Conducting Business and Assessing Results

Hopefully, we'll spend much more of our time with scenarios for "conducting business" and "assessing results" features. Why?

- These scenarios demonstrate higher-value features, desired outcomes in which domain experts have more of a vested interest (and will work hard to get it right).
- These scenarios help us discover additional classes and methods, improving overall results.

High-Value Scenarios Strategy: *Build scenario views that will exercise each "conducting business" and "assessing results" feature.*

1.3.4.2.1 Enter a reservation

Charlie's Charters example (Figure 1-9):

Enter a reservation.

Select a passenger.

Select a flight description.

Select a scheduled flight.

Invoke "add reservation."

If the scheduled flight is not full, add a reservation.

Action Sentence Strategy: *Describe the action in a complete sentence. Put the action in the object (person, place, or thing) that has the "what I know" and "who I know" to get the job done.*

Charlie's Charters example:

Complete sentence: Is the scheduled flight full?

Put the action in the object: scheduled flight.

What happens if more than one reservation is being made at the same time? Could we get into trouble here, overbooking without knowing it? We'll take a closer look at this concurrency issue in Chapter 4.

ReservationUI	ScheduledFlight	FlightDescription	Reservation
invokeAdd	tryToAddPassenger hasRoom addReservation	hasRoom	new

Name: Add a reservation.

ReservationUI	ScheduledFlight	FlightDescription	Reservation	Comments:
invokeAdd				
	→ tryToAddPassenger			(passenger ; result)
	-->hasRoom			(; hasRoom)
		→ hasRoom		(passengerCount ; hasRoom)
	IF			// IF it has room
	-->addReservation			(passenger ;)
	c - - - - - - - - - -	- - - - - - - - - -	→ new	(passenger ; reservation)
	ENDIF			

Figure 1-9. Add a reservation.

1.3.5 Build an Object Model

At this point, we've already developed a lot of content for an object model:

- PD classes
- UI classes
- Methods
- And some hints at object connections (unless the receiver comes along as a parameter, a sender needs an object connection to know to whom to send a message).

Indeed, it's good to build an object model in parallel with working out dynamics with scenarios. There is lot of synergy between an object model and its scenario views.

Here's the strategy:

Build an Object Model Strategy:

Start with scenario classes and methods.

Add attributes—content for methods.

Add attributes—content for the UI.

Add object connections—message paths for methods.

Add object connections—look-up paths for the UI.

1.3.5.1 Object Model—PD Component

Build an object model for the classes in the PD component (Figure 1-10):

- Class: Person

  attributes: name, address

  object connection: passenger

- Class: Passenger

  attribute: number, type (regular, gold, platinum)

  object connections (look-up paths): person, scheduled flight

- Class: Reservation

  attributes: date and time made, expiration date and time

  object connections (look-up paths): passenger, scheduled flight

- Class: Scheduled Flight

  methods:

    class methods (apply across the collection of objects in the class): new (add a new object to the collection of objects in the class)

    instance methods: try to add passenger, has room, add passenger

  attribute: date

  object connections (look-up paths): reservation, flight description

  object connection (message path): flight description

- Class: Flight Description

  methods:

    class methods: new

    instance methods: add scheduled flight, has room

  attributes: flight number, from, to, departure time, arrival time

  object connections (look-up paths): scheduled flight, airport

- Class: Airport

  attributes: (three-letter) code, description

  object connection (look-up path): flight description

Note that the methods in Figure 1-10 are exactly those methods we've added by working out dynamics with scenarios.

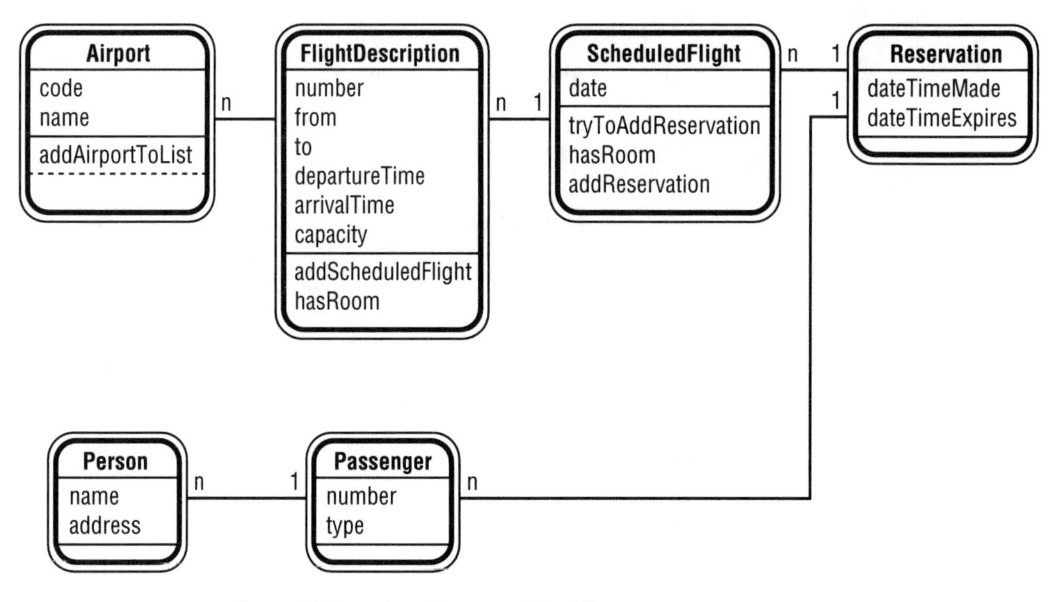

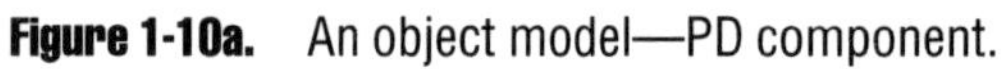

Figure 1-10a. An object model—PD component.

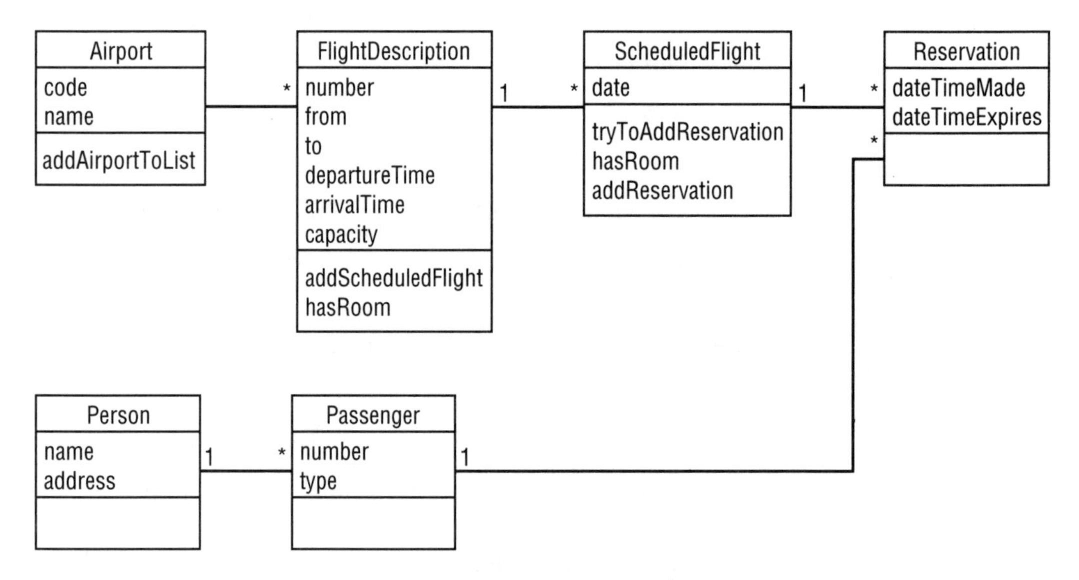

Figure 1-10b. An object model—PD component (UML notation).

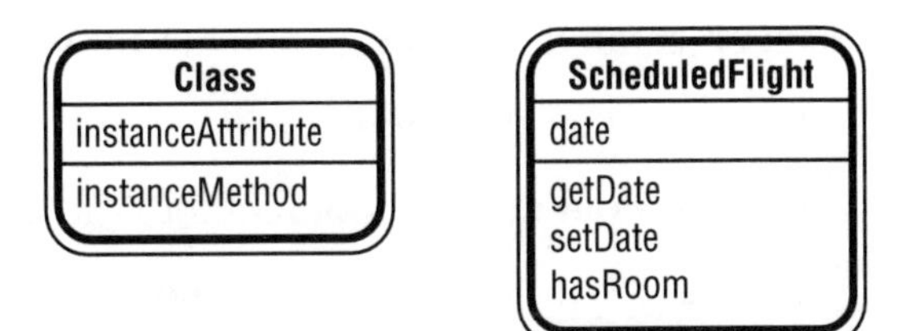

Figure 1-11. The basic "class with objects symbol" and an example.

Methods like new, get/set, add/remove, and delete apply to every class with objects. Normally, they should not be shown in an object model unless they are needed within a specific scenario view. Similarly, we are ignoring persistent storage mechanisms for the sake of clarity. Here too, common services like Save, Retrieve, Search, and so on, are not always shown for the sake of brevity.

1.3.5.2 Object-Model Notation

The following sections present some notes on Coad object-model notation.*

1.3.5.2.1 Basic "class with objects" symbol

Take a closer look at the symbol presented in Figure 1-11.

The inner rounded rectangle represents a class. The outer rounded rectangle represents one or some number of objects in a class.

By convention, class names are capitalized: the ScheduledFlight class. References to an object of a class, are not capitalized: a scheduled-flight object means an object instance of the class ScheduledFlight.

The class symbol is divided into three sections: class name, instance (object) attributes, and instance methods.

In these examples:

> Each object in the class Class
>
> holds its own value for instanceAttribute, and
>
> can carry out the instanceMethod.

*We also show many of the object model diagrams in UML notation for those more familiar with that notation.

Each object in the class ScheduledFlight will

hold its own value for date,

can carry out the accessor methods (getDate, setDate), and

can carry out the hasRoom method

We can express the design graphically (object models) or textually (in Java code itself).

So what does ScheduledFlight look like in Java? It looks like this:

```
public class ScheduledFlight extends Object {
✂
    // attributes / private
    private Date date;

    // methods / public / accessors for attribute values
    public Date getDate() { return this.date; }
    public void setDate(Date aDate) { this.date = aDate; }

    // methods / public / conduct business
    public boolean hasRoom() {
        /* code goes in here */ }
✂
}
```

The little scissors (✂) symbols designate Java *snippets*, small and to-the-point excerpts of Java code, illustrating key concepts along the way.*

*We prefer to limit access to all attributes, including class attributes; we make them private and insist upon using accessors. This method is consistent, easy to follow, and hard to foul up. Strict use of accessors is the convention that we follow in this book (this is not a religious tenet; it's just the way we prefer to program).

1.3.5.2.2 Expanded "class with objects" symbol

Now consider an expanded version of the same symbol (Figure 1-12).

The attributes section may be optionally divided into two sections: class attributes and instance (object) attributes. Class attributes have a value that applies across the collection of all of the objects in a class; if all flight descriptions had to abide by a "never to exceed" capacity, then we would need a class attribute. In practice, however, you will hardly ever find a need for a class attribute. (This generally occurs when your Problem Domain object model does not contain the "all-knowing" object whom you might be able to ask such collection-level questions.) Instance attributes are those attributes for which each object in a class can have its own values.

The methods section may be optionally divided into two sections: class methods and instance (object) methods. Class methods apply across the collection of all of the objects in a class; methods like new (create and initialize a new object and add it to the collection of all of the objects in that class), get list, and "find the object that matches this description" are class methods. Instance methods are those methods that each object in the class can do on its own.

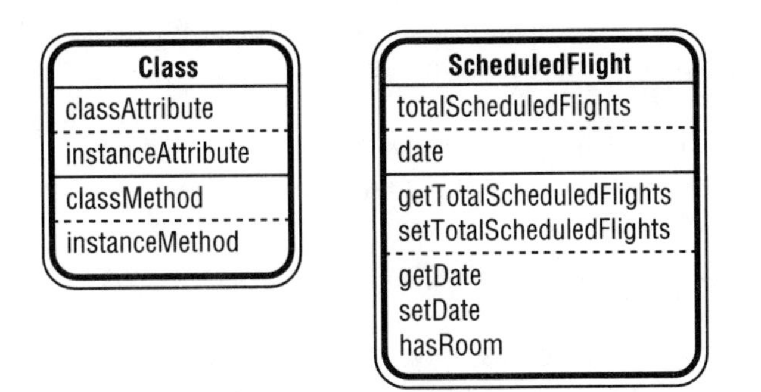

Figure 1-12. An expanded "class with objects" symbol and an example.

In these examples:

Each object in the class Class:

holds its own value for instanceAttribute, and

can carry out the instanceMethod.

In addition, the class Class:

holds its own value for classAttribute, and

can carry out the classMethod.

Each object in the class ScheduledFlight will:

hold its own value for date,

can carry out the accessor methods (getDate, setDate), and

can carry out the hasRoom method.

In addition, the class ScheduledFlight will:

holds its own value for totalScheduledFlights, and

can carry out getTotalScheduledFlights and setTotalScheduledFlights

(the "set" should be private, something that only the class itself can invoke).

Again, we can express the design graphically (object models) or textually (in Java code itself).

So, how can you express ScheduledFlight's class attribute and class methods in Java? Take a look:

```
public class ScheduledFlight extends Object {
✂
    // class attributes / private
    private static int totalScheduledFlights;

    // class methods / public / accessors for class attribute values
    public static int getTotalScheduledFlights() { return totalScheduledFlights; }
```

```
    // class methods / private / accessors for class attribute values
    private static void setTotalScheduledFlights(int total) {
        totalScheduledFlights = total; }
✂
}
```

1.3.5.3 "Object connection" lines

Object connections provide look-up paths and message paths. They establish the "who I know" aspect of an object's responsibilities.

If an object connection carries the added meaning of whole-part (assembly-part, container-contents, or group-member), it gets a little triangle at the midpoint of the line, pointing to the "whole."

Object connection constraints are placed next to the object that is being constrained, the object that will eventually implement that constraint. (This is the opposite of entity-relationship markings of rows in one table corresponding to rows in another table, yet it makes a lot of sense, when building effective object models. Worthwhile.)

Constraints include:

0-1	zero to one
1	one
n	many
1-n	one to many
[description] constraint	special constraint

One more time: you can express the design graphically (object models) or textually (in Java code itself).

Consider the object connection between scheduled flight and reservation (Figure 1-13).

So how can we show an object connection between a scheduled flight and its reservations in Java? Use something like this:

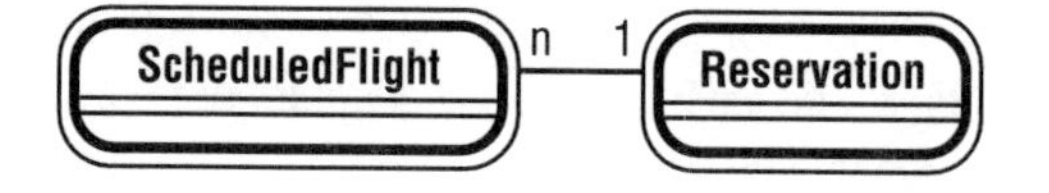

Figure 1-13. The object connection between scheduled flight and reservation.

```
public class ScheduledFlight extends Object {
✂
    // attributes / private / object connections
    private Vector reservations = new Vector();

    // methods / public / accessors for object connection values
    public void addReservation(Reservation aReservation) {
        this.reservations.addElement(aReservation); }
    public void removeReservation(Reservation aReservation) {
        this.reservations.removeElement(aReservation); }

    // methods / public / get enumeration of reservations vector
    public Enumeration getReservationList() {
        return this.reservations.elements(); }

    // methods / protected / accessor for object connection vector
    protected Vector getReservations() {
        return this.reservations; }
✂
}
```

Code note: We initialize the reservations variable as a Vector object, rather than null (the default). Alternatively we could initialize the variable with a constructor.

Code note: We limit visibility of getReservations to ScheduledFlight's subclasses. We let others gain access through an Enumeration.

```
public class Reservation extends Object {
✂
    // attribute / private / object connection
    private ScheduledFlight scheduledFlight;

    // methods / public / accessors for object connection values
    public void addScheduledFlight(ScheduledFlight aScheduledFlight) {
        this.scheduledFlight = aScheduledFlight; }
```

```
    public ScheduledFlight getScheduledFlight() { return this.scheduledFlight; }
    public void removeScheduledFlight() { this.scheduledFlight = null; }
✂
}
```

1.3.5.4 Object Model—UI Component

Build an object model for the classes for the UI component, by applying the same "Build an Object Model" strategy. Figure 1-14 shows the result.

Note that each window has attribute pairs: a list of objects and then a selected one (or selected ones, in contexts that warrant multiple selections).

Take a closer look at these attributes. A list of objects? A selected object? They sound like an association, an object connection. And that is what they are—object connections that are shown with text. That's the best way to show an object connection from UI objects to PD objects. Why? Well, UI objects show a view of the PD objects, and consequently tend to be very interconnected with some number of PD objects. Using text makes this interconnection easier to understand (a picture is worth a thousand words; though here a few words simplify the picture).

How do these UI objects get the values they need? For the *list attribute:* A UI object sends a message to a PD class, asking for a list

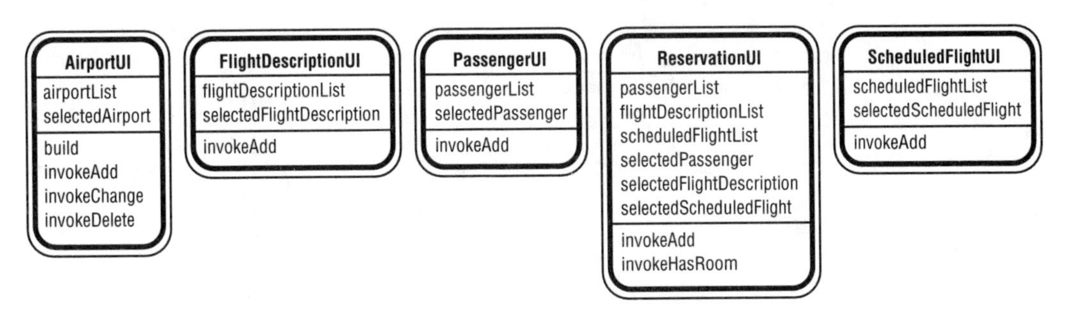

Figure 1-14. An object model—UI component.

of its objects. Then the UI object sends messages to each object in that class, to get the values it needs to display. For the *selection attribute:* Someone makes a selection, and then the UI object knows the selected object.

Most methods in these UI classes begin with "invoke," meaning, someone has just clicked on a button to invoke some corresponding set of actions.

1.3.5.5 Object Model for Charlie's Charters

At this point, the overall object model for Charlie's Charters looks like this (Figure 1-15).

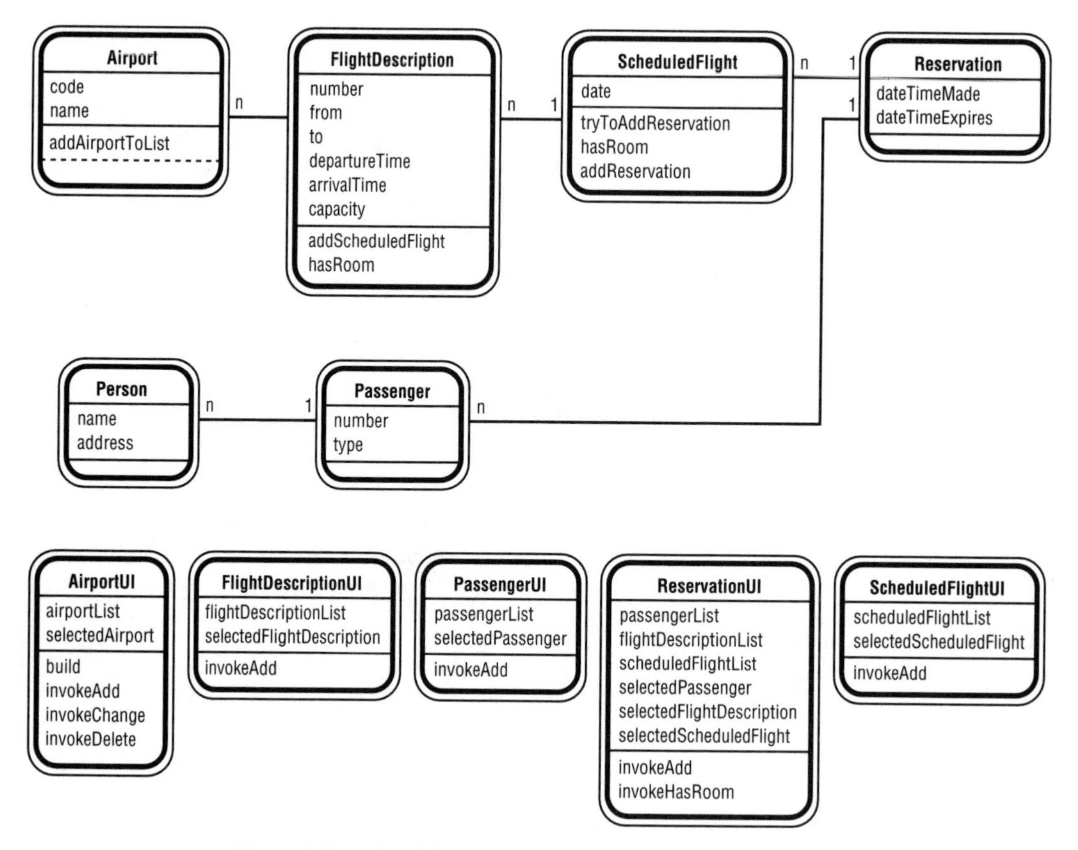

Figure 1-15. An object model for Charlie's Charters.

1.4 Zoe's Zones

A real-time example?

Please kindly note that by including a real-time example, we are not at all suggesting that we build *time-critical* real-time applications with Java—no way (not yet, anyway).

This book is about Java-inspired design, not about Java programming. The lessons learned here are applicable to design with other languages, too (notably C++, Smalltalk, and Object Pascal).

We include a real-time example here so we can (1) work with an example that engineers can more easily relate to, and (2) illustrate certain concurrency issues along the way.

The real-time example that runs throughout this book is called, "Zoe's Zones."

Zoe develops and delivers monitoring systems, consisting of zones and sensors and a centralized monitoring station.

A zone is a collection of sensors, typically located within a room, floor, assembly line, building, or facility.

A sensor is a data acquisition device that measures a given system variable and provides an output signal for other devices/systems to read. For example, different types of sensors might detect temperature, pressure, smoke level, or motion.

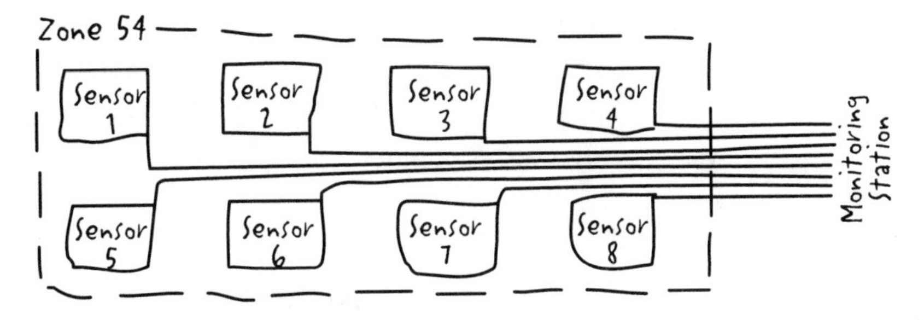

Figure 1-16. Zoe's Zones.

This example is streamlined, offering just a few comments along the way. It is a different problem domain, yet the same strategies apply.

Here we go.

1.4.1 Identify System Purpose and Features

1.4.1.1 Identify System Purpose

Apply the same set of strategies presented earlier in this chapter (the strategies are also listed at the end of the chapter and in Appendix A for easy reference).

This time, it's for Zoe's Zones. Apply the "identify purpose" strategy:

> Purpose: to monitor and track problem reports from sensors, grouped into zones.

1.4.1.2 Identify Features

Apply the "identify features" strategy to the Zoe's Zones application:

Setting up

1. Enter sensors.
2. Enter zones.

Conducting the business

3. Activate zones and sensors.
4. Record problem intervals.

Assess business results

5. Assess sensor reliability.

1.4.2 Select Classes

Apply the "select classes" strategy to the Zoe's Zones application (Figure 1-17):

Setting up

1. Enter sensors

   data acquisition device: sensor

2. Enter zones

   place, container: zone

Conducting the business

3. Activate zones and sensors

   data acquisition device: sensor

   place, container: zone

4. Record problem intervals

   transaction (moment or interval): problem interval

Assess business results

5. View problem intervals

   transaction (moment or interval): problem interval

6. Assess sensor reliability

   data acquisition device: sensor

   transaction (moment or interval): problem interval

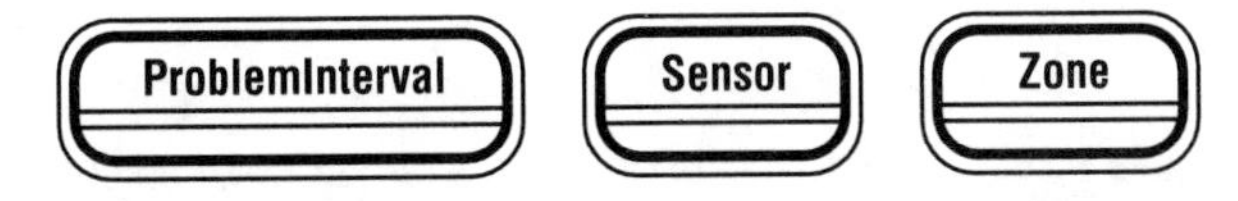

Figure 1-17. Problem-domain classes for Zoe's Zones.

The symbols in Figure 1-17 represent classes of objects for the software application that will serve the monitoring station.

Objects in these classes are *abstractions*, not the real thing.

A problem-interval object abstracts an interval of time between problem detection and problem correction. It is not an interval of absolute (or wall clock) time; instead, it is an abstraction of what the application knows and does about that interval of time.

A zone object abstracts a zone of sensors. It is not an actual zone; instead, it is an abstraction of what the application knows and does about each zone.

Similarly, a sensor object abstracts a sensor. It is not an actual sensor; instead, it is an abstraction of what the application knows and does to interact with an actual, physical sensor (Figure 1-18). In other words, model only those aspects necessary and sufficient to fulfill the system's purpose and features. It's clean. It's pragmatic. It's simpler. Cool.

Even though we might know a great deal about a physical object, we do our best to model only just what we need to get the job done—no more, no less.

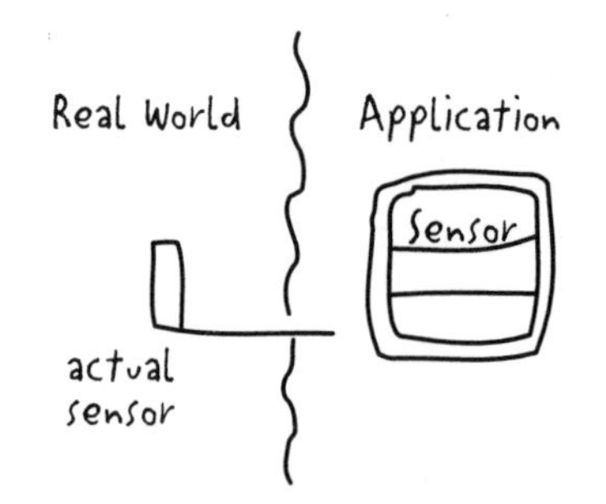

Figure 1-18. An actual sensor vs. an abstraction of an application's responsibilities for interacting with an actual sensor.

1.4.3 Sketch a UI

1.4.3.1 List the Key Ingredients

Apply the "UI content" strategy to the Zoe's Zones application:

1. Enter sensors

    primary selection and list: sensor, sensor list

    entry fields: number, interval

    actions: activate, assess reliability

2. Enter zones

    primary selection and list: zone, zone list

    secondary selection and list: sensor, sensor list

    entry fields:

      for zone: number, threshold

      for each sensor in the zone: number

    actions: activate, accept report (from a sensor)

3. View problem intervals

    list: problem interval list

1.4.3.2 Sketch It Out

Figure 1-19 depicts a sketch for entering sensors and zones.

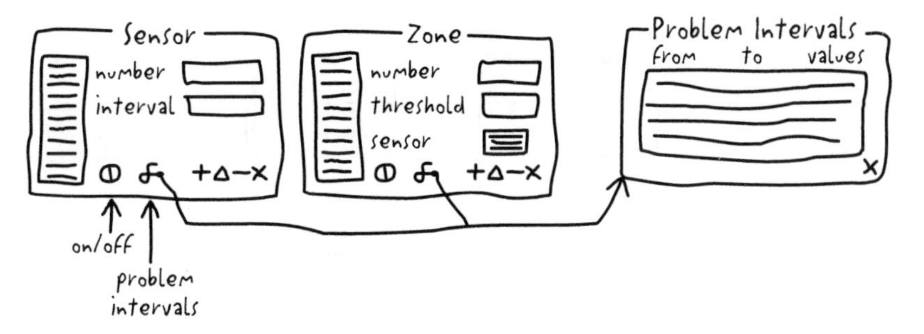

Figure 1-19. Mock-ups for entering sensor, entering zones, and looking at problem intervals.

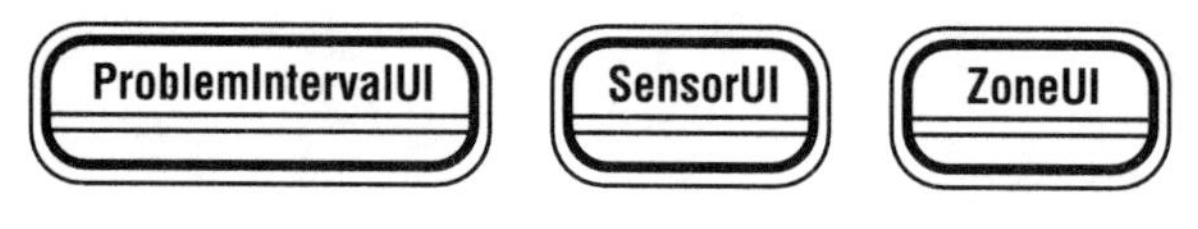

Figure 1-20. UI classes for Zoe's Zones.

Add the UI classes to the object model (Figure 1-20).

1.4.4 Build Scenario Views

1.4.4.1 Scenario Views for Setting Up

Work out the scenario views for setting up, to get things ready to go for monitoring sensors within zones.

1.4.4.1.1 Enter sensors

Figure 1-21 presents the "Add a sensor" scenario.

1.4.4.1.2 Enter zones

"Enter zones" follows the same basic pattern. The class names change to "ZoneUI" and "Zone." The parameters are: (number, threshold ; zone).

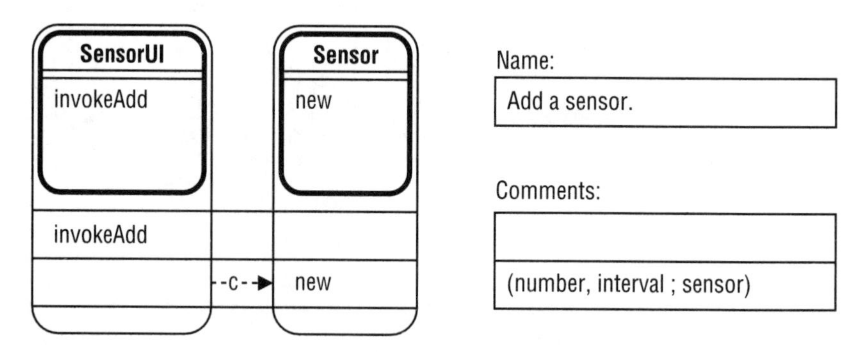

Figure 1-21. Add a sensor.

1.4.4.2 Scenario Views for Conducting Business and Assessing Results

Apply the "high-value scenarios" strategy to the Zoe's Zones application.

1. Activate a zone and its sensors. Hmmm. Apply the "action sentence" strategy here. We could tell a zone object to activate itself, and each zone object could tell each of its sensors to activate itself (Figure 1-22).
2. Record problem intervals (Figure 1-23).

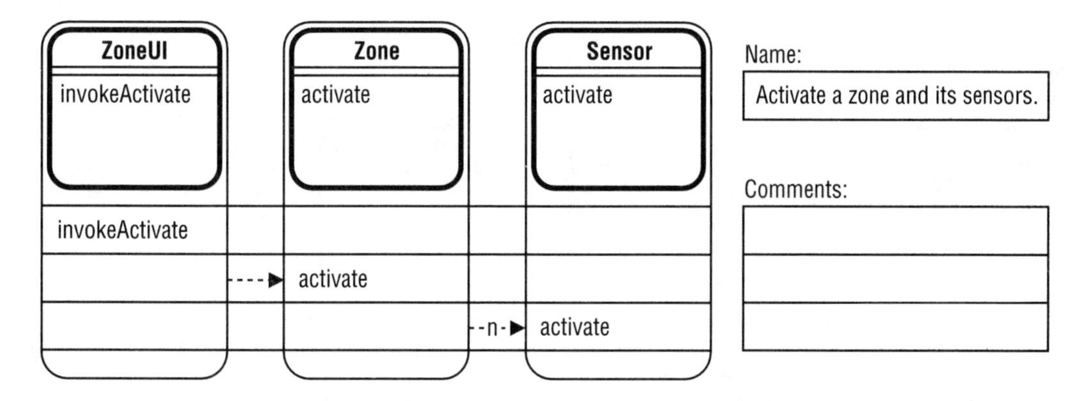

Figure 1-22. Activate a zone and its sensors.

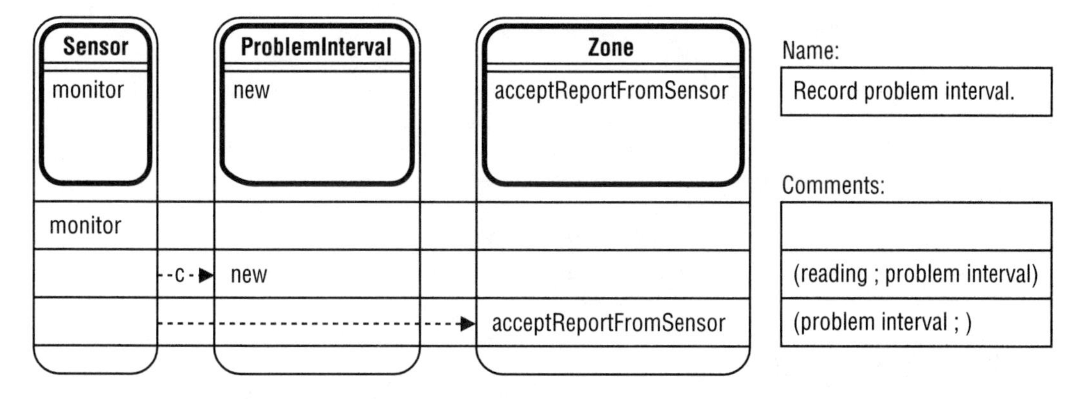

Figure 1-23. Record problem intervals.

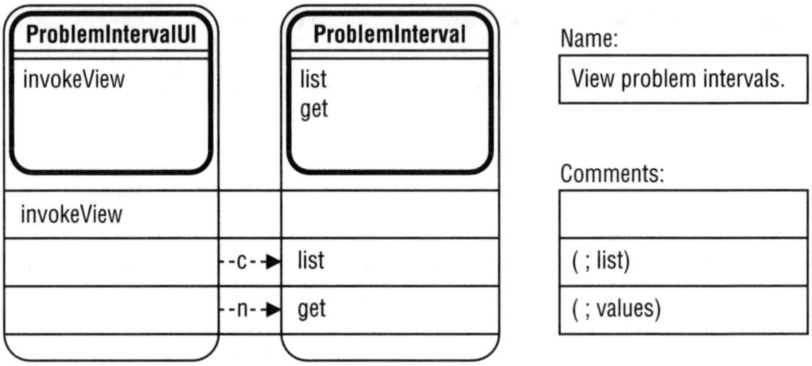

ProblemIntervalUI
invokeView

ProblemInterval
list
get

invokeView
-c-▶ list
-n-▶ get

Name:
View problem intervals.

Comments:
(; list)
(; values)

Figure 1-24. View problem intervals.

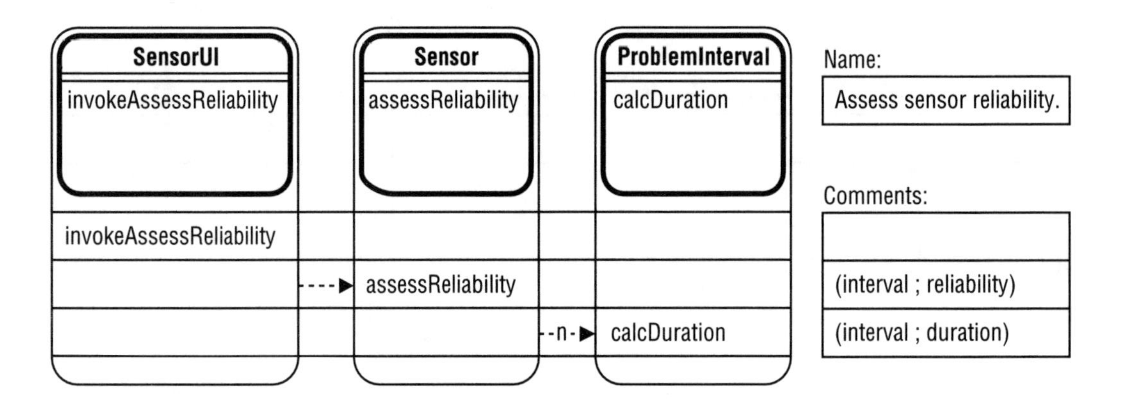

Figure 1-25. Assess sensor reliability.

3. View problem intervals (Figure 1-24).
4. Assess sensor reliability (Figure 1-25).

1.4.5 Build an Object Model

Apply the "build an object model" strategy to the Zoe's Zones application.

1.4.5.1 Content

Zoe's Zones:

- Sensor

  attribute: number, legal range, operational state

  (usually, a device object needs to keep track of its own operational state)

  object connection (look-up path): problem interval

  (if you needed the query: given a sensor, tell me its zone—then you'd need a look-up path from sensor to zone, too)

  object connection (message path): zone, problem interval

  actions: activate, monitor (on-going behavior), assess reliability

- Zone

  attribute: number, threshold

  object connection (look-up path): sensor, problem interval

  object connection (message path): sensor, problem interval

  actions: activate, monitor (on-going behavior), accept report (from a sensor)

- Problem interval

  attribute: date and time detected, worst value, date and time corrected

  object connection (look-up path): sensor or zone

  action: calculate duration

1.4.5.2 Object Model—PD Component

1.4.5.3 "Kinds of"—Some Notes

Should you consider two different *kinds of* problem intervals (Figure 1-26)?

- Sensor problem interval

  attribute: date and time detected, value, date and time corrected

  connection: sensor

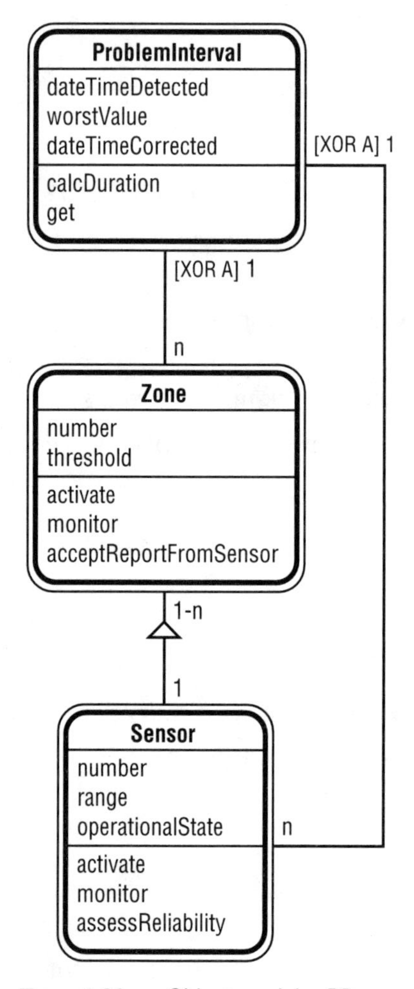

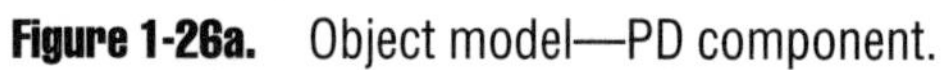
Figure 1-26a. Object model—PD component.

- Zone problem interval

  attribute: date and time detected, value, date and time corrected

  connection: zone

The two kinds of problem intervals are very similar. We could organize them with generalization-specialization, as shown in Figure 1-27.

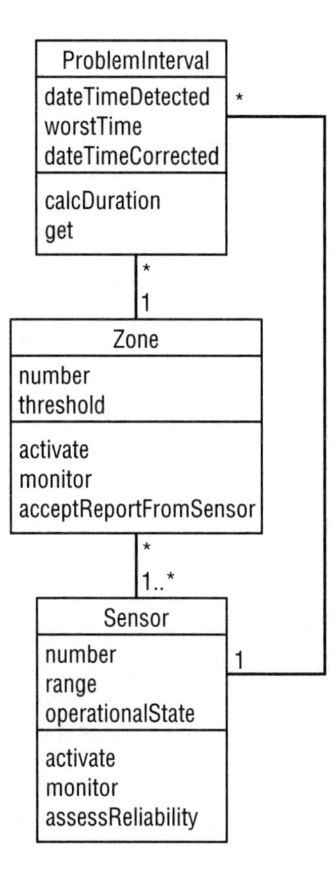

Figure 1-26b. Object model—PD component (UML notation).

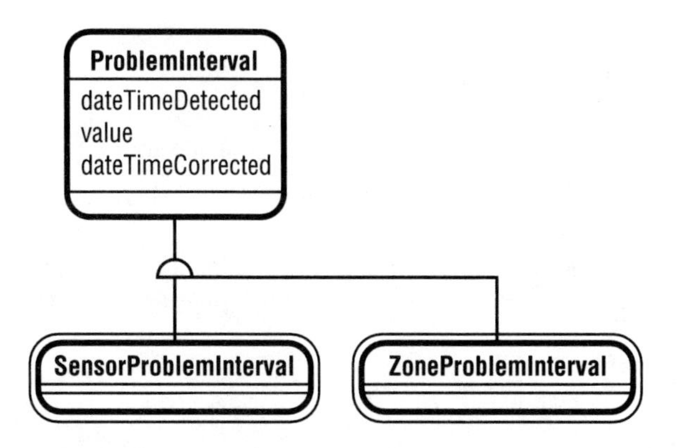

Figure 1-27. Kinds of problem reports.

However, the only difference between the two specialization classes is the kind of (sensor or zone).

Using specialization classes to describe what is nothing more than an enumeration of values is definitely overkill.

Hence, for now, a problem-interval class, as shown earlier in Figure 1-26, will do the trick:

- Problem interval

  attribute: date and time detected, value, date and time corrected

  connection: either sensor or zone, but not both.

1.4.5.4 Object Connections—Some Notes

The object connection between a problem report and its sensor or zone tells us what kind of problem report it is; so we don't even need an explicit "type" attribute. (If and when we need to know, we can ask the connecting object whether it is an instance of sensor or an instance of zone.)

Note the "[XOR A] 1" constraints in Figure 1-26a. Here, it indicates that each problem interval object has an object connection to a sensor or to a zone, not both (hence, the exclusive or notation).

```
public class ProblemInterval extends Object {
✂
    // attribute / private / object connection
    private Object reporter;

    // methods / public / accessors for object connection values
    public void addReporter(Object aReporter) {
        this.reporter = aReporter; }
    public Object getReporter() { return this.reporter; }
    public void removeReporter() { this.reporter = null; }
✂
}
```

Code notes: The reporter variable holds the connection to either a Zone or a Sensor. The class of object held in the connection can be determined by asking the object for its class.

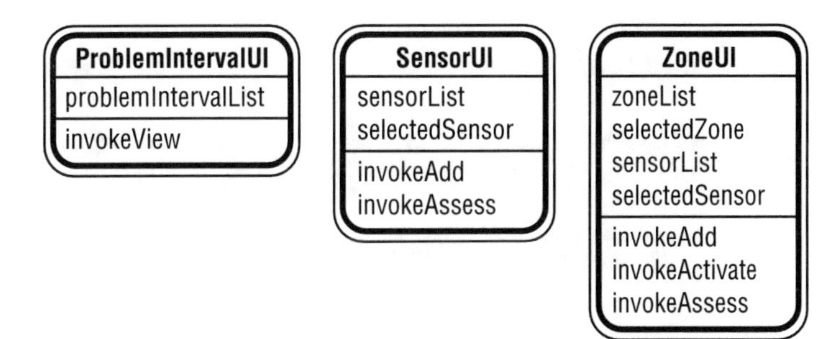

Figure 1-28. Object model—UI component.

1.4.5.5 Object Model—UI Component

Figure 1-28 depicts the UI component for Zoe's Zones.

1.5 Summary

In this chapter, you've worked with scenario views and object models for a business application (Charlie's Charters) and a real-time system (Zoe's Zones).

Along the way, you've learned and applied scenario-view notation (showing a time-ordered sequence of object interactions) and object-model notation (showing the responsibilities of each class of objects and each object within that class).

You've worked with these specific strategies for designing better apps:

Identify Purpose Strategy: *State the purpose of the system in 25 words or less.*

Identify Features Strategy: *List the features for setting up and conducting the business and assessing business results.*

Select Classes Strategy: *Feature by feature, look for: role-player, role, transaction (moment or interval), place, container, or catalog-like* *description. For real-time systems, also look for data acquisition and control devices.*

UI Content Strategy: *Feature by feature, establish content: selections, lists, entry fields, display fields, actions, assessments.*

High-Value Scenarios Strategy: *Build scenario views that will exercise each "conducting business" and "assessing results" feature.*

Action Sentence Strategy: *Describe the action in a complete sentence. Put the action in the object (person, place, or thing) that has the "what I know" and "who I know" to get the job done.*

Build an Object Model Strategy:

Start with scenario classes and methods.

Add attributes—content for methods.

Add attributes—content for the UI.

Add object connections—message paths for methods.

Add object connections—look-up paths for the UI.

We're on our way!

Chapter 2

Design with Composition, Rather than Inheritance

Composition and inheritance are both mechanisms for extending a design.

A number of years ago (and perhaps still, in the minds of some designers), inheritance was the only tool for extending responsibilities, and designers used it *everywhere.*

But extending responsibilities with inheritance is applicable only in very specific contexts. In nearly every case, extending the responsibilities with interfaces or with composition is more appropriate.

Use *composition* to extend responsibilities by delegating work to other more appropriate objects.

Use *inheritance* to extend attributes and methods. Note, however, with inheritance, encapsulation is inherently weak within a class hierarchy, so it's a good idea to use this mechanism only when certain criteria are met.

2.1 Composition

Composition extends the responsibilities of an object by delegating work to additional objects.

Composition is *the* major mechanism for extending the responsibilities of an object. Nearly every object in an object model is composed of, knows of, or works with other objects (composition).

2.1.1 Composition: An Example

Here's the strategy.

Composition Strategy: *Use Composition to extend responsibilities by delegating work to other objects.*

Figure 2-1 shows an example from Charlie's Charters. In this case, passenger objects need to have the ability to hold reservations.

This is an example of composition: a passenger object is a composition of some number of reservation objects.

How about in the other direction? A reservation object must have a single connection back to a passenger object.

Just a single connection? That's okay. We usually don't consider a single connection as a composition, though. So we would not expect to use composition had it been only a 1-1 connection.

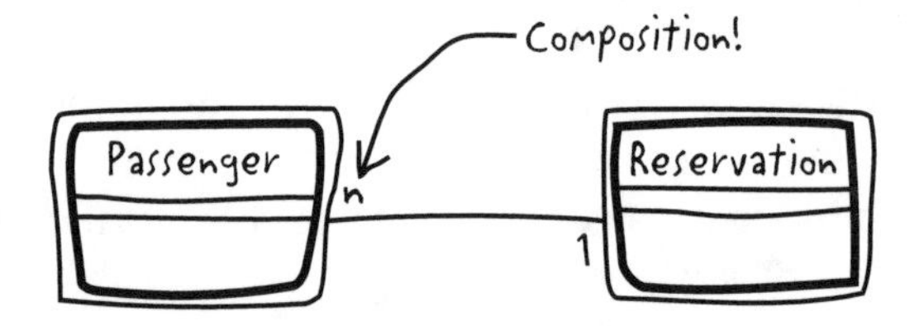

Figure 2-1. A passenger object is able to hold reservation objects.

So please note: composition is at work whenever you see an object connection constraint that is anything other than "1." For example,

0-1

2

n

1-n

all indicate composition is at work.*

2.2 Inheritance

Inheritance is a mechanism for extending the responsibilities defined in a class, meaning, to take the defined attributes, object connections, and methods of a base class and *add to them* in some way.

We can define basic common attributes, object connections, and methods in a superclass (generalization class). Then we can add to them in one or more subclasses (specialization classes).

A subclass inherits everything that is defined in its superclass, accepting the superclass' definitions as its own.

2.2.1 Inheritance vs. Interfaces

Inheritance extends the *implementation of a method*, not just its interface.

*A special kind of composition is called containment. It describes a composition in which the objects inside are hidden from all outsiders; access to what is inside is strictly limited to access via the container object. Most composition is *not* containment. A passenger object, with regard to its reservation objects, is composition, but not containment. A passenger object, with regard to its internal low-level objects such as strings, is often a container—a special kind of composition.

An interface establishes *useful sets of method signatures*, without implying an implementation of a method.

In Java, inheritance and polymorphism are expressed distinctly with different syntax.

In C++, both concepts are expressed with a single syntax blurring the distinction between these very different mechanisms.

2.2.2 Inheritance: An Example

Inheritance is great for showing a class that is always a special variant of its "parent" class. Within a PD component of an object model, inheritance most often occurs in three situations (Figure 2-2).

For example, consider transactions (notable moments or intervals of time). If our scope were to expand a bit at Charlie's Charters, we might discover that we need an object model like the one depicted in Figure 2-3.

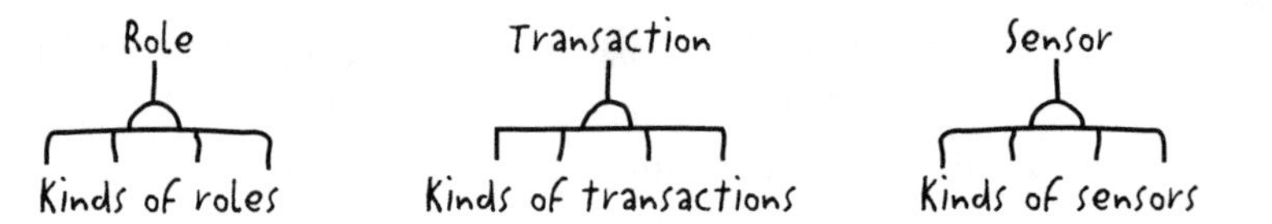

Figure 2-2. The three most likely kinds of inheritance within a PD component of an object model.

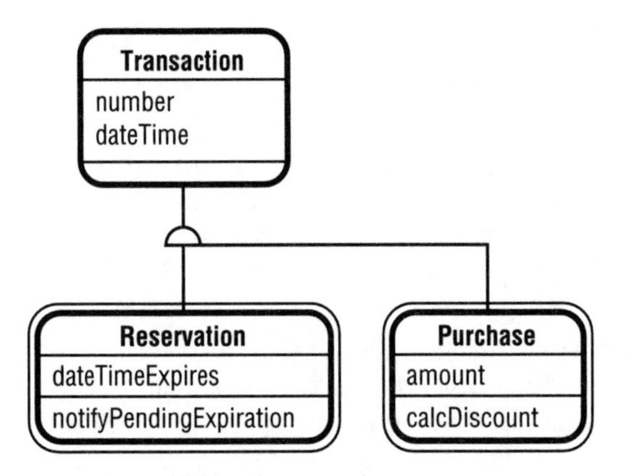

Figure 2-3. Kinds of transactions.

A reservation is a special kind of transaction. A purchase is a special kind of transaction. So far, so good.

2.2.3 Inheritance: Benefits

Inheritance explicitly captures commonality, taking a class definition (what's the same: attributes, method signatures, and methods) and extending it with a new class definition (what's different: attributes, method signatures, and methods).

Inheritance is explicitly shown in an object model and in source code—something very nice indeed; so it's good to use, when it's appropriate to do so.

So, what are the risks?

2.2.4 Inheritance: Risks

Yes, inheritance does have its risks. Let's take a closer look at them.

2.2.4.1 Weak Encapsulation Within

Risk #1 Inheritance connotes strong encapsulation with other classes, but weak encapsulation between a superclass and its subclasses.

The classes within a class hierarchy, with respect to each other, violate the spirit of encapsulation, a fundamental tenet of object-oriented design. Subclasses are not well shielded from the potential ripple effect of changes in superclasses.

If you change a superclass, we must check all of its subclasses to correct any rippling change effects (Figure 2-4). Here's why. If we change the implementation of a class that is a superclass, then we have effectively changed the implementation of all its subclasses (testers, please take note).

Figure 2-4. A change in a superclass ripples throughout its subclasses.

Obviating risk #1 We can obviate this risk by designing a cohesive class hierarchy. We make sure the subclass is indeed a special kind of the superclass, not merely

- a factoring-out of common method implementations (a hard-to-understand, even harder to reuse hacker's trick), or
- a role played by the superclass (composition is a more flexible, more scalable way to model roles played).

Also, we make sure that subclasses are indeed extensions. If we find the need to override or nullify inherited responsibilities, then we can

- introduce new superclasses (if you can), including one with exactly what you need to inherit (no more, no less), or
- define the class elsewhere. Then we use composition to invoke whatever responsibilities we might need from the class hierarchy we shunned. (If you'd like to interact exactly like the objects in that hierarchy, just add an interface [see Chapter 3].)

2.2.4.2 Clumsy Accommodation of Objects That Change Subclasses

Risk #2 Inheritance connotes weak accommodation of objects that change subclasses over time.

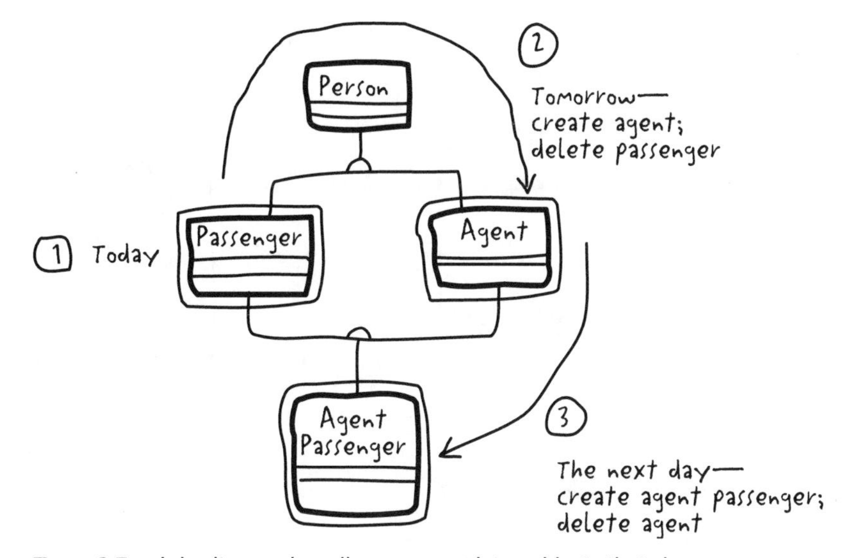

Figure 2-5. Inheritance clumsily accommodates objects that change subclasses.

For example, consider Person and its specializations, as shown in Figure 2-5.

What if we create an agent object, but later find out that we need an agent-passenger object? Consider the transition from an agent object to an agent-passenger object. Figure 2-6 illustrates what happens.

Every time an object in one subclass needs to change into an object in another class, we encounter the "transmute" problem: create an object in another class, copy values to the new object, then delete the old object.

When an object in our design transmutes, we might lose information. If the values are not needed in the new object, the old values go away.

Also, when an object transmutes, it loses all sense of history (even the question, "so how long have you been an agent?" is not easily answered, and requires additional classes to track such change over time). This makes change far more complex than it needs to be.

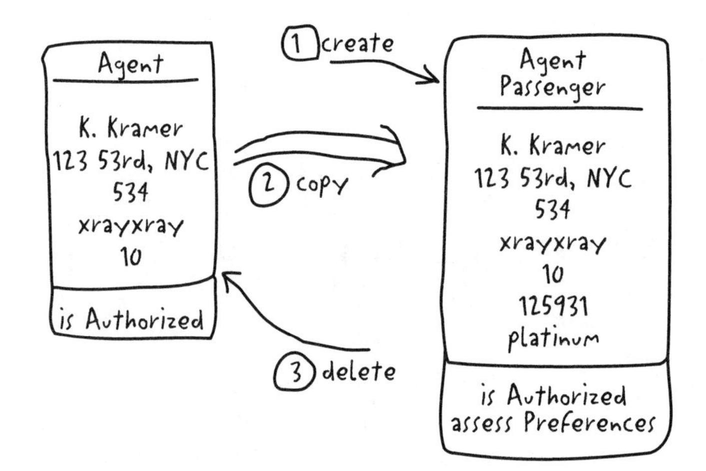

Figure 2-6. Create, copy, delete—"transmute."

Obviating risk #2 Use composition of roles to obviate the risk. Composition is far better suited to continual change.

When an object needs additional role-specific responsibilities, add another role object (composition).

Adding a new role is easy. In fact, with kinds of roles, we could apply composition (a person and its roles) *and* inheritance (person roles, specializing into special kinds of roles). See Figure 2-7.

2.2.5 Inheritance: When to Use It

In bibliographic classification, developers of classification methods strive to find a way to classify objects (publications) so that

1. a subclass expresses "is a special kind of," not "is a role played by a"
2. an object, once classified, will forever remain an object in that class.

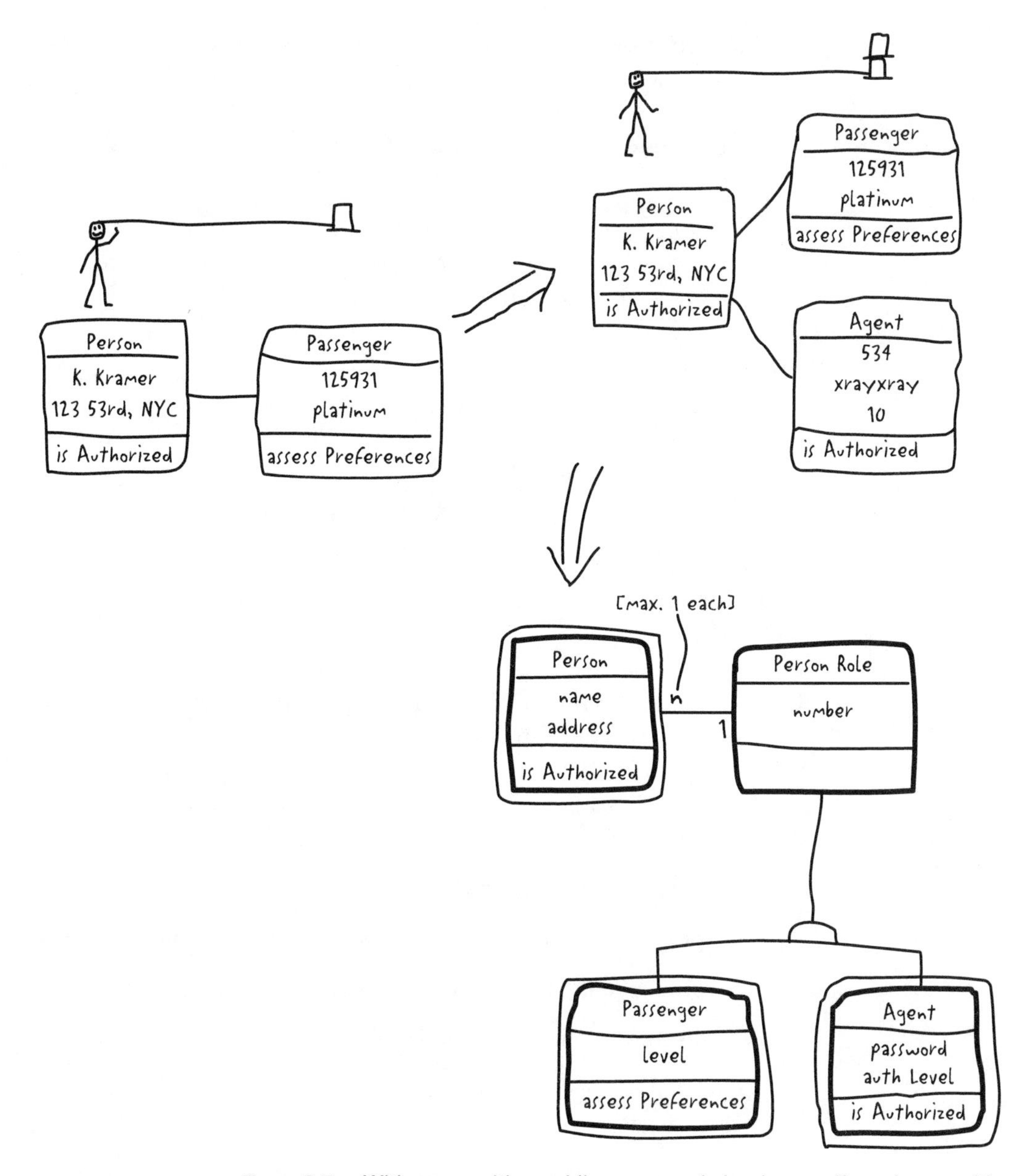

Figure 2-7. With composition, adding a new role is a breeze; if you have multiple kinds of roles, then inheritance can play along too.

In software classification, one strives to find a way to classify objects (publications) so that

1. subclass expresses "is a special kind of," not "is a role played by a"
2. an object, once classified, will forever remain an object in that class (it does not ever feel the need to transmute, to become an object in some other class).

In software classification, we add

3. a subclass extends, rather than overrides or nullifies, the responsibilities of its superclass
4. a subclass does not extend the capabilities of what is merely a utility class (useful functionality you'd like to reuse)
5. for PD classes, a subclass is a type of role played, transaction, or device.

Here's how item 5 fits in. We use inheritance in the PD component of an object model in three major ways:

- Role, specializing into special kinds of "participant" or "mission" roles

  a role that a person plays:

    person role (passenger, clerk, head clerk, manager, owner)

  a role that a facility or piece of equipment plays:

    aircraft mission (civilian mission, military mission)

- Transaction, specializing into special kinds of transactions (moments or intervals of time)

  customer transaction (membership, reservation, payment, refund)

- Device, specializing into special kinds of devices

  radar sensor (passive radar sensor, active radar sensor).

2.2.6 Inheritance: Checkpoints

The following strategy lists the five checkpoints for effective use of inheritance (Figure 2-8).

When to Inherit Strategy: *Inheritance is used to extend attributes and methods; but encapsulation is weak within a class hierarchy, so use of this mechanism is limited. Use it when you can satisfy the following criteria:*

1. *"Is a special kind of," not "is a role played by a"*
2. *Never needs to transmute to be an object in some other class*
3. *Extends rather than overrides or nullifies superclass*
4. *Does not subclass what is merely a utility class (useful functionality you'd like to reuse)*
5. *Within PD: expresses special kinds of roles, transactions, or devices*

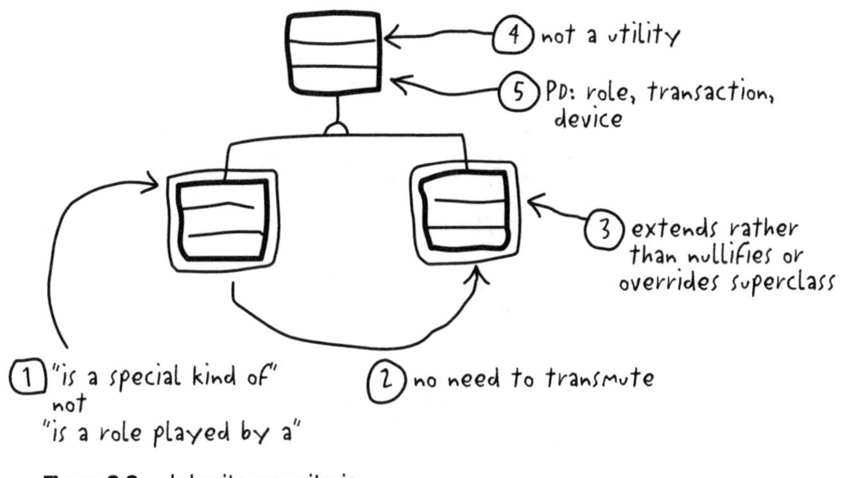

Figure 2-8. Inheritance criteria.

2.3 Example: Composition (the Norm)

Consider a person and the roles he or she plays, the hats he or she wears: passenger and agent. Composition is the norm rather than the exception.

However, could we apply inheritance with person as a superclass, plus passenger, agent, and agent-passenger as subclasses? (See Figure 2-9.)

Well, in Java we can't do that. It's a single-inheritance language, and the agent-passenger class inherits from more than one class—multiple inheritance.

Even if multiple inheritance were available, as it is in C++, is this an occasion to use inheritance, or would composition be better?

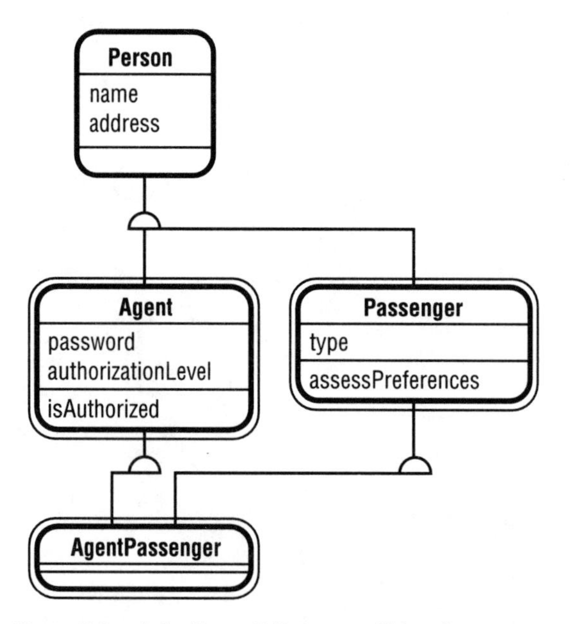

Figure 2-9. Inheritance? Not a good idea, here.

Apply the checkpoints strategy and check it out:

1. "Is a special kind of," not "is a role played by a"

   Fail. A passenger is not a kind of person; it's a role a person plays. An agent is not a kind of person; it's a role that a person plays.

2. Never needs to transmute to be an object in some other class

   Fail. It could change from passenger to agent to agent passenger, over time.

3. Extends rather than overrides or nullifies

   Pass. Okay here.

4. Does not subclass what is merely a utility class

   Pass. Okay here.

5. Within PD: Expresses special kinds of roles, transactions, or devices

   Fail. This is not a kind of role, transaction, or device.

Inheritance? No way. Composition applies here as is true in most cases of building better object models. It's the norm.

Take a look at Charlie's Charters. We could pick any association in the object model and find composition hard at work. Figure 2-10 provides an example (with a couple of methods, for good measure).

In Java, it looks like this:

```
public class Person extends Object {
✂
    // attributes / private / object connections
    private Passenger passenger;
    private Agent agent;

    // methods / public / accessors for object connection values
    public void addPassenger(Passenger aPassenger) {
        this.passenger = aPassenger; }
```

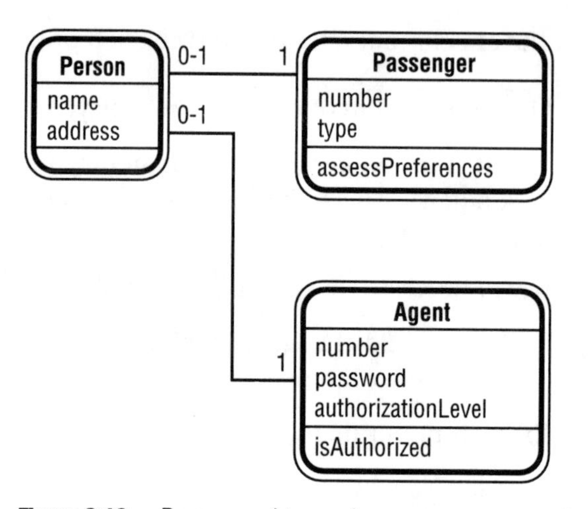

Figure 2-10. Person and two roles: passenger, agent.

```
    public void removePassenger() { this.passenger = null; }
    public Passenger getPassenger() { return this.passenger; }
    public void addAgent(Agent anAgent) {
        this.agent = anAgent; }
    public void removeAgent() { this.agent = null; }
    public Agent getAgent() { return this.agent; }
✂
}
public class Passenger extends Object {
✂
    // attributes / private / object connections
    private Person person;

    // methods / public / accessors for object connection values
    public Person getPerson() { return this.person; }

    // constructors
    // notice that there is no *default* constructor; a passenger must have
    // a corresponding person object.
    public Passenger(Person aPerson) {
        // implicit call to superclass constructor super();
        this.person = aPerson; }
✂
}
```

```
public class Agent extends Object {
✂
    // attributes / private / object connections
    private Person person;


    // methods / public / accessors for object connection values
    public Person getPerson() { return this.person; }

    // constructors
    // note that there is no *default* constructor; an agent must have
    // a corresponding person object.
    public Agent(Person aPerson) {
        // implicit call to superclass constructor super();
        this.person = aPerson; }
✂
}
```

Code notes: Each passenger object and agent object requires a corresponding person object. Therefore, for Passenger and Agent, we create a constructor that requires a person object, but we purposely do not provide a default constructor.

2.4 Example: Both Composition and Inheritance

Yes, passenger and agent are special kinds of person roles.

So, we can apply composition (person and its roles) in tandem with inheritance (person roles and special kinds of person roles), as shown in Figure 2-11.

If we check the inheritance usage criteria this time, we find:

1. "Is a special kind of," not "is a role played by a"

   Pass. Passenger and agent are special kinds of person roles (not roles that a "person role" plays).

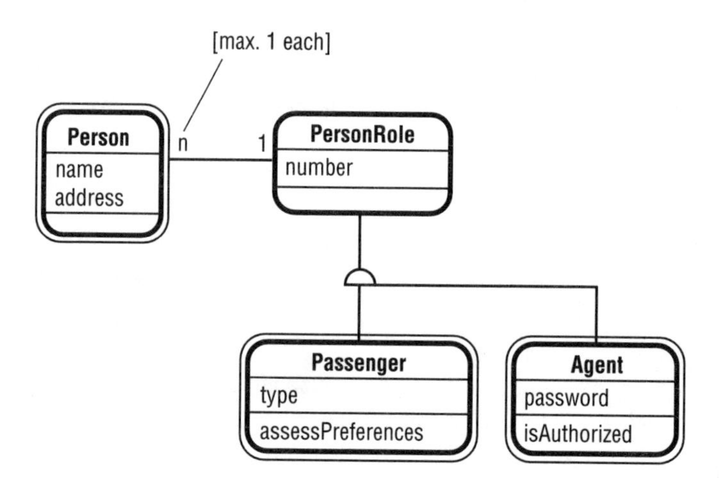

Figure 2-11. A person and its roles (composition); roles and special kinds of roles (inheritance).

2. Never needs to transmute to be an object in some other class

   Pass. A passenger object forever stays a passenger object; there is no need to transmute it to an object in some other class; the same is true for agent.

3. Extends rather than overrides or nullifies

   Pass. Both subclasses extend the responsibilities defined in the superclass.

4. Does not subclass what is merely a utility class

   Pass. Okay here.

5. Within PD: Expresses special kinds of roles, transactions, or devices.

   Pass. Now we have special kinds of roles. All is well.

A nice combination! Cool.

In Java, it looks like this:

```
public class Person extends Object {
✂
    // attributes / private / object connections
    private Vector roles = new Vector();
```

```
    // methods / public / accessors for object connection values
    public void addRole(PersonRole aRole) {
        this.roles.addElement( aRole); }
    public void removeRole(PersonRole aRole) {
        this.roles.removeElement(aRole); }
    public Enumeration getRoles() {
        return this.roles.elements(); }
✂
}
```

Code notes: The above code does not check for an existing role when a role is added. That is, a person can add many agent roles to its list of roles.

```
public abstract class PersonRole extends Object {
✂
    // attributes / private / object connections
    private Person person;

    // methods / public / accessors for object connection values
    public Person getPerson() { return this.person; }

    // constructors
    // note that there is no *default* constructor; a person role must have
    // a corresponding person object.
    public PersonRole(Person aPerson) {
        // implicit call to superclass constructor super();
        this.person = aPerson; }
✂
}

public class Passenger extends PersonRole {
✂
    // constructors
    // notice that there is no *default* superclass constructor;
    // an explicit call to the superclass constructor is required.
    public Passenger(Person aPerson) { super( aPerson); }
✂
}
```

```
public class Agent extends PersonRole {
✂
    // constructors
    // notice that there is no *default* superclass constructor;
    // an explicit call to the superclass constructor is required.
    public Agent(Person aPerson) { super( aPerson); }
✂
}
```

Code notes: Since Java implicitly creates a default constructor for a class without a constructor, and since the default constructor includes an implicit call to the superclass' default constructor, both Passenger and Agent require a constructor that calls PersonRole's nondefault constructor.

2.5 Example: Inheritance (the Exception)

Consider an example for Charlie's Charters. Suppose that we expand the context for the moment to include both reservations and purchases.

Extend the responsibilities expressed by the model to include purchases. We have two special kinds of transactions to deal with: reservation and purchase. Add a generalization class, called "transaction." Then extend it with two specialization classes, reservation and purchase.

Now we have two special kinds of transactions (moments or intervals of time): reservation and purchase. Some reservation objects will have a corresponding purchase object.

Figure 2-12 illustrates this concept in object-model notation.

But is this a good use of inheritance? After all, we could use composition (Figure 2-13).

However, we'd like to get the benefit of inheritance in those special cases where it is applicable. After all, explicitly capturing commonality in an object model and in source code is a very attractive thing.

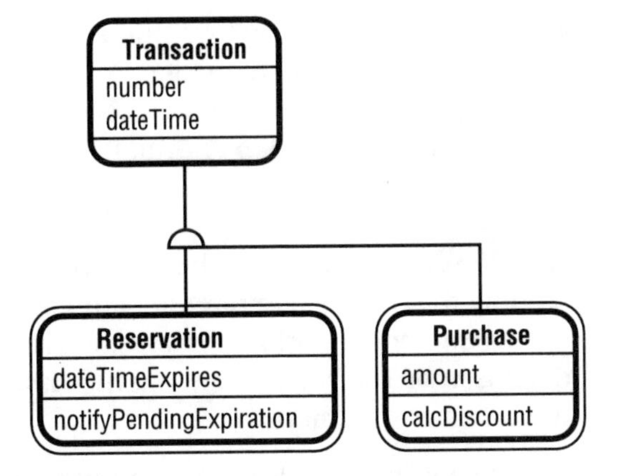

Figure 2-12. Special kinds of transactions.

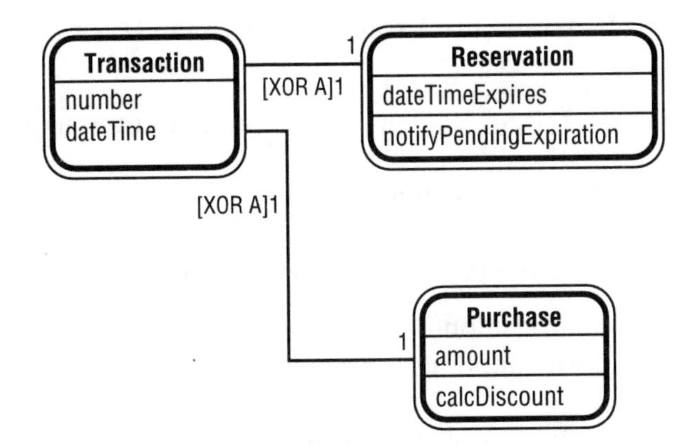

Figure 2-13. Use composition instead? Not here.

So check out this use of inheritance, using the five-part checklist:

1. "Is a special kind of," not "is a role played by a"

   Pass. Reservation is a special kind of Transaction (not a role that a transaction plays); Purchase is a special kind of Transaction (not a role that a transaction plays).

2. Never needs to transmute to be an object in some other class

   Pass. A reservation object stays a reservation object, even if we create a corresponding purchase object at some point along the way. In fact, a reservation object might need to know its corresponding purchase object. (Egad! That means composition between objects in the subclasses. Composition is indeed the norm; it is nearly everywhere.)

3. Extends rather than overrides or nullifies

   Pass. Reservation extends the definition of Transaction (adding the dateTimeExpires attribute and the notifyPendingExpiration method); Purchase extends the definition of Transaction (adding the amount attribute and the calcDiscount method).

4. Does not subclass what is merely a utility class

   Pass. Okay here.

5. Within PD: Expresses special kinds of roles, transactions, or devices.

   Pass. Here, it's special kinds of transactions.

We could use both inheritance and composition here:

- inheritance—for special kinds of transactions
- composition—a reservation object is composed of a corresponding purchase object.

See Figure 2-14 for the result.

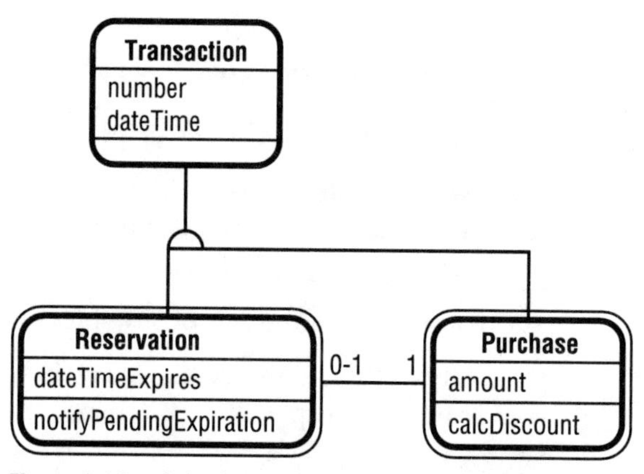

Figure 2-14. Inheritance with a little composition too.

Here's how it looks in Java:

```
public class Transaction extends Object {
✂
    // attributes / private
    private int number;
    private Date dateTime;

    // methods / public / accessors for attribute values
    public int getNumber() { return this.number; }
    public void setNumber(int aNumber) { this.number = aNumber; }
    public Date getDate() { return this.dateTime; }
    public void setDate(Date aDateTime) { this.dateTime = aDateTime; }
✂
}

public class Reservation extends Transaction {
✂
    // attributes / private
    private Date dateTimeExpires;

    // attributes / private / object connections
    private Purchase purchase;

    // methods / public / accessors for attribute values
    public Date getDateTimeExpires() { return this.dateTimeExpires; }
    public void setDateTimeExpires(Date aDateTime) {
        this.dateTimeExpires = aDateTime; }

    // methods / public / accessors for object connection values
    public void addPurchase(Purchase aPurchase) {
        this.purchase = aPurchase; }
    public void removePurchase() { this.purchase = null; }
    public Passenger getPurchase() { return this.purchase; }
✂
}

public class Purchase extends Transaction {
✂
    // attributes / private
    private float amount;
```

```
// attributes / private / object connections
private Reservation reservation;

// methods / public / accessors for attribute values
public float getAmount() { return this.amount; }
public void setAmount(float anAmount) { this.amount = anAmount; }

// methods / public / accessors for object connection values
public Reservation getReservation() { return this.reservation; }

// constructors
// note that there is no *default* constructor; a purchase must have
// a corresponding reservation.
public Purchase(Reservation aReservation) {
    // implicit call to superclass constructor super();
    this.reservation = aReservation; }
✂
}
```

2.6 Example: Inheritance in Need of Adjustment

Let's consider another possibility. Switch over to Zoe's Zones for this one.

Remember the sensor class? Figure 2-15 illustrates this as well as the object connection to some number of problem intervals, to round out this example.

Now we find out that we will be working with remote sensors too. Instead of activating and monitoring a remote sensor, all we can do is request a reading from it (getting back a value and its operational state).

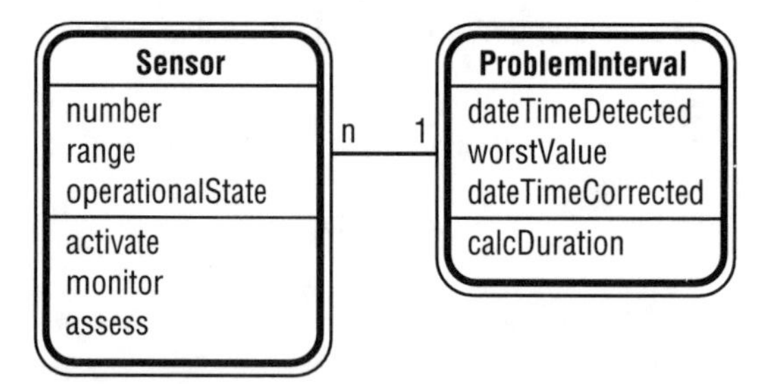

Figure 2-15. A sensor and its problem intervals.

Extend the responsibilities expressed by the model to include a new kind of sensor. Extend the Sensor class with one specialization class, RemoteSensor.

But for a remote sensor object we don't need an object connection to a problem interval. Nor do we need activate, monitor, or assess for interacting with a remote sensor. The X's in the figure mark the things a remote sensor nullifies; they're not needed, and are never used.

We could add a subclass (Figure 2-16).

Maybe we were a bit hasty in our subclassing. Was this a good use of inheritance? Pull out the checklist one more time:

1. "Is a special kind of," not "is a role played by a"

   Pass. Remote Sensor is a special kind of Sensor (not a role that a sensor plays)

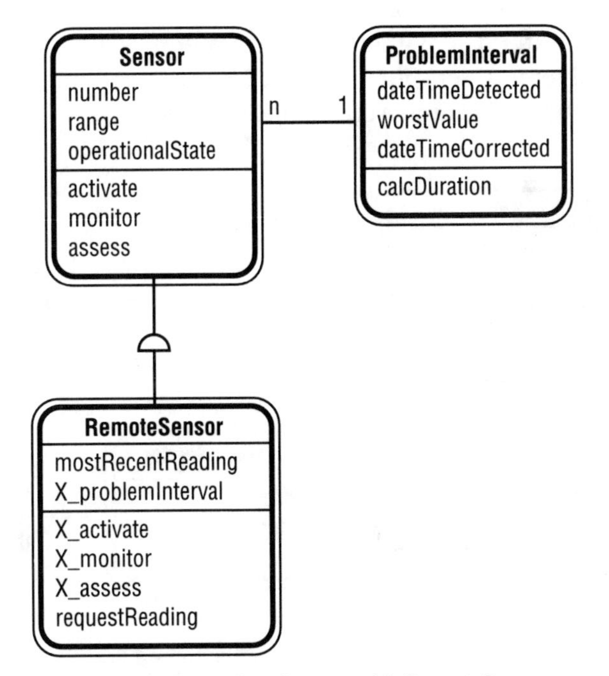

Figure 2-16. Extending Sensor with RemoteSensor.

2. Never needs to transmute to be an object in some other class

   Pass. A remote sensor remains a remote sensor that is not under our direct control.

3. Extends, rather than overrides or nullifies

   Fail. Ahhh, here's the catch. The remote sensor class nullifies, has no use for a connection to problem interval or the method trio (activate, monitor, assess).

4. Does not subclass what is merely a utility class

   Pass. Okay here.

5. Within PD: Expresses special kinds of roles, transactions, or devices.

   Pass. Here, it's a special kind of device.

We're close. Inheritance does apply, we just need to rearrange the hierarchy a bit.

Try this: extend the responsibilities expressed by the model to include activatable sensors and remote sensors. We have two special kinds of sensors to deal with: activatable sensors and remote sensors. We can keep a generalization class, called "sensor." Then we can extend it with two specialization classes, activatable sensor and remote sensor (Figure 2-17). The ProblemInterval remains connected only at the ActivatableSensor level.

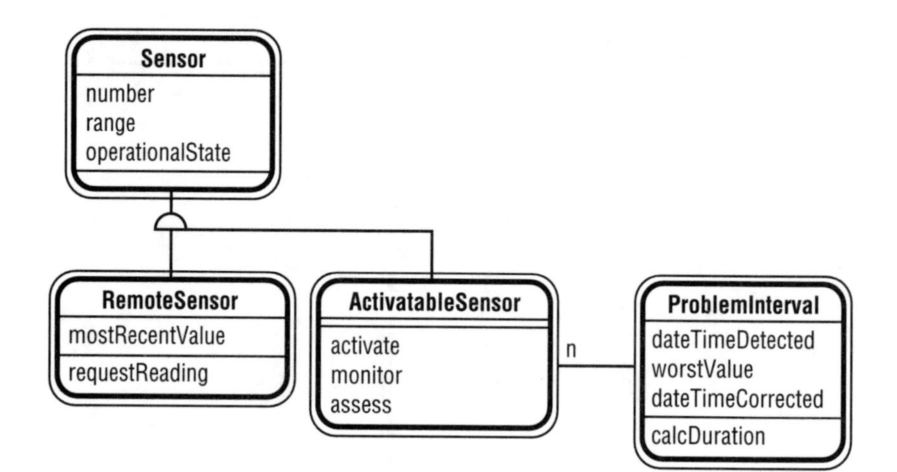

Figure 2-17a. Rearranging the class hierarchy a bit.

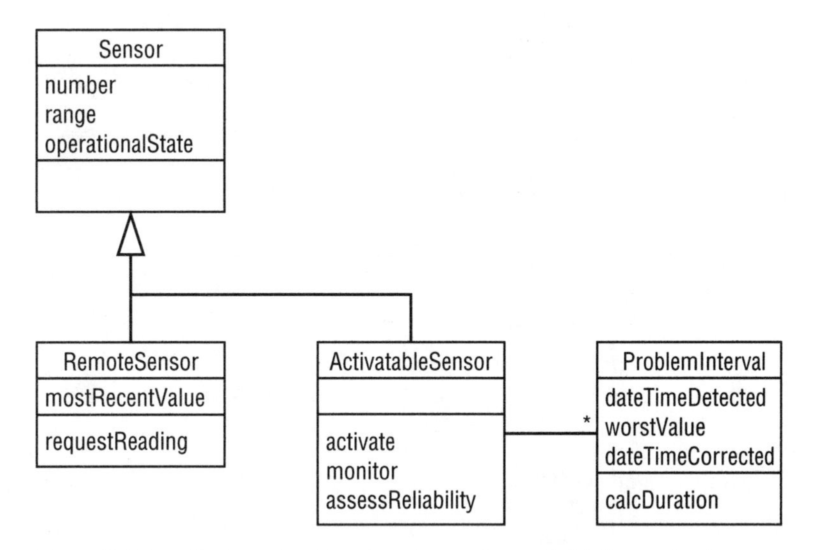

Figure 2-17b. Rearranging the class hierarchy a bit (UML notation).

Now checklist criterion number 3 is satisfied (extends, rather than nullifies) along with the others. We've made it—good inheritance!

2.7 Example: Thread

Suppose we want to add a thread (a copy of a program, running with the same data as other copies of that program) to an object model.

Is it time for composition, or inheritance? (See Figure 2-18.)

The outer rounded rectangle around the superclass indicates that one might have objects of that class, too. (In other words, it's a concrete class, not an abstract class.)

In Java, it looks like this:

```
public class Sensor extends Thread {
✂
    // attributes / private
    private int number;
    private int range;
```

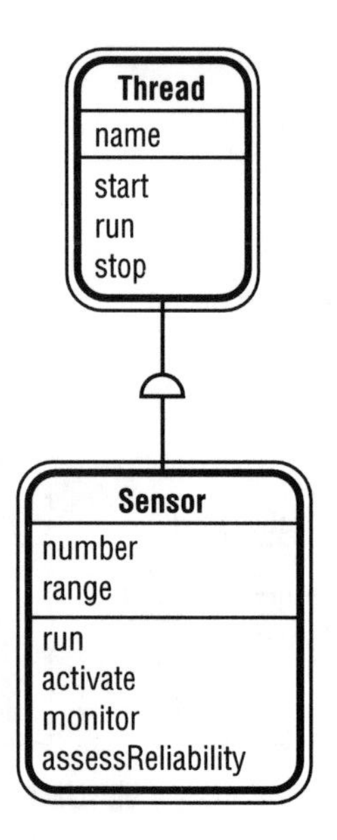

Figure 2-18. A kind of thread?

```
    // methods / public / override
    public void run () { /* code goes here */ }
✂
}
```

Again, consider the exception: inheritance. Is a sensor a kind of thread? Does specialization apply here?

1. "Is a special kind of," not "is a role played by a"

   Fail. A sensor is not a kind of thread.

2. Never needs to transmute to be an object in some other class

   Pass. Okay here.

3. Extends, rather than overrides or nullifies

   Pass. Okay here.

4. Does not subclass what is merely a utility class

   Pass. Okay here.

5. Within PD: Expresses special kinds of roles, transactions, or devices.

Not applicable (Thread is an infrastructure class, not a PD class)

Composition to the rescue. Here's how it works. The Java runtime system manages threads. We define a sensor class with a "run" method. We create a sensor object; we create a thread object. Finally, we send the sensor object to the thread object, asking it to run what we are passing to it.

Extend the responsibilities of a sensor object with a thread object (Figure 2-19).

The Thread class comes with Java. Here's what the Sensor class looks like in Java:

```
public class Sensor extends Object implements Runnable {
✂
    // attributes / private
    private int number;
    private int range;

    // attributes / private / object connections
    private Thread monitorThread;
    private Thread assessThread;

    // methods / public / Runnable implementation
    public void run() { /* code goes here */ }
✂
}
```

We'll spend more time on threads in Chapter 4.

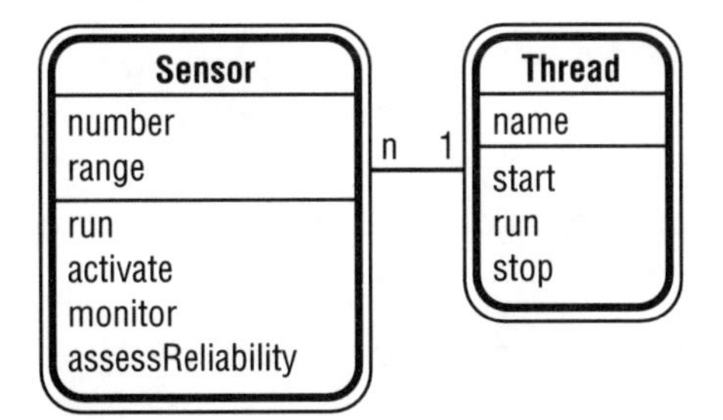

Figure 2-19. A sensor and its threads.

2.8 Example: Applet

Now take a look at the Applet class in Java.

Inheritance chain: Applet is a special kind of Panel is a special kind of Container is a special kind of Component is a special kind of Object (Figure 2-20).

Is this a good use of inheritance? Check it out:

1. "Is a special kind of," not "is a role played by a"

   Pass. Applet is a special kind of Panel, is a special kind of Container, is a special kind of Component, is a special kind of Object—not a role played.

2. Never needs to transmute to be an object in some other class

   Pass. An applet remains an applet.

3. Extends, rather than overrides or nullifies

   Pass. An applet extends what a panel is all about.

4. Does not subclass what is merely a utility class

   Pass. Okay here.

5. Within PD: Expresses special kinds of roles, transactions, or devices.

   Not applicable (applet is an infrastructure class, not a PD class)

So, yes, this is a good use of inheritance.

When we extend (inherit from) Applet, we get all the goodies for gluing together what we need in an applet. Typically,

- we use some methods as they are (for example: getAudioClip, getImage, play)
- other methods are specific to our applet (for example: init, start, resize, stop, destroy).

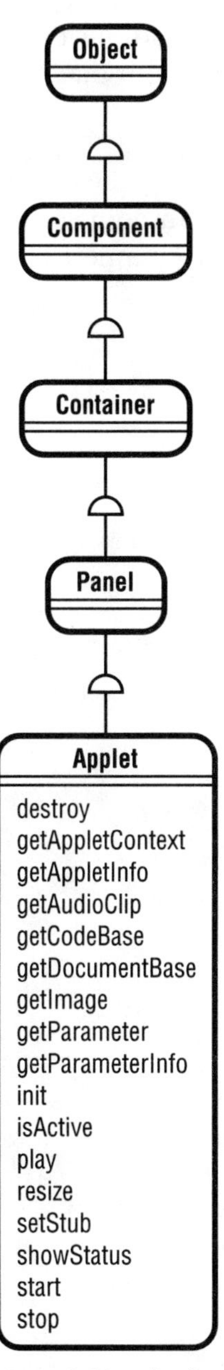

Figure 2-20. Applet and its superclasses.

What happens when we want to add our own special kind of applet? Whoops! By now, the wording of that question should tip us off—"a special kind of."

Add specializations that are indeed special kinds of applets, for example, a "ReservationUI" applet. In doing so, we'll extend the responsibilities of the applet class with inheritance (Figure 2-21).

Here's what it looks like in Java:

```
public class ReservationUI_Applet extends Applet {
✂
    // methods / public / Applet override
    public void init() {
        /* initialization code goes here */ }
✂
}
```

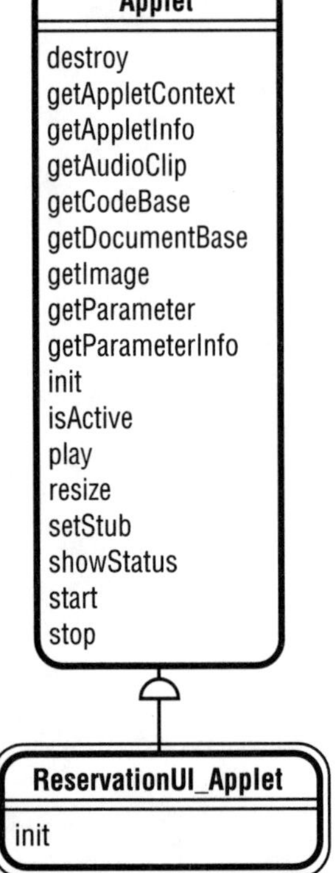

Figure 2-21. A special kind of applet.

2.9 Example: Observable

Now consider the Observable class in Java (Figure 2-22).

Observable is a class that is used in notification. Or at least, it is supposed to be used that way.

Observable consists of a number of methods that make it easier for an observable object to notify other objects about a state change.

Suppose that we make Reservation a subclass of Observable, so it acts as an observable (Figure 2-23). That way, a reservation object can notify other objects (notably UI objects) whenever it changes.

Is this a good use of inheritance? Check it out:

1. "Is a special kind of," not "is a role played by a"

   Fail. A reservation is not a special kind of observable. (Well, maybe, in a real abstract sense. Somehow it doesn't feel right. Let's check the other criteria.)

2. Never needs to transmute to be an object in some other class

   Pass. A reservation object remains a reservation object.

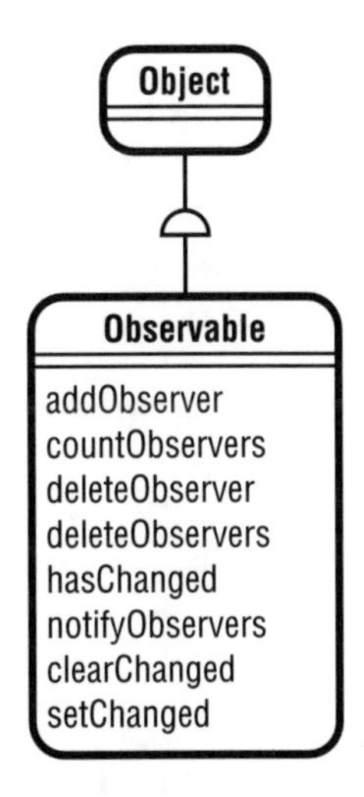

Figure 2-22. Observable and its superclass.

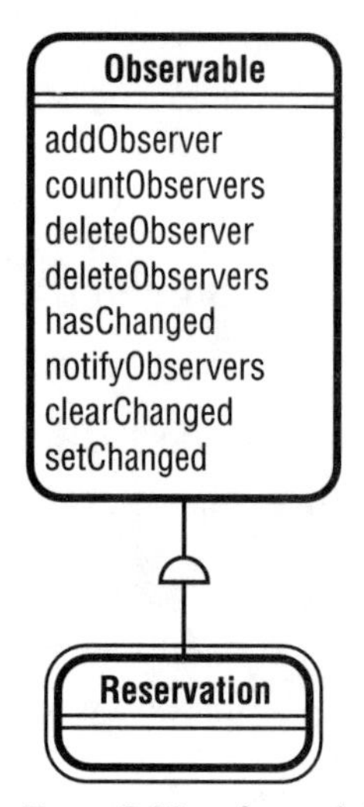

Figure 2-23. A special kind of observable.

3. Extends, rather than overrides or nullifies

   Pass. Reservation extends what Observable is all about.

4. Does not subclass what is merely a utility class

   Fail. Observable is a utility class, a collection of useful methods—nothing more.

5. Within PD: Expresses special kinds of roles, transactions, or devices.

   Not applicable (Observable is a utility class, not a PD class).

So inheritance does *not* apply here, even though it's set up that way in Java.

Don't worry, though. There is an excellent alternative that is discussed in subsequent chapters.

2.10 Summary

We've explored two mechanisms for extending a design: composition and inheritance.

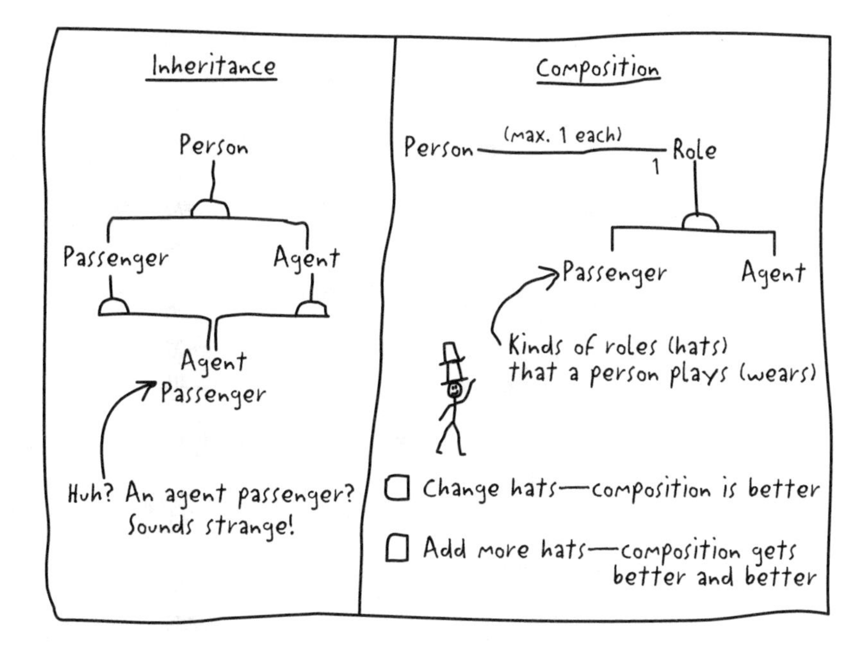

Figure 2-24. Summary: inheritance vs. composition.

Inheritance is useful in limited contexts. Composition is useful in nearly every context (Figure 2-24).

Inheritance was all the rage in the early days of object-oriented development. But over time, designers have discovered that inheritance is effective only within certain contexts.

Composition, in tandem with interfaces (Chapter 3), is far more common, far more generally useful, and much closer to the heart of good object-oriented design.

Here are the strategies that you've learned and applied in this chapter:

Composition Strategy: *Use Composition to extend responsibilities by delegating work to other objects.*

When to Inherit Strategy: *Inheritance is used to extend attributes and methods; but encapsulation is weak within a class hierar-*

chy, so use of this mechanism is limited. Use it when you can satisfy the following criteria:

1. *"Is a special kind of," not "is a role played by a"*
2. *Never needs to transmute to be an object in some other class*
3. *Extends rather than overrides or nullifies superclass*
4. *Does not subclass what is merely a utility class (useful functionality you'd like to reuse)*
5. *Within PD: expresses special kinds of roles, transactions, or devices*

Chapter 3

Design with Interfaces

In this chapter we explore Java-style interfaces: what they are, why they are important, and the four major contexts in which you'll find them helpful.

3.1 What Are Interfaces?

Interfaces are the key to pluggability, the ability to remove one component and replace it with another. Consider the electrical outlets in your home: the interface is well-defined (plug shape, receptacle shape, voltage level, polarity for each prong); you can readily unplug a toaster and plug in a java-maker, and continue on your merry way.

Design with interfaces? Yes!

An *interface* is a collection of method signatures that you define for use again and again in your application. It's a listing of method signatures alone. There is neither a common description, nor any source code behind these method signatures.*

An interface describes a standard protocol, a standard way of interacting with objects in classes that implement the interface.

Working with interfaces requires that we (1) specify the interface and (2) specify that classes implement that interface.

Let's begin with a simple interface, called IName (Figure 3-1). IName consists of two method signatures, the accessors getName and setName.

By convention, interface names are capitalized: the IName interface. References to an object of a class that implements an interface

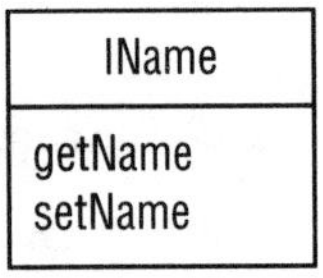

IName
getName setName

Figure 3-1. An interface.

*Java expresses inheritance and polymorphism distinctly with different syntax. C++ expresses both concepts with a single syntax; it blurs the distinction between these very different mechanisms, resulting in overly complex, overly deep class hierarchies. (We design with interfaces regardless of language; Java makes it easier for us to express that design in source code.)

In Smalltalk, interfaces (called protocols) are agreed upon by convention and learned by reading source code. In C++, interfaces are implemented as classes with no default implementation (everything inside is declared as being "pure virtual").

Java interfaces can also include constants. This provides a convenient way to package useful constants when programming, but it has no impact on effective design.

are not capitalized: a name object, meaning, an object in a class that implements IName.

By convention, Java interface names end with the suffix "-able," "-ible," or (occasionally) "-er."*

By convention in SOM and in ActiveX, interface names begin with the prefix "I."

By convention in this book, interface names begin with the prefix "I" and are followed by

- a noun, if it's an accessor interface
- a verb, if it's a calculation interface, or
- a noun or a verb, if it's a combination of interfaces.**

In Figure 3-1 the interface name is "I" + a noun.

In Java, an IName interface might look something like this:

```
public interface IName {
    String getName();
    void setName(String aName); }
```

---

*Requiring interface names to end in -able or -ible is a bit too complicated a convention. However, if you'd like to adopt this convention, take note of the following English-language spelling rules:

1. Drop a silent "e" before adding "-able."
2. Check a dictionary. If the spelling is not listed, look at other forms of the word to see which letter might make sense. (Again, this is a bit too complicated for day-to-day use.)

**Choose whatever prefix convention you prefer: I, I_, Int_; whatever. We prefer "I" (as long as it does not conflict with other prefix conventions of the project).

Person
name
IName

Figure 3-2. A class that promises to implement the IName interface.

A class that implements the IName interface promises to implement the "get name" and "set name" methods in a way that is appropriate for that class. The "get name" method returns the name of an object. The "set name" method establishes a new name for an object (Figure 3-2).

The IName interface describes a standard way to interact with an object in any class that implements that interface.

This means that as an object in any class, you could hold an IName object (that is, objects within any number of classes that implement the IName interface). And you could ask an IName object for its name without knowing or caring about what class that object happens to be in.

3.2 Why Use Interfaces?

3.2.1 The Problem

Over the years, we've encountered a classic barrier to:

- flexibility (graciously accommodating changes in direction)
- extensibility (graciously accommodating add-ons), and
- pluggability (graciously accommodating pulling out one class of objects and inserting another with the same method signatures).

Yes, this is a barrier within object-oriented design.

Some background is in order. All objects interact with other objects to get something done. An object can answer a question or calculate a result all by itself, but even then some other object does the asking. In short, objects interact with other objects. That's why scenario views are so significant, because they model time-ordered sequences of interactions between objects.

The problem in object models and scenario views is that an object must be within a specified class.

What is the element of reuse? It's not just a class; objects in that class are interconnected with objects in other classes. It's some number of classes, the number of classes in a scenario, or even worse, the total number of classes contained in overlapping scenarios.

What's the impact, in terms of pluggability? If you want to add another class of objects, one that can be plugged in as a substitute for an object in another class already in a scenario view, you are in trouble. There is no pluggability here. Instead, you must add object connections, build another scenario view, and implement source code behind it all.*

The problem is that each object connection and each message-send is hardwired to objects in a specific class (or class hierarchy), impeding pluggability, as well as extensibility and flexibility.

Traditionally, objects in a scenario view are hardwired to each other. But if the "what I know" (object connections) and "who I interact with" (object interactions) are hardwired to just one class of objects, then pluggability is nonexistent; adding a new class means adding the class itself, object connections, and scenario views, in addition to making changes to other classes in the design and in source code.

---

*In C++, developers often implement monolithic class hierarchies with a base class that does nothing more than allow the ease of "pluggability" via base class pointers. This is a bulky and limited workaround compared to the elegance of Java interfaces.

3.2.2 A Partial Solution

We'd like a more flexible, extensible, and pluggable approach, one that would let us add in new classes of objects with no change in object connections or message-sends.

There is a partial solution.

If you want to add a new class that is a subclass of one of the classes of objects participating in a scenario, you can do so without any problems. You can add a specialization class to your object model by adding a comment to your scenario view indicating that objects from the specialization class are applicable too, and you are ready to go.

However, if inheritance does not apply, or if you have already used inheritance in some other way (keeping in mind that Java is a single inheritance language), then this partial solution is no solution at all.

3.2.3 Flexibility, Extensibility, and Pluggability— That's Why

Interfaces enhance, facilitate, and even make possible the flexibility, extensibility, and pluggability that we so desire.

Interfaces shift one's thinking about an object and its connections with other objects.

Challenge Each Object Connection Strategy: *Is this connection hardwired only to objects in that class (simpler), or is this a connection to any object that implements a certain interface (more flexible, extensible, pluggable)?*

For an object and its connections to other objects ask, "Is this connection hardwired only to objects in that class, or is this a connection to any object that implements a certain interface?" If it's the latter, you are in effect saying, "I don't care what kind of object I am connected to, just as long as that object implements the interface that I need."

Interfaces also shift one's thinking about an object and the kinds of objects that it interacts with during a scenario.

Challenge Each Message-Send Strategy: *Is this message-send hardwired only to objects in that class (simpler), or is this a message-send to any object that implements a certain interface (more flexible, extensible, pluggable)?*

For each message-send to another object ask, "Is this message-send hardwired only to objects in that class, or is this a message-send to any object that implements a certain interface? If it's the latter, you are in effect saying, "I don't care what kind of object I am sending messages to, just as long as that object implements the interface that I need."

So, when you need flexibility, specify object connections (in object models) and message-sends (in scenario views) to objects in *any* class that implements the interface that is needed, rather than to objects in a *single* class (or its subclasses).

Interfaces loosen up coupling, make parts of a design more interchangeable, and increase the likelihood of reuse—all for a (very) modest increase in design complexity.

Interfaces express "is a kind of" in a very limited way, "is a kind that supports this interface." This gives us the categorization benefits of inheritance; at the same time, it obviates the major weakness of inheritance: weak encapsulation within a class hierarchy.

Interfaces give composition a much broader sphere of influence. With interfaces, composition is flexible, extensible, and pluggable (composed of objects that implement an interface), rather than hardwired to just one kind of object (composed of objects in just one class).

Interfaces reduce the otherwise compelling need to jam many, many classes into a class hierarchy with lots of multiple inheritance. In effect, using interfaces streamlines how one uses inheritance: use interfaces to express generalization-specialization of method signatures (behavior); use inheritance to express generalization-specialization of interfaces implemented—along with additional attributes and methods.

Interfaces give you a way to separate method signatures from method implementations. So you can use them to separate UI method signatures from operating-system dependent method implementations; that's exactly what Java's Abstract Windowing Toolkit (AWT) does. You could do the same for data management, separating method signatures from vendor-dependent method implementations. You also can do the same for problem-domain objects, as you'll see later in this chapter.

Sound-bite summary: Why use interfaces? Interfaces give us a way to establish object connections and message-sends to objects in any class that implements a needed interface, without hardwiring object connections or hardwiring message-sends to a specific class of objects.

The larger the system and the longer the potential life span of a system, the more significant interfaces become.

3.3 Four Major Contexts

Factoring out every method signature into a separate interface would be overkill—you'd make your object models more complex and your scenario views rather abstract.

In what contexts should you apply interfaces?

You can factor out method signatures into interfaces in a variety of contexts, but the following are the four major contexts in which interfaces really help:

Factor out repeaters

Factor out to a proxy

Factor out for analogous apps

Factor out for future expansion.

3.4 Factor Out Repeaters

We begin with the simplest use of interfaces: to factor out common method signatures to bring a higher level of abstraction (and an overall visual simplification) to an object model. This is a modest yet important use of interfaces.

Factor Out Repeaters Strategy: *Factor out method signatures that repeat within your object model. Resolve synonyms into a single signature. Generalize overly specific names into a single signature. Reasons for use: to explicitly capture the common, reusable behavior and to bring a higher level of abstraction into the model.*

Look for repeating method signatures and factor them out.

Example: calcTotal in one class, calcTotal in another class.

Factor out that method signature into an ITotal interface.

Label each class as one that implements the ITotal interface.

Now look for method signatures that are synonyms. Pick a common method signature and factor it out.

Example: calcTotal in one class, determineTotalAmount in another class. Same behavior.

Pick a synonym: calcTotal.

Factor out that method signature, into an ITotal interface.

Label each class as one that implements the ITotal interface.

Next take each method signature and generalize it. (But be careful not to generalize to the point of obscurity; a method name like “process it” or “calculate it” would not be very helpful, would it?)

Then look for method signatures that are synonyms; finally, pick a common method signature and factor it out.

> Example: calcSubtotal in one class, calcTotal in another class, calcGrandTotal in another class
>
> Pick a synonym: calcTotal.
>
> Factor out that method signature into an ITotal interface.
>
> Label each class as one that implements the ITotal interface.

When factoring out interfaces, you also need to consider the return types and the parameter types; they must match up, too. In fact in an object model, you could include a complete method signature:

return type + method name + parameter types + exceptions

But, no matter how well intentioned, this is usually a mistake. It takes up far too much screen real estate. It is far better to have an effective object model of the design plus source code with details, side by side.

3.4.1 Example: The Lunch Counter at Charlie's Charters

Okay then, let's see if we can discover interfaces by applying the "Factor Our Repeaters" strategy. Consider a point-of-sale application for the lunch counter at Charlie's Charters (Figure 3-3).

In Java, it looks like this:

```
public Customer extends Object {
✂
    // methods / public / conducting business
    public float howMuch() { /* code goes here */ }
✂
}
public Sale extends Object {
✂
    // methods / public / conducting business
    public float calcTotal() { /* code goes here */ }
```

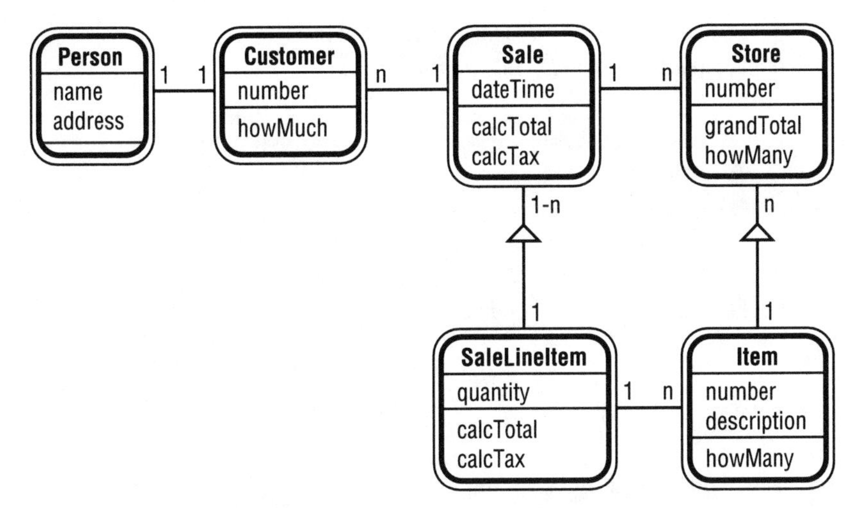

Figure 3-3a. Repeating method signatures.

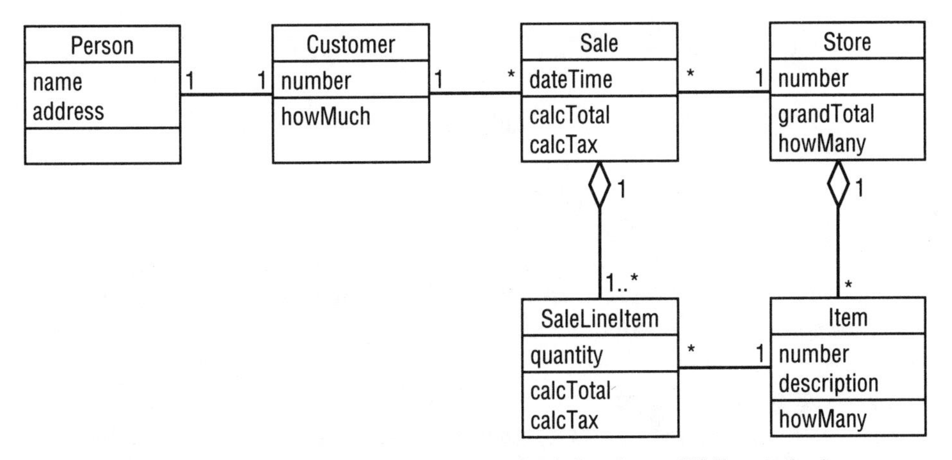

Figure 3-3b. Repeating method signatures (UML notation).

```
}
public SaleLineItem extends Object {
```

```
    // methods / public / conducting business
```

```
    public float calcTotal() { /* code goes here */ }
    public float calcTax() { /* code goes here */ }
✂
}
public Store extends Object {
✂
    // methods / public / conducting business
    public float grandTotal() { /* code goes here */ }
    public int howMany() { /* code goes here */ }
✂
}
public Item extends Object {
✂
    // methods / public / conducting business
    public int howMany() { /* code goes here */ }
✂
}
```

Applying the "factor out repeaters" strategy:

You can factor out calcTotal without any problem.

Now look for synonyms.

The methods calcTotal and howMany could be synonyms, but they have distinct meanings here (adding monetary units versus tallying some items, respectively).

Moreover, the return types don't match. This is a problem. We could check the return types to see if they too are synonyms; or we could try generalizing each return type to see if that helps. In this case, however, calcTotal returns a floating-point number; howMany returns an integer. You cannot combine different method signatures into one interface.

Let's keep looking. The calcTotal and howMuch methods are synonyms, and the return types match (both return a floating-point value). One or the other will do just fine; choose calcTotal and factor it out.

Looking further, grandTotal is a specialized name for calcTotal. Use calcTotal for both.

What are the common method signatures? Let's see.

- howMany—occurs twice
- calcTax—occurs twice
- calcTotal, how much (synonyms here)—occurs four times.

We can factor out those common method signatures, using these interfaces:

- ICount—how many
- ITax—calcTax
- ITotal—calcTotal.

We can go a step further. What common interface combinations are we using?

- ITotal, ITax—occur together, twice.

So we can combine those two interfaces, with this result:

- ISell—ITotal, ITax.

The result? See Figure 3-4.

In Java, it looks like this:

```
public interface ICount {
    int howMany(); }

public interface ITotal {
    float calcTotal(); }

public interface ITax {
    float calcTax(); }

public interface ISell extends ITotal, ITax {}
```

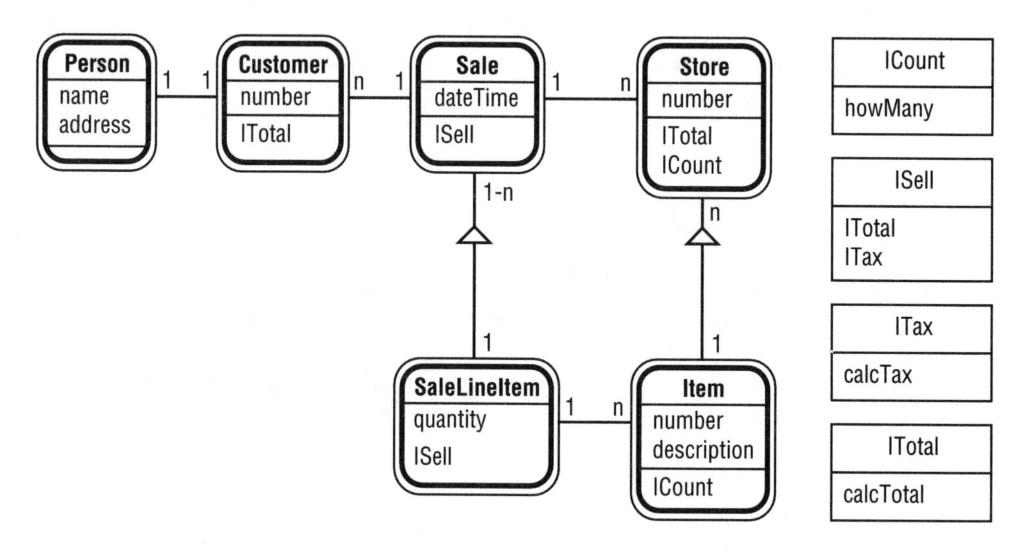

Figure 3-4a. Factor out repeating method signatures.

```
public Customer extends Object implements ITotal {
✂
    // methods / public / ITotal implementation
    public float calcTotal() { /* code goes here */ }
✂
}
public Sale extends Object implements ISell {
✂
    // methods / public / ISell implementation
    public float calcTotal() { /* code goes here */ }
    public float calcTax() { /* code goes here */ }
✂
}
public SaleLineItem extends Object implements ISell {
✂
    // methods / public / ISell implementation
    public float calcTotal() { /* code goes here */ }
    public float calcTax() { /* code goes here */ }
✂
}
public Store extends Object implements ITotal, ICount {
✂
    // methods / public / ITotal implementation
```

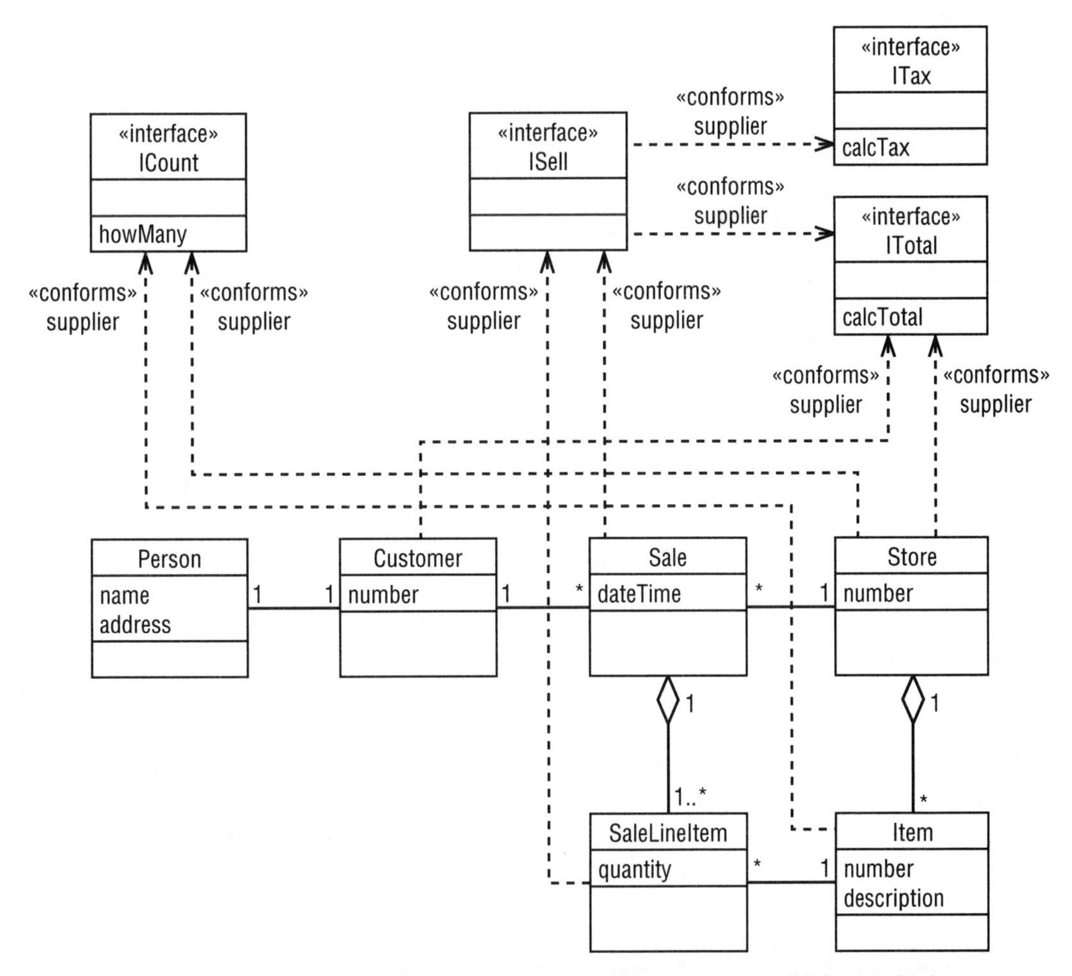

Figure 3-4b. Factor out repeating method signatures (UML notation).

```
    public float calcTotal() { /* code goes here */ }
    // methods / public / ICount implementation
    public int howMany() { /* code goes here */ }
✂
}
public Item extends Object implements ICount {
✂
    // methods / public / ICount implementation
    public int howMany() { /* code goes here */ }
✂
}
```

Especially note this:

```
public interface ISell extends ITotal, ITax {}
```

Here, an interface extends two other interfaces. Is this Multiple inheritance?

Well, yes and no.

Yes, the new interface is a combination of the other two interfaces. Yes, ISell is a special kind of ITotal and a special kind of ITax.

No, it's not inheritance; only method signatures are involved. There is absolutely no implementation behind these method signatures.

We don't really want to think of it as inheritance, either.

We think of interfaces as useful method-signature descriptions, ones that we can conveniently mix and match with the "extends" keyword to provide pluggability.

One way to visualize it is to picture a stack of index cards; each card has an interface name and its method signatures on it; grab whatever combination is useful to you (ITotal, ITax); name that useful combination (ISell)—especially if it is reusable.

3.4.2 Example: Simplify and Identify Object-Model Patterns

Together with David North, we have cataloged 31 object-model patterns: templates of objects with stereotypical responsibilities and interactions. Those patterns are documented at www.oi.com/handbook and (more thoroughly) in the book, *Object Models: Strategies, Patterns, and Applications*.

One of the more puzzling matters has been how to show these patterns within source code. Some have proposed adding extra classes of objects to manage each pattern, but that seemed like overkill to us.

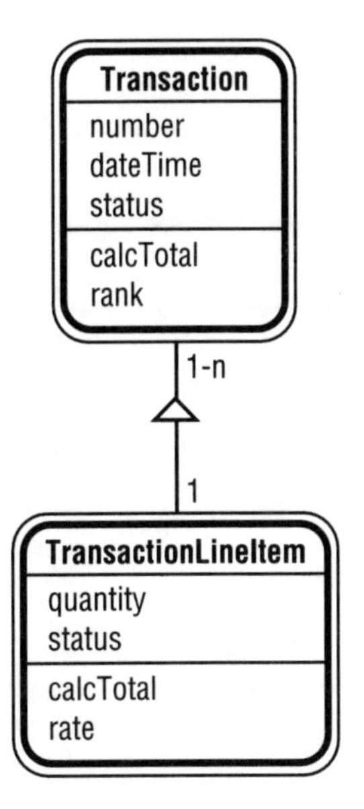

Figure 3-5. The transaction-transaction line item object-model pattern.

Interfaces offer an interesting twist. And the simplest use of interfaces, factoring out common method signatures, takes on some added significance.

Consider the transaction pattern called "transaction-transaction line item" (Figure 3-5).

Other patterns use attributes and services with exactly the same names. So everything can be factored out into interfaces.

For full impact, first add in attribute accessors (Figure 3-6).

In Java, it looks like this:

```
public class Transaction extends Object {
✂
    // attributes / private
    private int number;
    private Date dateTime;
    private String status;
```

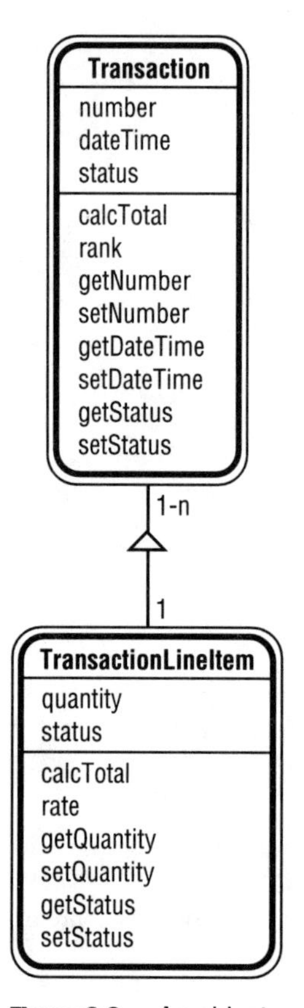

Figure 3-6. An object-model pattern with attribute accessors.

```
// attributes / private / object connections
private Vector transactionLineItems = new Vector();

// methods / public / conducting business
public float calcTotal() { /* code goes here */ }
public Enumeration rank() {
    /* return an enumeration with ranked transaction line items*/
    /* code goes here */ }

// methods / public / accessors for attribute values
public int getNumber() { return this.number; }
public void setNumber(int aNumber) { this.number = aNumber; }
public Date getDateTime() { return this.dateTime; }
```

```
    public void setDateTime(Date aDateTime)
        { this.dateTime = aDateTime; }
    public String getStatus() { return this.status; }
    public void setStatus(String aStatus) { this.status = aStatus; }
✂
}

public class TransactionLineItem extends Object {
✂
    // attributes / private
    private int quantity;
    private String status;

    // attributes / private / object connections
    private Transaction transaction;

    // methods / public / conducting business
    public float calcTotal() { /* code goes here */ }
    public int rate() { /* code goes here */ }

    // methods / public / accessors for attribute values
    public int getQuantity() { return this.quantity; }
    public void setQuantity(int aQuantity) { this.quantity = aQuantity; }
    public String getStatus() { return this.status; }
    public void setStatus(String aStatus) { this.status = aStatus; }
✂
}
```

Second, apply the "factor out repeaters" strategy (Figure 3-7).

In Java, it looks like this:

```
public interface IRank {
    Enumeration rank(); }

public interface IRate {
    int rate(); }

public interface ITotal {
    float calcTotal() ; }
```

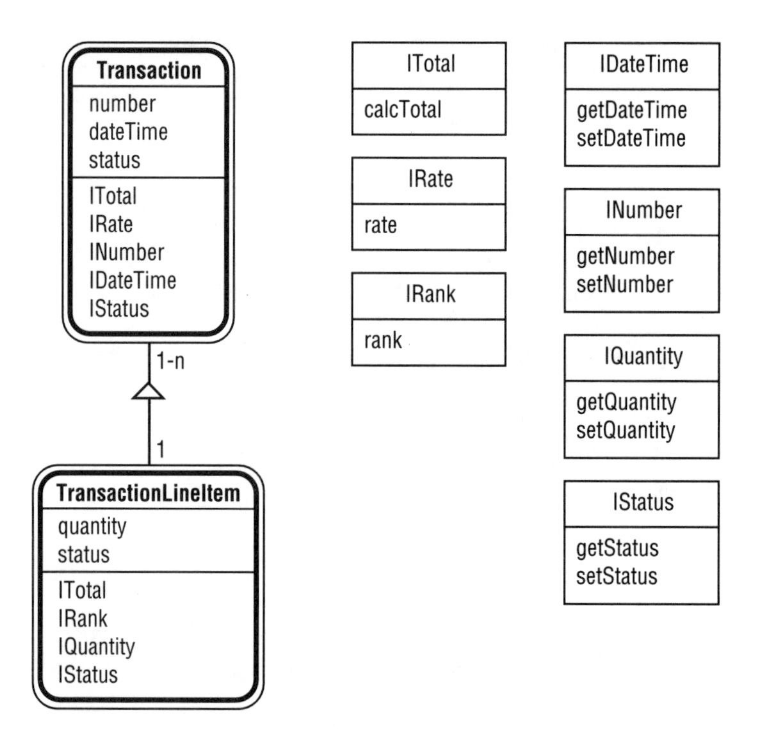

Figure 3-7. Factor out repeaters.

```
public interface INumber {
    int getNumber();
    void setNumber(int aNumber); }

public interface IDateTime {
    Date getDateTime();
    void setDateTime(Date aDate); }

public interface IQuantity {
    int getQuantity();
    void setQuantity(int aQuantity); }

public interface IStatus {
    String getStatus();
    void setStatus(String aStatus); }

public class Transaction extends Object
    implements IRank, ITotal, INumber, IDateTime, IStatus {
```

```
        // class definition here
✂
}

public class TransactionLineItem extends Object
    implements IRate, ITotal, IQuantity, IStatus {
✂
        // class definition here
✂
}
```

Now, go for the gold: factor out the interfaces within each "pattern player," making pattern players explicit in the design (and ultimately, in source code). See Figure 3-8.

In Java, it looks like this:

```
public interface ITransaction
    extends ITotal, IRank, INumber, IDateTime, IStatus {}

public interface ILineItem
    extends ITotal, IRate, IQuantity, IStatus {}

public class Transaction extends Object
    implements ITransaction {
```

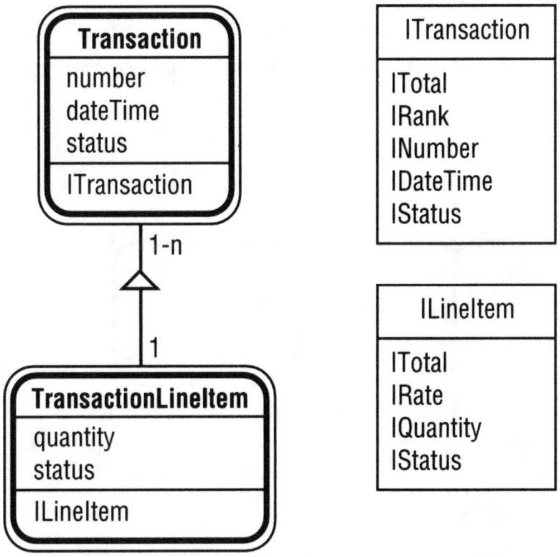

Transaction
number dateTime status
ITransaction

1-n

1

TransactionLineItem
quantity status
ILineItem

ITransaction
ITotal IRank INumber IDateTime IStatus

ILineItem
ITotal IRate IQuantity IStatus

Figure 3-8. Factor out completely, so you can mark out pattern players.

```
✂
        // class definition here
✂
}

public class TransactionLineItem extends Object
    implements ILineItem {
✂
        // class definition here
✂
}
```

If you glance back at the original object model and source code, you'll appreciate just how clean this is.

3.5 Factor Out to a Proxy

Factor Out to a Proxy Strategy: *Factor out method signatures into a proxy, an object with a solo connection to some other object. Reason for use: to simplify the proxy within an object model and its scenario views (Figure 3-9).*

3.5.1 Recognizing a Proxy

Another way to bring interfaces into your design is to factor out method signatures into a proxy. A proxy is one who acts as a sub-

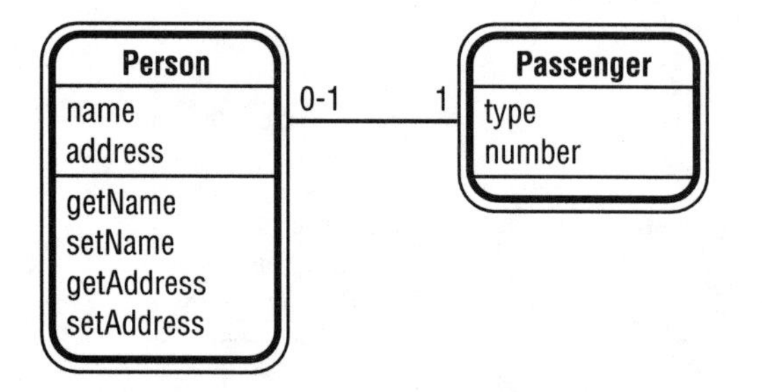

Figure 3-9. Person with accessors.

stitute. Consider person and passenger in Charlie's Charters' reservation system, this time with get and set accessors included (Figure 3-9).

In Java, it looks like this:

```
public class Person extends Object {
✂
    // attributes / private
    private String name;
    private String address;

    // attributes / private / object connections
    private Passenger passenger;

    // methods / public / accessors for attribute values
    public String getName() { return this.name; }
    public void setName(String aName) { this.name = aName; }
    public String getAddress() { return this.address; }
    public void setAddress(String anAddress)
        { this.address = anAddress; }

    // methods / public / accessors for object connection values
    public void addPassenger(Passenger aPassenger) {
        this.passenger = aPassenger; }
    public void removePassenger() { this.passenger = null; }
    public Passenger getPassenger() { return this.passenger; }
✂
}

public class Passenger extends Object {
✂
    // attributes / private
    private int number;
    private String type;

    // attributes / private / object connections
    private Person person;

    // methods / public / accessors for attribute values
    public String getNumber() { return this.number; }
```

```
    public void setNumber(int aNumber) { this.number = aNumber; }
    public String getType() { return this.type; }
    public void setType(String aType)
        { this.type = aType; }

    // methods / public / accessors for object connection values
    public Person getPerson() { return this.person; }

    // constructors
    // notice that there is no *default* constructor; a passenger must have
    // a corresponding person object.
    public Passenger(Person aPerson) {
        // implicit call to superclass constructor super();
        this.person = aPerson; }
✂
}
```

Passenger has a "one and only one" connection with a person object. Whenever an object (Passenger) has a "one and only one" connection with another object (Person), then that object (Passenger) can act as a proxy for the other (Person).

3.5.2 Life without a Proxy

Proxy? Why bother? Well, consider this "before" picture, where we don't have one object acting as a proxy for another. Suppose that you've identified a passenger object, and would like to know its name and address. What does the scenario view look like? (Figure 3-10.)

3.5.3 Life with a Proxy

A proxy answers questions on behalf of another, and it provides a convenient interface. See Figure 3-11.

The scenario view as seen from the perspective of a reservation object is shown in Figure 3-12.

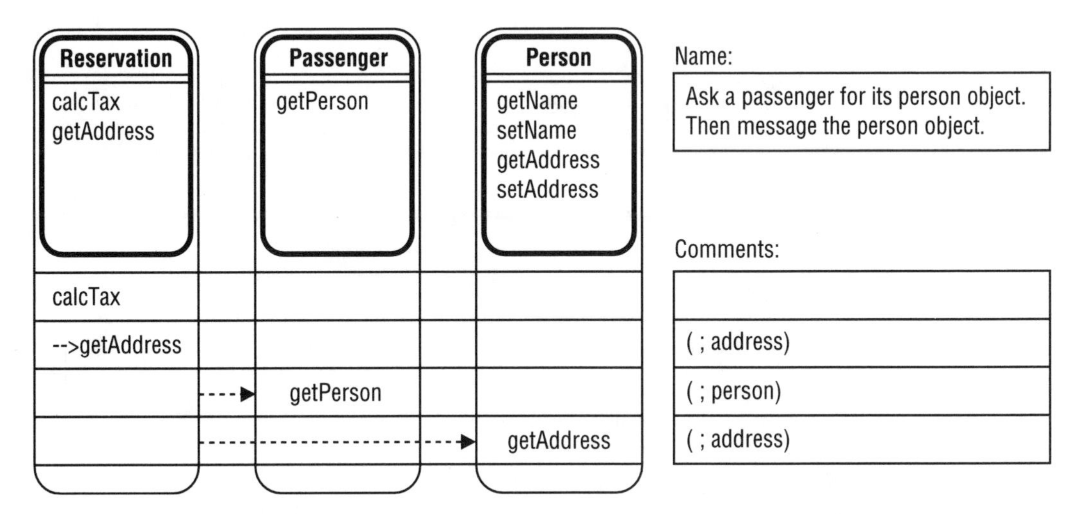

Figure 3-10. Asking a passenger for its person object, then asking a person object for its name and address.

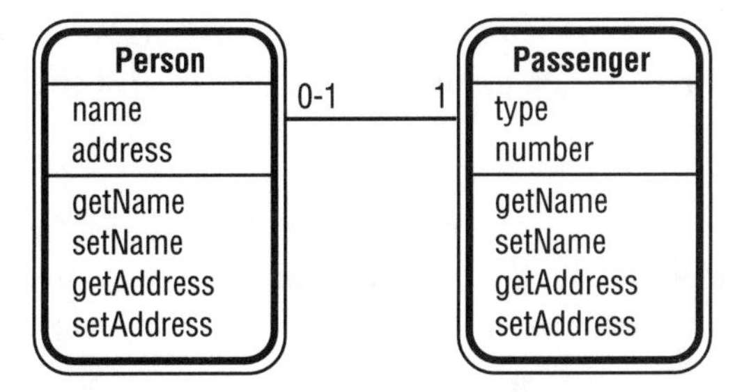

Figure 3-11. Person and Passenger, both with accessors.

In Java, it looks like this:

```
public class Passenger extends Object {
✂
    // methods / public / accessors for Person's attribute values
    public String getName() { return this.person.getName(); }
    public void setName(String aName) { this.person.setName(aName); }
    public String getAddress() { return this.person.getAddress(); }
    public void setAddress(String anAddress)
        { this.person.setAddress(anAddress); }
✂
}
```

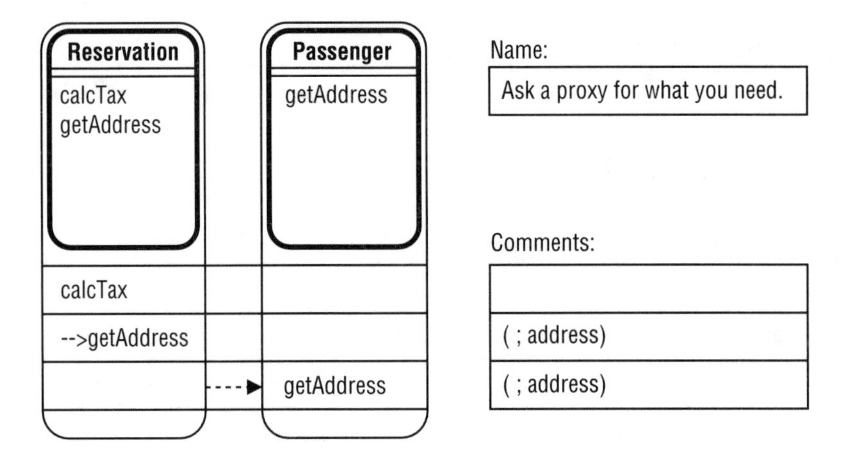

Figure 3-12. Asking a proxy for what you need.

Now you can ask a passenger for its name and address rather than asking a passenger for its person object and then interacting with that person object.

Yes, a passenger object still privately interacts with its person object. We could show that interaction, as illustrated in a separate scenario view (Figure 3-13).

But that really is rather boring and not something we would normally sketch out.

Hence, with a proxy, scenario views become simpler; the details about whomever is being represented by the proxy are shielded from view, letting the important stand out, improving effective communication—a good thing.

3.5.4 Introducing a Proxy Interface

Okay, so now let's bring interfaces into the picture. Factoring out commonality yields Figure 3-14.

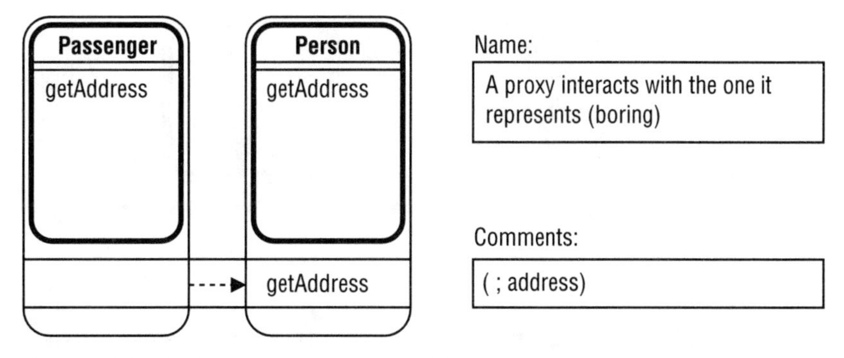

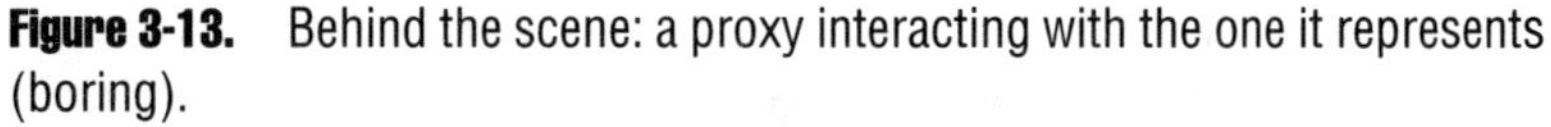

Figure 3-13. Behind the scene: a proxy interacting with the one it represents (boring).

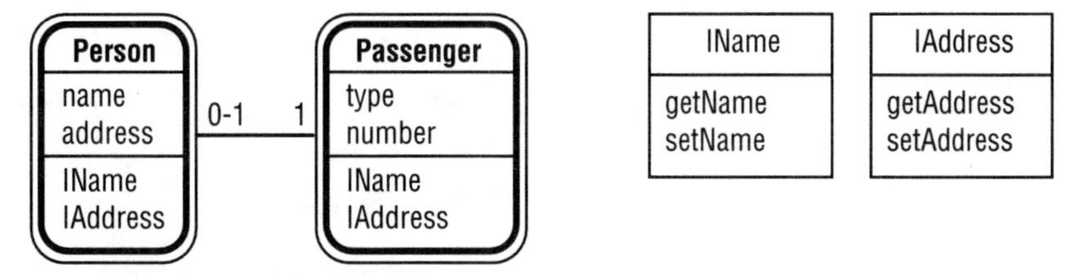

Figure 3-14. Person and Passenger, with common interfaces.

In Java, it looks like this:

```
public interface IName {
    String getName();
    void setName(String aName);
}

public interface IAddress {
    String getAddress();
    void setAddress(String anAddress);
}

public class Person extends Object implements IName, IAddress {
✂
    // class definition here
✂
}
```

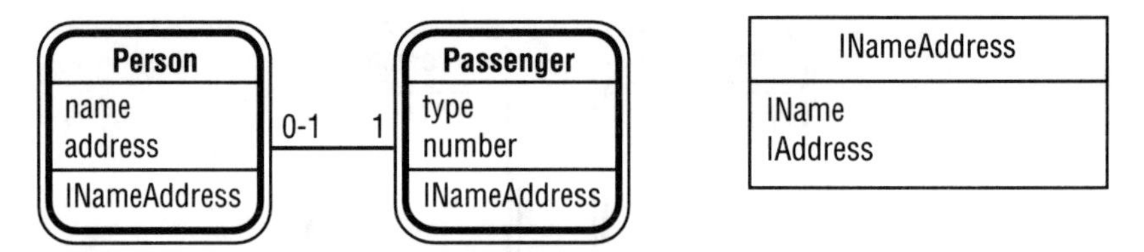

Figure 3-15. Person and Passenger with a single, combined interface.

```
public class Passenger extends Object implements IName, IAddress {
✂
    // class definition here
✂
}
```

We can combine these two interfaces as shown in Figure 3-15.

In Java, it looks like this:

```
public interface INameAddress extends IName, IAddress {}

public class Person extends Object implements INameAddress {
✂
    // class definition here
✂
}

public class Passenger extends Object implements INameAddress {
✂
    // class definition here
✂
}
```

Now bring agent into the picture (Figure 3-16).

In Java, it looks like this:

```
public class Person extends Object
    implements INameAddress {
```

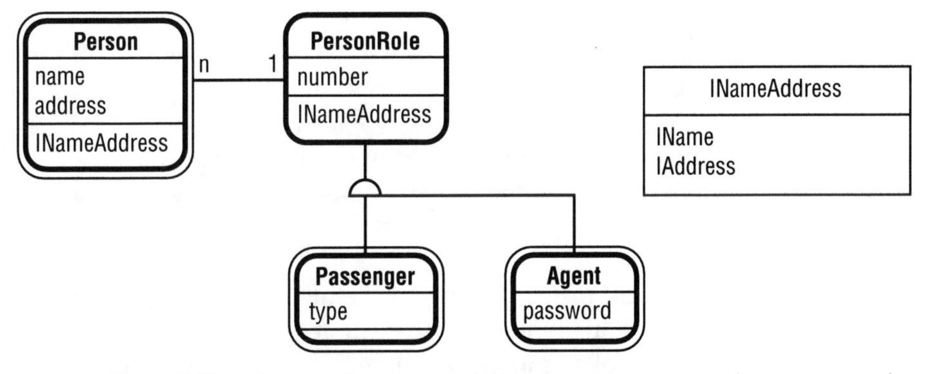

Figure 3-16. A person is composed of one or more person roles; a person role specializes into different kinds of person roles.

```
✂
        // class definition here
✂
}

public abstract class PersonRole extends Object implements INameAddress {
✂
        // class definition here
✂
}

public class Passenger extends PersonRole {
✂
        // class definition here
✂
}

public class Agent extends PersonRole {
✂
        // class definition here
✂
}
```

Now consider a NameAddressUI object.

It's a user interface (UI) object, one that contains a number of smaller, handcrafted or GUI-builder-generated UI objects: text fields, buttons, scrollable lists, and the like.

In addition, and more importantly (from an object-modeling perspective), a NameAddressUI object knows some number of objects in classes that implement the INameAddress interface.

The real power is that the NameAddressUI is not hardwired to objects in just one class. Instead, it works with objects from any class that implements the INameAddress interface (Figure 3-17).

In Java, it looks like this:

```
public class NameAddressUI {
✂
    // attribute / private / object connection
    private Vector nameAddresses = new Vector();

    // method / public / accessor for object connection values
    public void addNameAddress(INameAddress aNameAddress) {
        // only add objects of the type INameAddress to the vector
        this.nameAddresses.addElement(aNameAddress) ; }
✂
}
```

Impact: interfaces change the very nature of an object connection, of one object knowing other objects. As an object, one's perspective shifts from, "I hold a collection of sale objects" to "I hold a collection of ISell objects," meaning, objects in *any* class that implements the ISell interface. Intriguing!

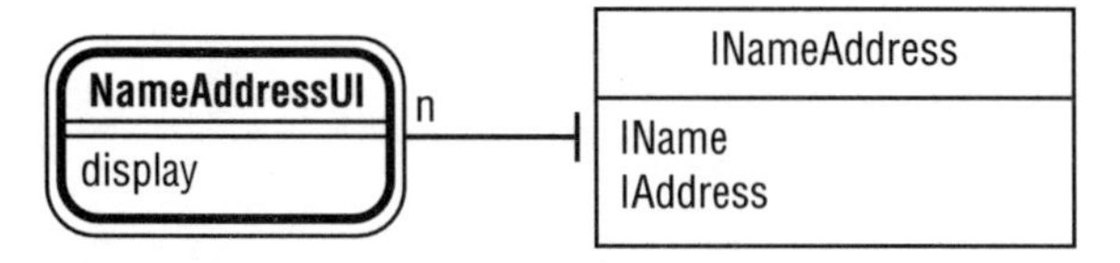

Figure 3-17. Each name-address UI object is composed of a collection of INameAddress objects.

Here a UI object holds a collection of objects from any class that implements a specific interface. This shifts an object-model builder's attention to "what behavior does that object need to provide?" rather than "what class(es) of objects should I limit myself to?"

With interfaces an object model gains better abstraction and simpler results. The implementation also benefits from this simplification.

Now, take a look at the corresponding scenario view (Figure 3-18).

Additional impact: interfaces change the heart and soul of working out dynamics with scenarios. A scenario is a time-ordered se-

NameAddressUI		INameAddress Implementer	Name: Name and address
displayName displayAddress invokeSetName invokeSetAddress		getName setName getAddress setAddress	Comments:
displayName			
	---▶	getName	(; name)
displayAddress			
	---▶	getAddress	(; address)
invokeSetName			
	---▶	setName	(name ;)
invokeSetAddress			
	---▶	setAddress	(address ;)

Figure 3-18. A name-address UI object, interacting with an INameAddress object.

quence of object interactions. Now, as an object in a scenario, one's perspective shifts from, "I send a message to a sale object" to "I send a message to an ISell object," meaning, an object in *any* class that implements the ISell interface. Doubly intriguing!

In this scenario, a UI object sends a message to any object in a class that implements the needed interface. For the receiving object, it no longer matters where its class is in the class hierarchy, and it no longer matters if its class spells out a different implementation (time vs. size tradeoffs will always be with us).

With interfaces, your attention shifts from "what class of objects am I working with now?" to "what's the interface and what's the behavior that I need from whatever kind of object I might work with, now or in the future?"

With interfaces, you spend more time thinking about the behavior that you need, rather than who might implement that behavior.

With interfaces, each scenario view delivers more impact within each scenario and reduces redundancy across related scenarios.

What's the impact of interfaces? Reuse within the current app and greater likelihood of reuse in future apps. In addition, we gain simplified (easier to develop and maintain) models that are flexible, extensible, and support pluggability.

A nice outcome for a relatively modest effort.

3.6 Factor Out for Analogous Apps

Factor Out for Analogous Apps Strategy: *Factor out method signatures that could be applicable in analogous apps. Reason for use: to increase likelihood of using and reusing off-the-shelf classes.*

You can use the "factor out repeaters" strategy to increase the level of abstraction within the object model and its scenario views within the problem domain you are currently working.

This "factor out for analogous apps" strategy takes an even broader perspective. You can use this strategy to achieve use and reuse across a family of analogous applications.

Here's how.

3.6.1 Categorize to Your Heart's Content

You can categorize business apps in different ways. If inheritance were your only categorization mechanism, you could go absolutely crazy. How could you decide upon just one or just a few ways to categorize what you are working on?

Now you have interfaces. You can use them to categorize classes of objects in multiple ways, across a variety of dimensions.

Consider business apps. Two key (yet certainly not all inclusive) categories are sales and rentals. In a sales system, some goods are sold for a price. So we could categorize certain classes of objects as being sellable, perhaps reservable, too.

In a rental system, talent, equipment, or space is rented for a date or for an interval of time; the goods are still there, and are rented again and again and again. Here, we could classify certain classes of objects as being rentable, and perhaps reservable, too.

3.6.2 Categorize Charlie's Charters Business

How do we categorize Charlie's Charters business? Charlie's Charters is in the rental business: it rents space on a scheduled flight for a specific date.

For a flight description on Charlie's Charters, we can reserve space on a scheduled flight. We can ask it if a seat is available; we can ask it to reserve a seat; and we can ask it to cancel a reservation (Figure 3-19).

Now consider a UI object who knows one or more flight description objects. Without interfaces, it looks like Figure 3-20.

Figure 3-19. Methods for reserving space on a scheduled flight.

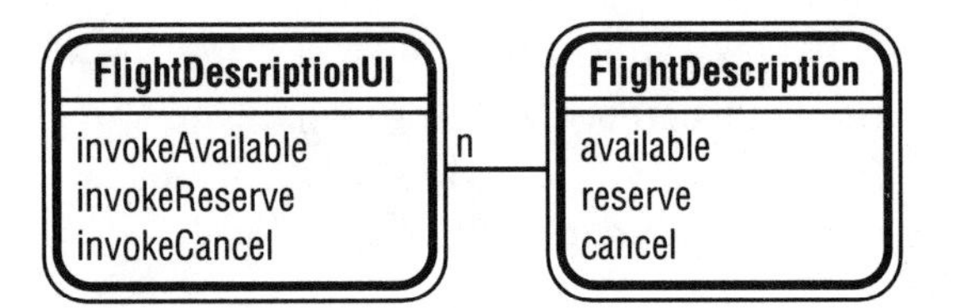

Figure 3-20. A UI class, custom crafted for a flight description.

The corresponding scenario view is shown in Figure 3-21.

3.6.3 How Can Interfaces Help in This Context?

Charlie's Charters is a no-frills airline. It reserves space on a scheduled flight; it does not reserve specific seat numbers. (Adding SeatMap, Seat, and SeatAssignment classes would take care of that—not a big deal.)

For the Charlie's Charters app, we are interested in reserving space for a given date. We could use an interface called IDateReserve (Figure 3-22).

We need to add the passenger as a parameter for reserve and cancel. However, since we want this interface to be general, the parameter type should be that of an Object. Let's give it the name "reserver,"—and so we have:

reserve (date, reserver) and

cancel (date, reserver).

FlightDescriptionUI		FlightDescription
invokeAvailable invokeReserve invokeCancel		available reserve cancel
invokeAvailable		
	---▶	available
invokeReserve		
	---▶	reserve
invokeCancel		
	---▶	cancel

Name:

Interacting with objects in just one class

Interacting with objects in just one cla

Comments:

(date ; available)
(date, reserver ; reservation)
(date, reserver ;)

Figure 3-21. UI objects, interacting with objects in just one class (hardwired object interactions).

Here is what it looks like in Java:

```
public interface IDateReserve {
    boolean available(Date aDate);
    Object reserve(Date aDate, Object reserver);
    boolean cancel(Date aDate, Object reserver); }
```

Code notes: available and cancel return boolean results. Reserve returns an object, keeping the interface flexible (we aren't needlessly limiting the interface to objects in a specific class or its subclasses). The object that gets that returned object must cast the result into whatever kind of object it expects to get back.

IDateReserve
available (date) reserve (date, reserver) cancel (date, reserver)

Figure 3-22. The IDateReserve interface.

Note that the method signatures are generalized a bit, so they can be applied within any system that has IDateReserve elements within it.

Why bother extracting this analogous interface? Simply put, we are looking for an interface that makes it easy for objects that know how to interact with that interface to "plug in" and make use of that interface. Having off-the-shelf UI components that sport commonly used interfaces saves design, development, and testing time. Very nice indeed.

For example, if we have an object that knows how to interact with an object in any class that implements IDateReserve, then I can use and reuse that object in any app with IDateReserve objects in it. Note that all we care about is the interface; we are free from having to consider the specific class or classes of objects that we might want to interact with. This gives us new-found freedom within object-oriented design.

3.6.4 An Aside: Some Related Interfaces

A variation on this theme is IDateTimeReserve, which is not needed here because a flight description specifies a time of departure. However, if we needed it, it would look like Figure 3-23.

Let's consider analogous systems such as other rental businesses.

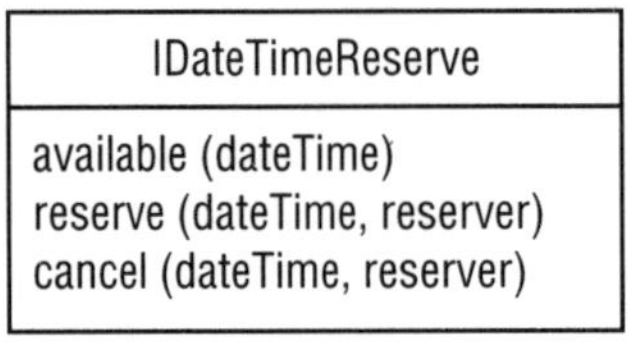

IDateTimeReserve
available (dateTime) reserve (dateTime, reserver) cancel (dateTime, reserver)

Figure 3-23. The IDateTimeReserve interface.

For video rentals, we'd reserve a title for a date (for example, this Saturday). This is another case in which we could use that same IDateReserve interface.

For hotel rooms, we'd be interested in reserving a certain kind of room (concierge level) for an interval of time (for example, from the fifth to the ninth). We could use an interface called IDateIntervalReserve (Figure 3-24).

For car rentals, we'd reserve a certain kind of car (full-size four-door) for an interval of time (for example, from the fifth at 5 PM until the ninth at 9 PM). We could use an interface called IDateTimeIntervalReserve (Figure 3-25).

3.6.5 Using IDateReserve for Charlie's Charters

For Charlie's Charters we need an IDateReserve interface as shown in Figure 3-26.

IDateIntervalReserve
available (from date, to date) reserve (from date, to date, reserver) cancel (from date, to date, reserver)

Figure 3-24. The IDateIntervalReserve interface.

IDateTimeIntervalReserve
available (from dateTime, to dateTime) reserve (from dateTime, to dateTime, reserver) cancel (from dateTime, to dateTime, reserver)

Figure 3-25. The IDateTimeIntervalReserve interface.

Figure 3-26. The flight description class implements the IDateReserve interface.

We can use or reuse any object that knows how to interact with an object in a class that implements the IDateReserve interface.

For example, a "date reservation" user interface could interact with an object in any class that implements IDateReserve—a flight reservation object, a video title object, and so on.

With interfaces we get new found flexibility. Now UI objects can connect with an object in any class that implements the correct interface (Figures 3-27 and 3-28).

With interfaces our attention shifts from "what class of objects can I interact with?" to "what's the interface that I can interact with?"

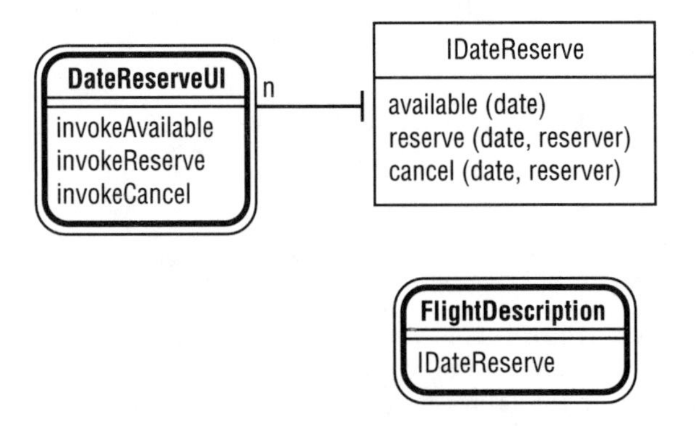

Figure 3-27. UI objects, connected to objects in classes that implement a given interface (flexible object connections).

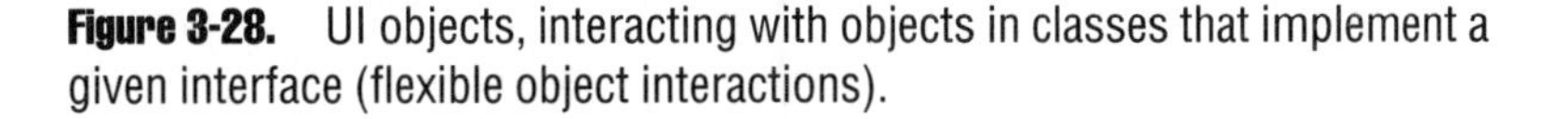

Figure 3-28. UI objects, interacting with objects in classes that implement a given interface (flexible object interactions).

3.6.6 Using IDateReserve in Other Apps

Let's consider another date reservation example. Suppose you are designing a system for a temporary help business in which each worker and each piece of equipment is reservable for a date. In this case, a "daily work order" object can interact with any objects in classes that implement the IDateReserve interface (Figures 3-29 and 3-30).

Today, a daily work order might be a collection of workers and pieces of equipment. Next year, it might be a collection of workers, pieces of equipment, and workspace.

What is the impact of change ?

Add a new class to your object model: Workspace. Be sure it implements the IDateReserve interface. Connect it with whatever object connections it might need (Figure 3-31).

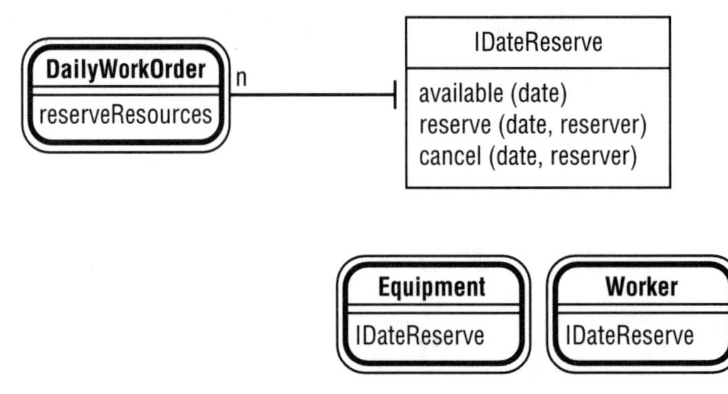

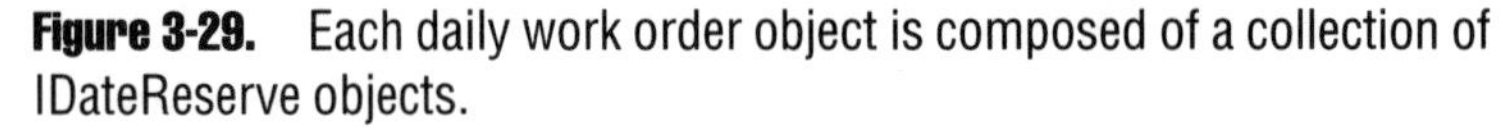

Figure 3-29. Each daily work order object is composed of a collection of IDateReserve objects.

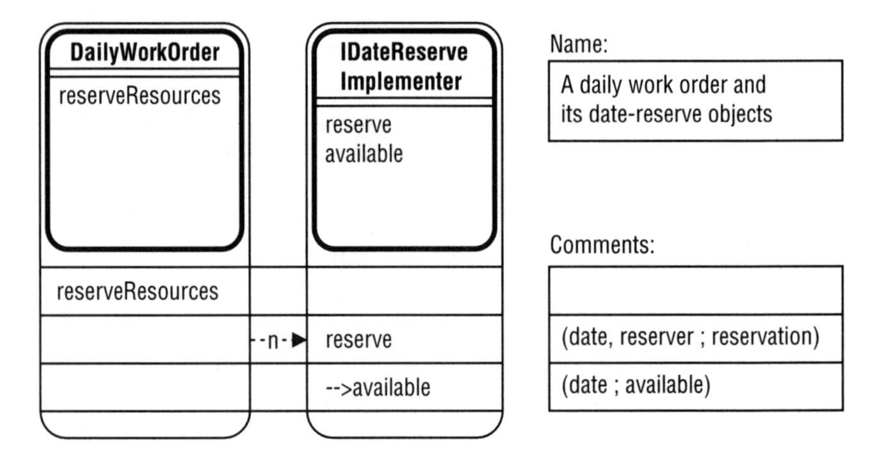

Figure 3-30. Each daily work order object interacts with IDateReserve objects.

No change to your scenario view is needed. The interaction between a daily work order and its IDateReserve objects remains exactly the same.

A daily work order holds a collection of IDateReserve objects. What if it also holds other objects in that collection, objects from classes that don't implement IDateReserve? In this case, a daily work order object can ask an object if it is an instance of IDateRe-

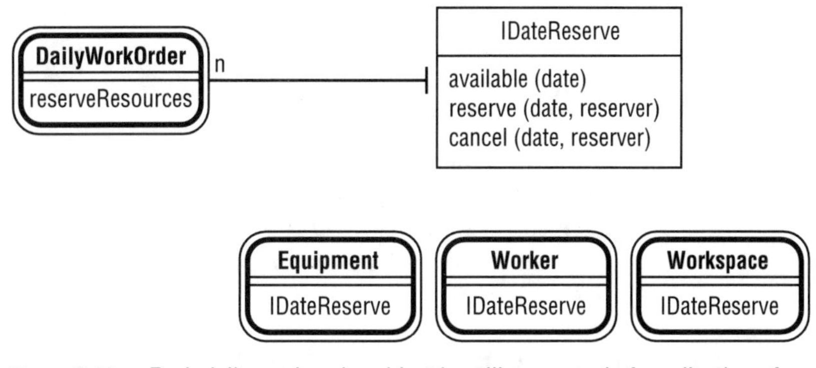

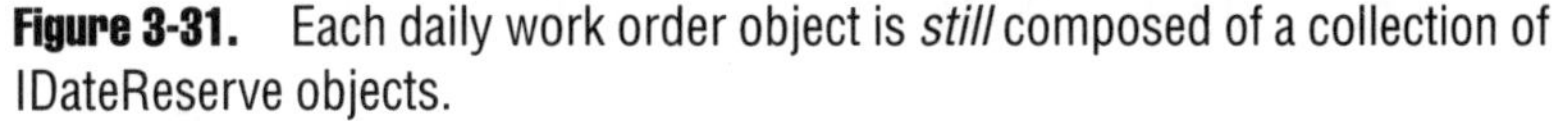

Figure 3-31. Each daily work order object is *still* composed of a collection of IDateReserve objects.

serve. If it is, the daily work order object can then use the interface to interact with that object.*

The point of all this is expandability. By using interfaces, your object model and scenario views are organized for change. Instead of being hardwired to a limited number of classes of objects, your design can accommodate objects from present or future classes, just as long as these classes implement the interface(s) that you need.

3.7 Factor Out for Future Expansion

Factor Out for Future Expansion Strategy: *Factor out method signatures now, so objects from different classes can be graciously accommodated in the future. Reason for use: to embrace change flexibility.*

You can use interfaces as a futurist, too. What if you are wildly successful on your current project? Simply put, the reward for work well done is more work.

*In C++, information about what class an object is in is called run-time type information (RTTI). In Smalltalk, information about what class an object is in is a standard query that can be asked of any object.

So what is next? What other objects might you deal with in the future, objects that could "plug in" more easily, if you could go ahead and establish a suitable interface now?

You can add such interfaces to improve model understanding now and point to change flexibility for the future (hey, this might even get you a pay raise). And you can demonstrate to your customer that your model is ready for expansion—just send more money!

3.7.1 Factoring Out for the Future of Zoe's Zones

Take a look at a zone and its sensors (Figure 3-32).

Factor out common method signatures into a new interface (Figure 3-33).

Now adjust the object model, so a zone holds a collection of IActivate objects (Figure 3-34).

Go even further: an IActivate object consists of other IActivates (Figure 3-35).

However, this is going a bit too far. An IActivate is an interface; it has no attributes, it has no object connections. So showing an object

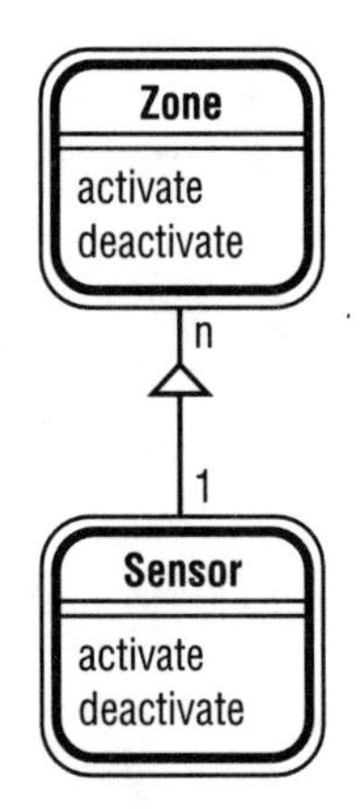

Figure 3-32. A zone and its sensors.

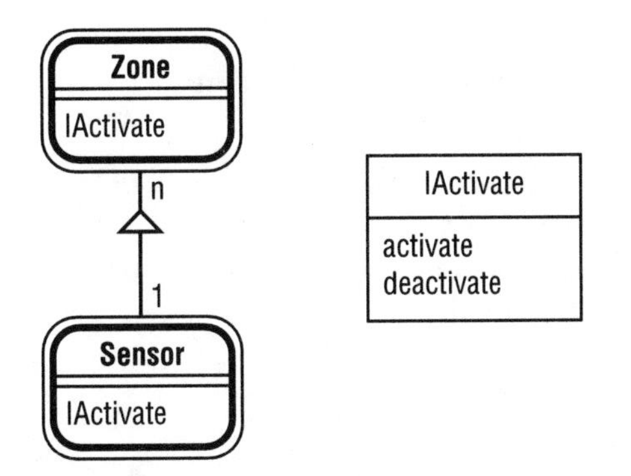

Figure 3-33. Factoring out a common interface.

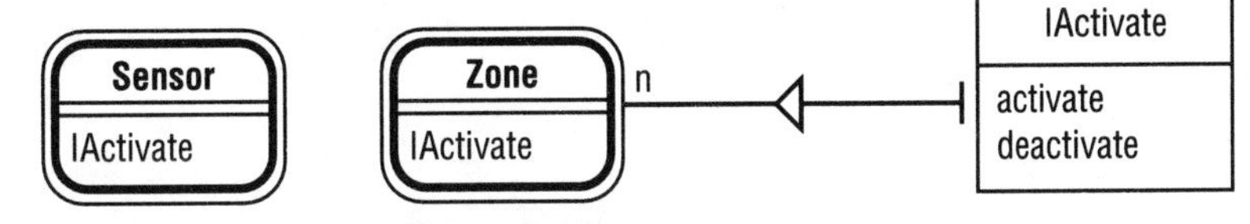

Figure 3-34. A zone and its collection of IActivates.

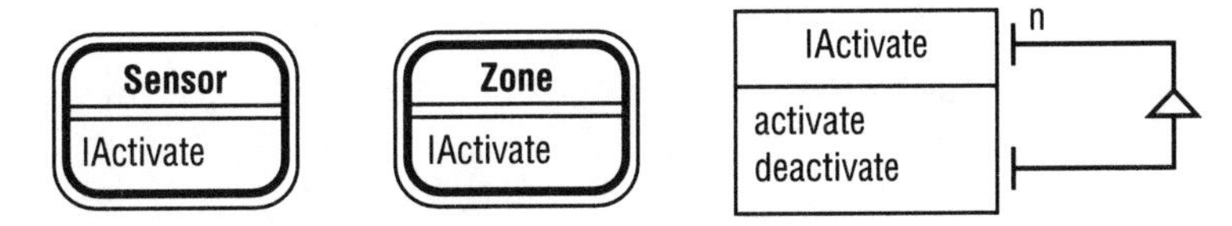

Figure 3-35. An IActivate and its collection of IActivates.

connection with a constraint on an interface really is going a bit too far. We cannot require an interface to implement an object connection.

Now, what we *can* do is use method naming conventions that imply attributes and services:

- get/set method signatures imply attributes

  getStatus and setStatus

- add/remove method signatures imply object connections

  addIActivate and removeIActivate.

By using the add/remove naming convention, we end up with a new, improved IActivate interface (Figure 3-36).

Figure 3-37 depicts a corresponding scenario view, showing add, activate, and deactivate.

In Java, it looks like this:

```
public interface IActivate {
    void activate();
    void deactivate(); }

public interface IActivateGroup extends IActivate {
    void addIActivate(IActivate anIActivate);
    void removeIActivate(IActivate anIActivate); }
```

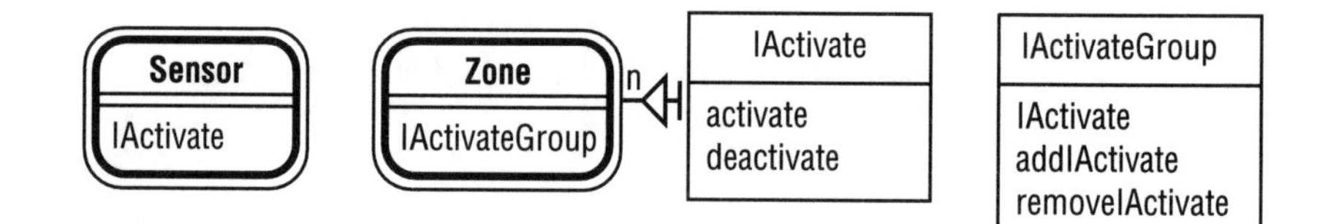

Figure 3-36a. An IActivate and adding/removing IActivates.

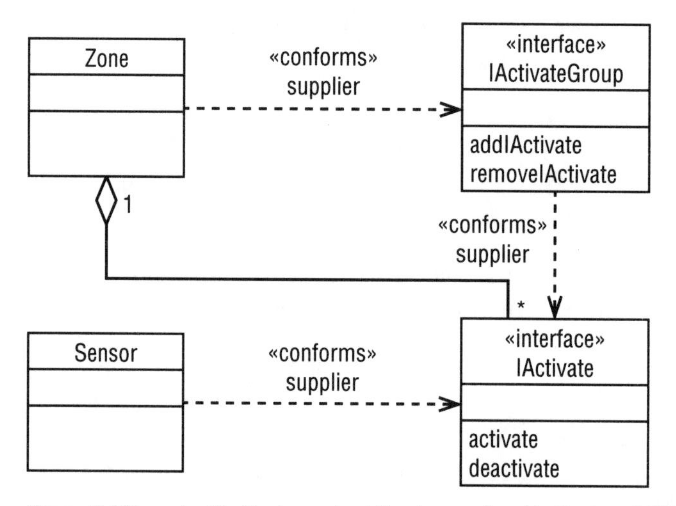

Figure 3-36b. An IActivate and adding/removing IActivates (UML notation).

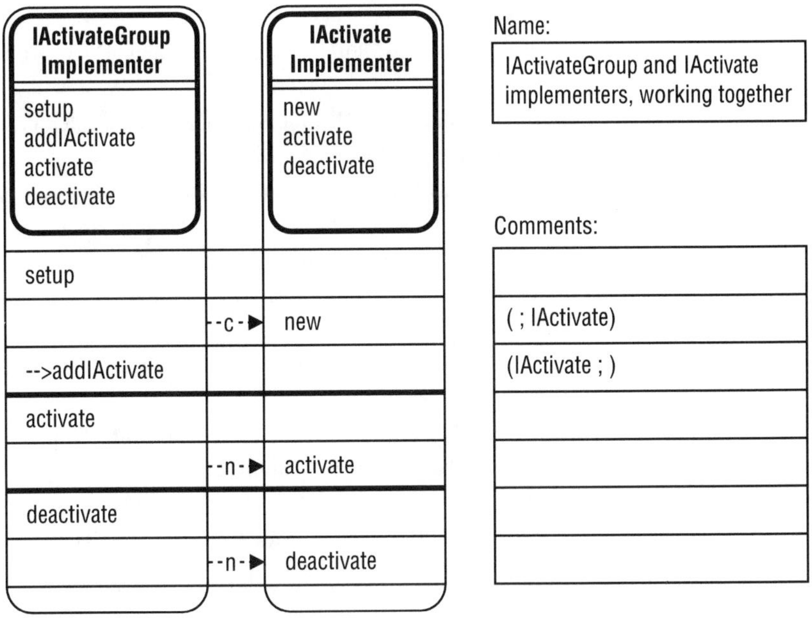

IActivateGroup Implementer		IActivate Implementer
setup addIActivate activate deactivate		new activate deactivate
setup		
	-c-▶	new
-->addIActivate		
activate		
	-n-▶	activate
deactivate		
	-n-▶	deactivate

Name:

IActivateGroup and IActivate implementers, working together

Comments:

(; IActivate)
(IActivate ;)

Figure 3-37. An IActivateGroup interacting with its IActivates.

```
public class Sensor extends Object implements IActivate {
✂
    // methods / public / IActivate implementation
    public void activate() { /* code goes here */ }
    public void deactivate() { /* code goes here */ }
✂
}

public class Zone extends Object implements IActivateGroup {
✂
    // attributes / private / object connections
    private Vector activates = new Vector();

    // methods / public / IActivateGroup implementation
    public addIActivate(IActivate anIActivate) {
        this.activates.addElement(anIActivate); }
    public removeIActivate(IActivate anIActivate) {
        this.activates.removeElement(anIActivate); }
```

```
public void activate() {
    // iterate through the vector of "activates" and tell each iActivate to
    // activate
    Enumeration activateList = this.activates.elements();
    while (activateList.hasMoreElements()) {
        // must cast the element to IActivate
        IActivate anIActivate = (IActivate)activateList.nextElement();
        anIActivate.activate(); }
    }
public void deactivate() {
    // iterate through the vector of "activates" and tell each iActivate to
    // deactivate
    Enumeration activateList = this.activates.elements();
    while (activateList.hasMoreElements()) {
        // must cast the element to IActivate
        IActivate anIActivate = (IActivate)activateList.nextElement();
        anIActivate.deactivate(); }
    }
✂
}
```

3.7.2 Flexibility, Extensibility, and Pluggability for Zoe's Zones

One aspect of flexibility, extensibility, and pluggability is being able to combine objects that you are already working with in new ways—combinations that you might not have anticipated at first.

Now a zone could be a collection of other zones, which could be a collection of sensors. And a sensor could be a collection of other sensors. Nice.

A sensor could be a collection of zones, but this would probably not make much sense. Interfaces allow us to express what kind of behavior must be supported. However, reasonableness applies when it comes to deciding what to plug together!

Another aspect of extensibility is being able to add in new classes of objects: ones that you can anticipate now, and ones that may surprise you in the future.

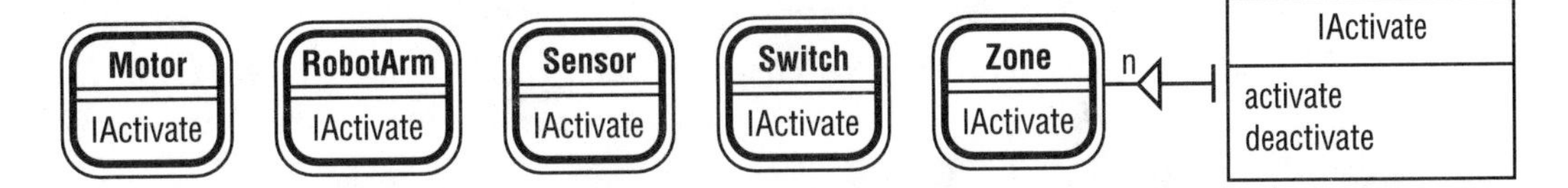

Figure 3-38. Adding in some new IActivates—flexibility, extensibility, pluggabililty.

Look at the interfaces that you are establishing and consider what other classes of objects might implement that same interface at some point in the future.

For zones and sensors, we might look ahead to additional IActivates: switches, motors, conveyor belts, and robot arms (Figure 3-38).

Just add the new classes to the object model.

The scenario view stays exactly the same as before; no change is required.

3.8 Summary

In this chapter you've worked with interfaces: common sets of method signatures that you define for use again and again in your application.

Designing with interfaces is the most significant aspect of Java-inspired design because it gives you freedom from object connections that are hardwired to just one class of objects and freedom from scenario interactions that are hardwired to just one class of objects. For systems in which flexibility, extensibility, and pluggability are key issues, Java-style interfaces are a must. Indeed the larger the system and the longer the potential life span of a system, the more significant interface-centric scenario development becomes.

In this chapter, you've learned and applied the following specific strategies for designing better apps:

Challenge Each Object Connection Strategy: *Is this connection hardwired only to objects in that class (simpler), or is this a connection to any object that implements a certain interface (more flexible, extensible, pluggable)?*

Challenge Each Message-Send Strategy: *Is this message-send hardwired only to objects in that class (simpler), or is this a message-send to any object that implements a certain interface (more flexible, extensible, pluggable)?*

Factor Out Repeaters Strategy: *Factor out method signatures that repeat within your object model. Resolve synonyms into a single signature. Generalize overly specific names into a single signature. Reasons for use: to explicitly capture the common, reusable behavior and to bring a higher level of abstraction into the model.*

Factor Out to a Proxy Strategy: *Factor out method signatures into a proxy, an object with a solo connection to some other object. Reason for use: to simplify the proxy within an object model and its scenario views.*

Factor Out for Analogous Apps Strategy: *Factor out method signatures that could be applicable in analogous apps. Reason for use: to increase likelihood of using and reusing off-the-shelf classes.*

Factor Out for Future Expansion Strategy: *Factor out method signatures now, so objects from different classes can be graciously accommodated in the future. Reason for use: to embrace change flexibility.*

Chapter 4

Design with Threads

This chapter is about concurrency—doing more than one thing at a time.

4.1 Threads

4.1.1 What Is a Thread?

A thread is a single stream of program execution—one statement after the next after the next (Figure 4-1).

Multiple threads are more than one stream of program execution running in parallel, or concurrently. The program runs one statement after the next after the next—and then switches to a different part of the program and runs one statement after the next after the next—and then switches to a different part of the program and runs one statement after the next after the next, and so on.

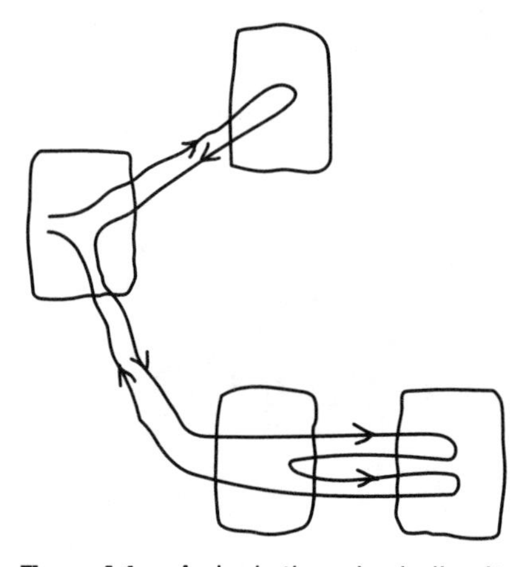

Figure 4-1. A single thread, winding its way through some objects.

A multiple threads might follow the same path (Figure 4-2) or different paths (Figure 4-3) as they wind their way through a program.

4.1.2 How Do Threads Get Started?

How do threads get started, and with how many threads am I working?

Here's one way to start a thread: begin with a UI object (Figure 4-4). Each client has its own thread, so with multiple clients you have multiple threads; your design must account for this.

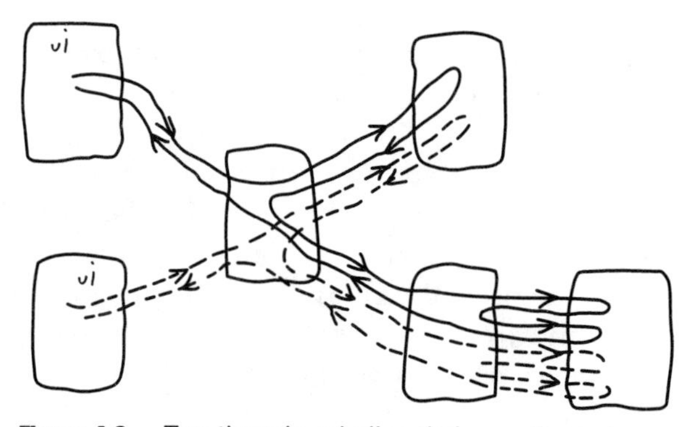

Figure 4-2. Two threads, winding their way through some objects.

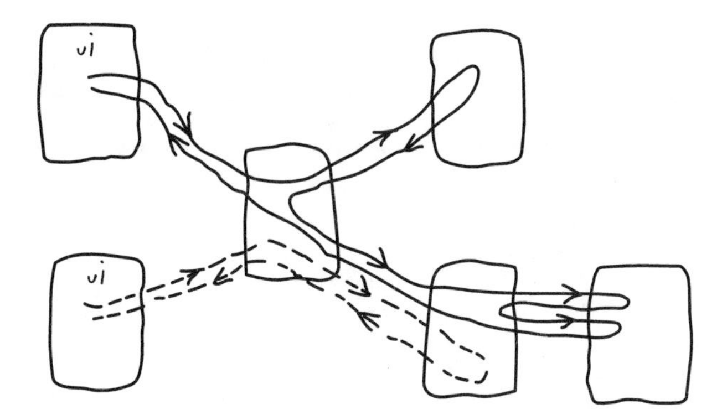

Figure 4-3. Two threads, winding their way on different paths through some objects.

Here's another way to start a thread: begin with a thread object (Figure 4-4). Thread objects, you say? Yes. In Java, there is a class called Thread. You can ask the class to create a new thread object for you. Then you can tell that thread object to start—and (along with other threads) that thread will begin (at whatever starting point you give it) and wind its way through objects in your app.

Cool, huh?

So you add thread objects when you need additional program streams above and beyond a single programming stream for each client. Why? If you need to give the appearance of doing more than one thing at a time, thread objects are the tools you need to use to get the job done. For example, at Zoe's Zones, we could run monitoring at a high level of priority, yet let assessing of reliability run at a lower level of priority.

It's helpful to think of a *thread object* like any other object when commanding a thread to start, stop, and the like.

It's helpful to visualize a *thread* as something that starts from a client or a thread object and then winds its way through your application.

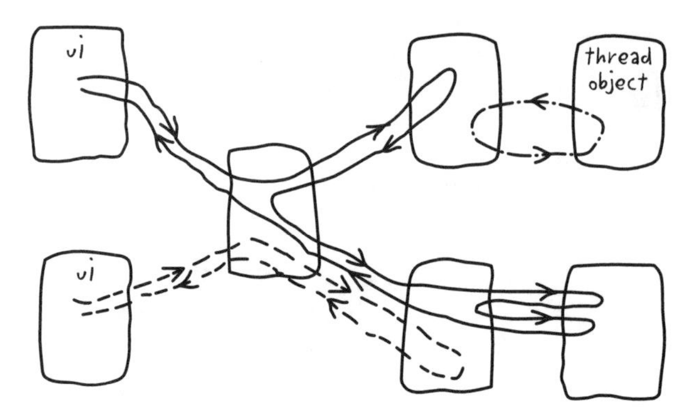

Figure 4-4. Two threads beginning from UI objects, one thread beginning from a thread object.

4.1.3 Why Use Multiple Threads?

Most designs must account for multiple streams of program execution; this chapter shows how to do that safely.

Multiple threads let you give the appearance of doing more than one thing at a time. For example, your application can serve multiple clients at the same time, or you can spawn a background printing thread.

Threads also give you a clean, simple way to design in the main thing you want your application to do, along with other things that you'd like it to be aware of or check on from time to time (like a background calculation or some other mundane chore).

Threads simplify a design when you need to give the appearance that you are doing more than one thing at a time (Figure 4-5). Threads also improve response time when a higher priority part of an application needs to run.

4.1.4 If You Don't Need Multiple Threads, Don't Use Them

If you don't need to give the appearance of doing more than one thing at a time, don't use multiple threads.

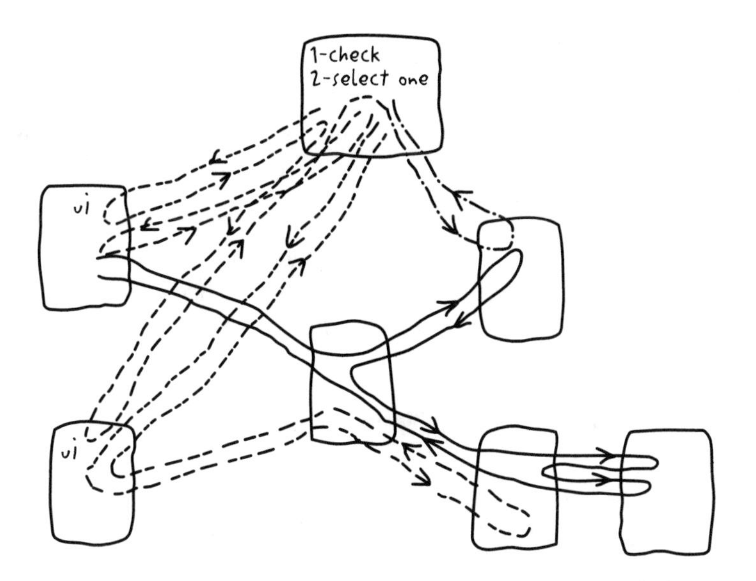

Figure 4-5. Without threads, designing in the appearance that you are doing more than one thing at a time gets complicated in a hurry!

Why?

First and foremost, keep your design simple. By doing one thing at a time and not creating conflicts between shared resources, all will be well.

Secondly keep your overhead down. Multiple threads add processing overhead, the time it takes to change from one thread to the next; it's called context switch time. Your app eats up some microseconds each time it switches from one thread to another. It adds up.

4.1.5 Sync

In Java, a "sync'd" method is *synchronized* in the following way:

- only one thread is allowed in at a time
- only one thread is allowed in any sync'd method within a given object

- a thread within a sync'd method can invoke nonsync'd methods
- a thread within a sync'd method can invoke sync'd methods within the same object, immediately entering into that method without delay
- a thread within a sync'd method can invoke sync'd methods in another object, but if another thread is already inside, it must wait in a queue just like any other thread.

4.1.6 Sync: A Guarantee and a Nonguarantee

A sync guarantees that only one thread will run within *a method* for *an object*, making it "thread-safe."

However, a sync has a nonguarantee when it comes to good service: any other threads that come along to invoke sync'd methods within that object wait in a queue, standing by until the earlier threads exit the sync'd method (Figure 4-6).

Other threads, running in other objects, even running in the same object (winding their way through nonsync'd methods), continue to run. Those other threads get turns running, perhaps even before the thread that was running in a sync'd method gets the opportunity to complete ending that sync.

Hence, a sync *does not* guarantee that a thread will run to completion before being interrupted by another thread somewhere else in the application.

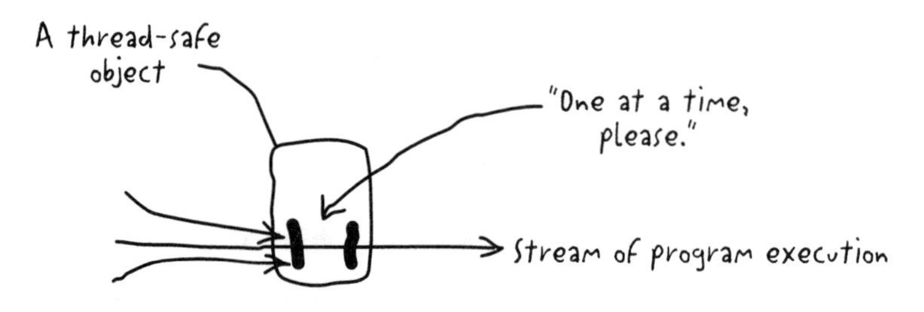

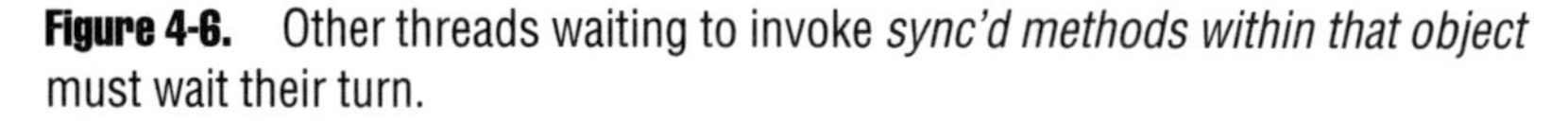

Figure 4-6. Other threads waiting to invoke *sync'd methods within that object* must wait their turn.

4.1.7 Sync: Scope

You can sync an instance method so that just one thread at a time can enter and work with the values of its instance variables.

You can sync a class method so that just one thread at a time can enter and work with the values of its class variables.*

4.1.8 Shared Value (and Keeping Out of Trouble)

Threads and tasks (real-time processes) are very similar. Okay then, in what few ways are they different? Threads share the same set of values in a running program; each task has its own set of values (Figure 4-7).

Consequently, the overhead for threads is lower. All newer operating systems support threads; it's the trendy way to support concurrency.

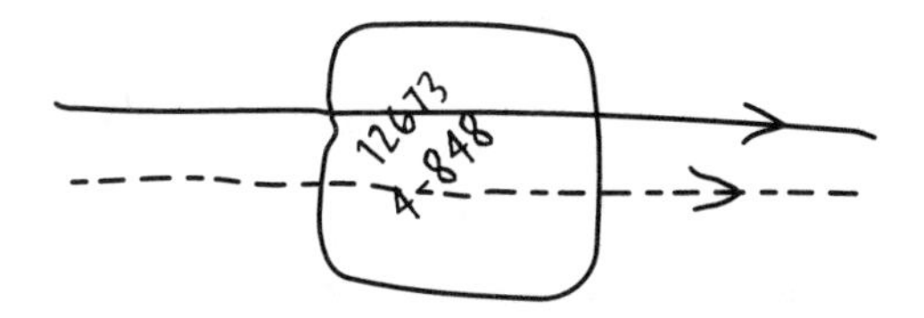

Figure 4-7. Threads share the same internal values.

---

*In Java, you can even sync a block of code within a method. A better idea is to put that code in a separate method because you'll end up with smaller, more cohesive methods (a good idea) and harder-to-miss sync's (also a good idea).

An object with one or more sync'd methods has a lock. When a thread enters one of its sync'd methods, the lock for that object is set (no other thread can enter that sync'd method or any other sync'd method for that object). When a thread exits a sync'd method, the lock for that object is reset. (Similarly, this is true for a class with one or more sync'd class methods.)

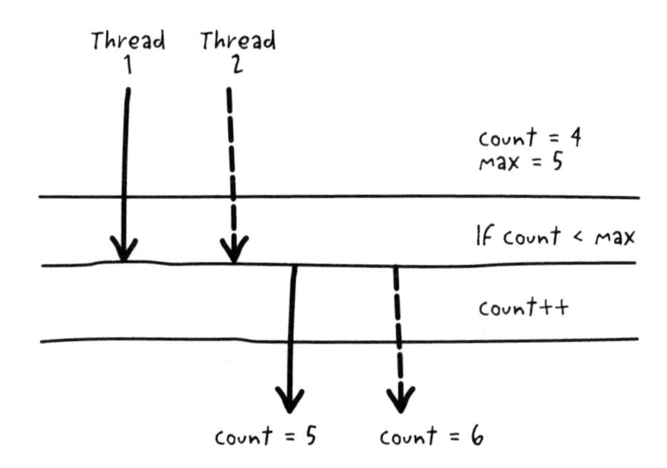

Figure 4-8. Why methods that work with internal values must be sync'd.

Consequently, as designers we have to make sure that multiple threads don't work with the same values at the same time. Otherwise, we might get unexpected results (Figure 4-8).

In Figure 4-8:

- Internal values of the object are set to count = 4, max = 5
- Thread 1 executes the first part of the statement:

  if 4 < 5 (count < max)

- Thread 2 gets a turn and executes the first part of the same statement:

  if 4 < 5 (count < max)

- Thread 1 executes the second part of the statement:

  5 = 4 + 1 (count ++)

- Thread 2 gets a turn and executes the same statement:

  6 = 5 + 1 (count ++)

Yes, a thread might get through just part of a statement. Why? Because each Java statement becomes some number of bytecodes. The Java virtual machine executes one bytecode at a time. Most often, threads *are* interrupted in the middle of a Java statement.

And so, in this case, the count ends up with a value greater than max, which is not at all what we expected.

How do we get around this problem?

Methods that work with internal values must be sync'd (sometimes referred to as "locked"), meaning that such methods should allow just one thread in at a time.

Syncs add processing overhead, so it's not a good idea to sync everything in sight.

However, keep in mind that if you don't sync up something that you should, values can become corrupted, leading to erroneous results.

Checking your design for being "thread-safe" is an important aspect of designing with multiple threads.

Sync Access to Values Strategy: *When multiple threads compete for values(s) within an object—and you try other thread paths but cannot avoid competition for these values—use sync'd methods to limit access (one thread at a time). For multithreaded objects, sync each method that compares, operates on, gets, or sets internal values.*

4.1.9 Don't Sync Longer Than You Have To

The idea in a multithreaded design is to let multiple threads run through your application.

When you sync a method and a thread enters that sync, then *no other thread can enter any sync'd method in that object* until that sync method runs to completion. It's similar to a multilane highway that suddenly squeezes down to just one lane: if traffic is light, no problem; if traffic is heavy, the queue stretches out for miles and miles.

This means that it's a good idea to streamline a sync'd method, including just those steps that must be sync'd.

Zoom In and Sync Strategy: *Zoom in on exactly what you need to sync, factor it out into a separate method, and sync that method. Why? Sync for as little time as possible so other (potentially higher priority) threads waiting at the start of other sync methods for that object will get to run sooner rather than later.*

4.1.10 Shared Resource (and Keeping Out of Trouble)

Too many syncs can hang your application.

Watch out for a sync'd method that extends its reach to other methods. If that thread hits another sync'd method in some other object and another thread is inside, then it must wait—and might be stuck forever.* Welcome to the wonderful world of deadlock (Figure 4-9).

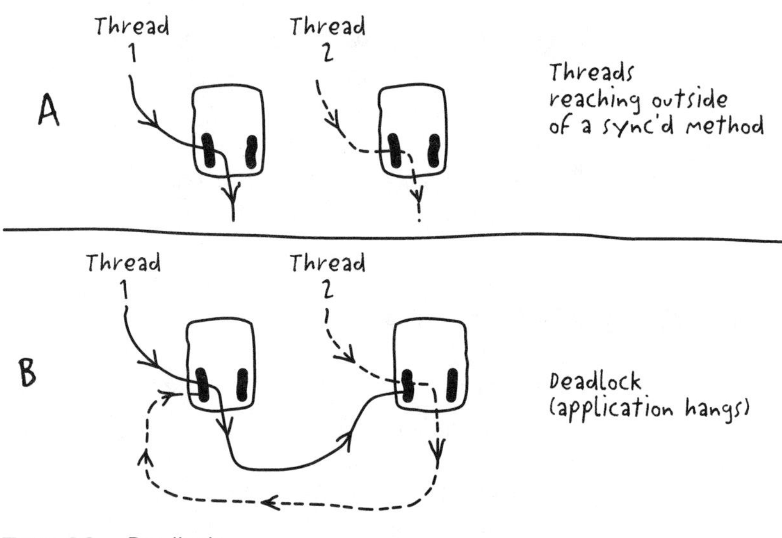

Figure 4-9. Deadlock.

*A thread can re-acquire a lock on an object that it already locked, even if others are waiting. This avoids any possibility of a circular deadlock, and allows synchronized methods within the same object to call one another.

Here's how deadlock happens:

Thread 1 enters a sync'd method. Then, before exiting that sync'd method, it follows a method call outside of that object.

Thread 2 enters a sync'd method. Then, before exiting that sync'd method, it follows a method call outside of that object.

Thread 1 arrives at the sync'd method that Thread 2 already entered, and waits for Thread 2 to exit that method.

Thread 2 arrives at the sync'd method that Thread 1 already entered, and waits for Thread 1 to exit that method.

You can find deadlock in everyday life (for example, TCP/IP), although usually someone gives in and allows it to end (Figure 4-10).

A pair of strategies is needed here, analogous to "when to sync access to values" and "how to sync access to values."

This time, it's at a bit higher level of abstraction.

Sync Access to Objects Strategy: *When multiple threads compete for entry into each other's sync'd methods, use a gatekeeper to control access one thread at a time, and make sure the objects that the gatekeeper protects have no sync methods.*

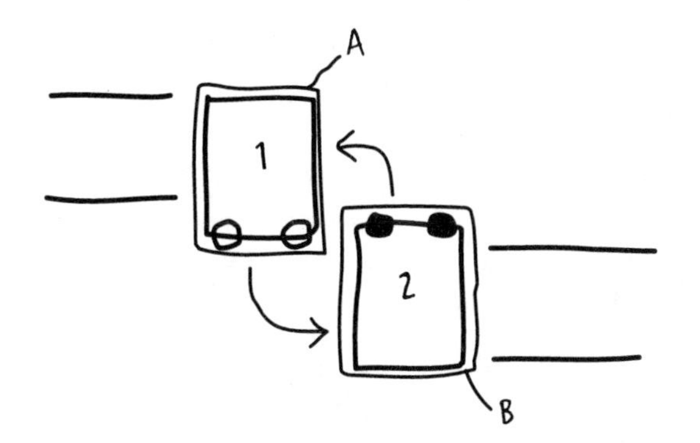

Figure 4-10. Deadlock at the mall, each car sync'd one space, then waited at each other's sync'd space (with some drivers, this deadlock could last forever).

What can you do about deadlock like the one shown in Figure 4-10? Add an object that acts as a gatekeeper; design the object interactions so that each thread first sync's on a gatekeeper's method, followed by exclusive sync'd access to the objects that the gatekeeper protects.

In a parking lot, you can add a gatekeeper by (1) adding a very stern parking attendant or (2) slanting the parking slots to encourage one-way travel down the rows in the parking lot (one-way streets in large cities have a similar effect).

4.2 Multiple Clients, Multiple Threads within an Object

Back to Charlie's Charters and its reservation system.

As soon as the reservation system has more than one agent making reservations at the same time, then we have multiple clients and multiple threads.

Here it's not a matter of whether or not to use multiple threads; multiple threads are definitely part of the design.

Here, it's a matter of using multiple threads safely. Hmmm. It sounds like it is time for a couple of strategies:

Value Gatekeeper Strategy: *Look for a method that increments or decrements a count of a limited resource. Sync that method; give it exclusive access to that count.*

Object Gatekeeper Strategy: *Look for a method that reserves or issues a limited resource, represented by the objects in that collection. Sync that method and give it exclusive access to that collection of objects.*

Apply these strategies to Charlie's Charters.

What limited resource are we working with? Space on a scheduled flight.

Do we manage a counter or a collection of objects? If we had a seat map and made seat assignments, then we'd have a collection of objects. But at Charlie's Charters, all we have is a counter, the count of the number of reservations on the flight.

So, based upon the "value gatekeeper" strategy, we'd expect to sync a method within the ScheduledFlight class.

Figure 4-11 illustrates what the object model looks like.

Sync the method responsible for comparing the current number of reservations against the capacity and adding in the new reservation. It's the "try to add reservation" method.

Figure 4-12 depicts the scenario view.

In Java, it looks like this:

```
public class ScheduledFlight extends Object {
✂
    // attributes / private / object connections
    private Vector reservations = new Vector();

    // methods / public / conducting business
    public synchronized
```

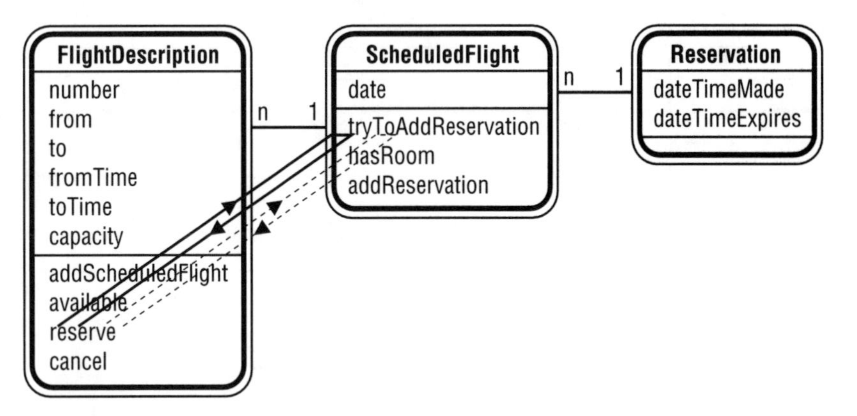

Figure 4-11a. Multiple threads could lead to inadvertent overbooking. You need to sync here.

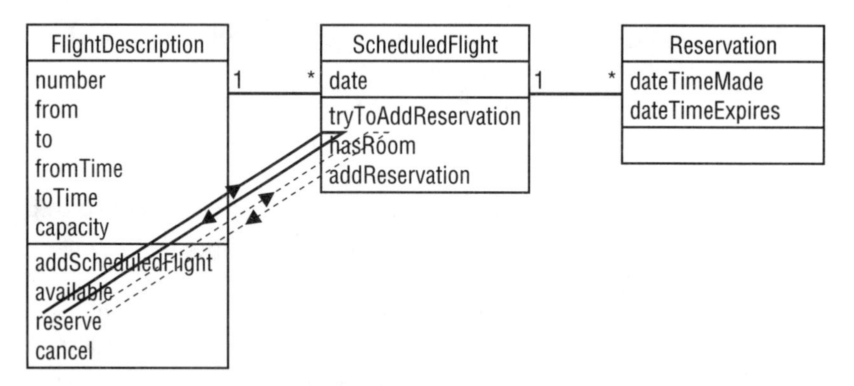

Figure 4-11b. Multiple threads could lead to inadvertent overbooking. You need to sync here (UML notation).

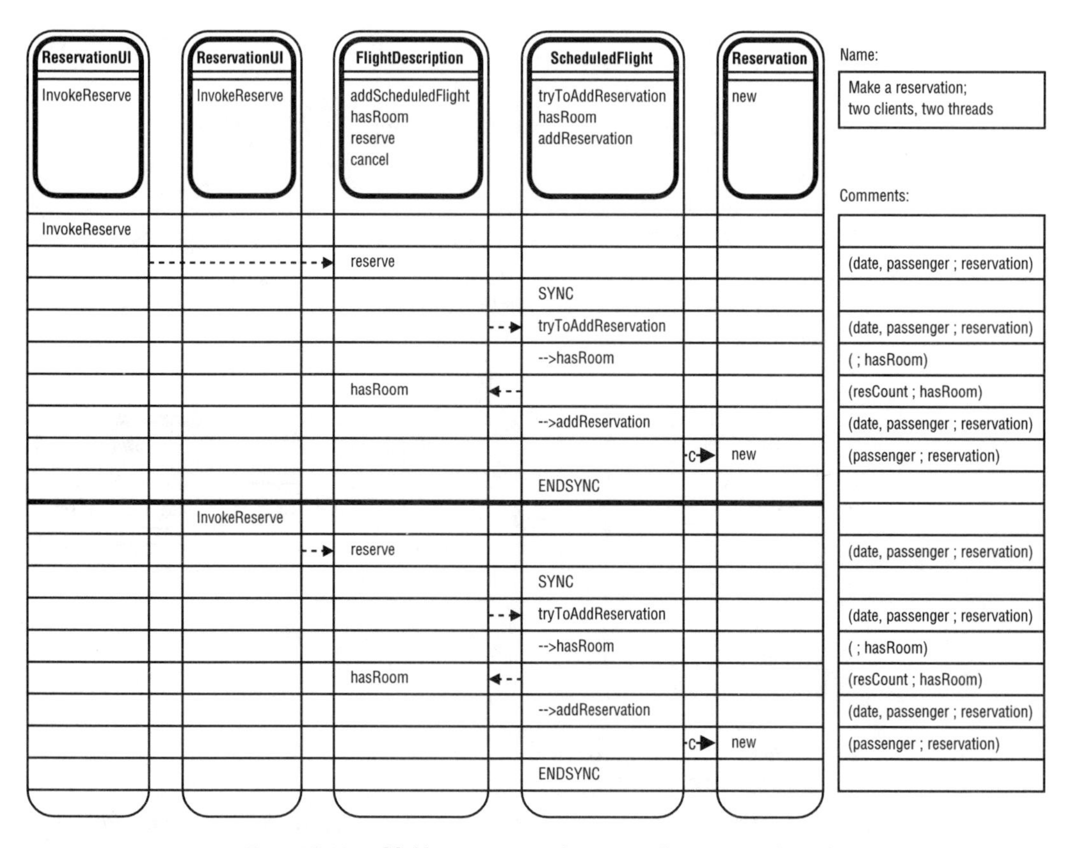

Figure 4-12. Making a reservation: two clients, two threads.

```
            Reservation tryToAddReservation(
                        Date aDate, Passenger aPassenger) {
               // code goes here
               if (this.hasRoom())
               // code goes here
                        this.addReservation(aDate, aPassenger);
               /* code goes here */ }

   // methods / protected / conducting business
   protected boolean hasRoom() {
            /* code goes here */ }
   protected Reservation addReservation (
            Date aDate, Passenger aPassenger) {
            /* code goes here */ }
✂
}
```

Code notes: We limit the visibility of hasRoom and addReservation and only call them within a synchronized method. If at some point we need to add a reservation without first having to check if there's room, then we will synchronize addReservation. The reservations vector is the resource that we need to protect.

4.3 Multiple Thread Objects, Multiple Threads within an Object

Now let's take a look at Zoe's Zones.

We're working with zones and sensors. This time, we're beginning with just one thread and considering when and if we might add additional threads. Here is a helpful strategy:

Four Thread Designs Strategy: *Apply these thread designs, looking for the simplest one that will satisfy your performance requirements. From simplest to most complex, consider: (1) single thread, (2) prioritized-object threads, (3) prioritized-method threads, (4) prioritized-method prioritized-object threads.*

4.3.1 Single Thread

The simplest solution is a single-thread design.

It's not high-tech sexy. After all, threads and concurrency are really fun things to mess around with. But wait a minute. We're not in a classroom. We're not considering a group of dining philosophers who like sharing their eating utensils with each other. We're designing an application.

A simpler design is a better design provided that it gets the job done within time, budget, and resource constraints.

Could a single-thread solution work here? Let's take a closer look (Figure 4-13).

Thread		Zone		Sensor		ProblemReport
start		run monitor		readAndCheckValue readValue checkValue logProblem assessReliability		new

Name: Single thread

Thread		Zone		Sensor		ProblemReport	Comments:
start							
	- - -▶	run					
		DO					// do again and again for each zone
		-->monitor					
			-n-▶	readAndCheckValue			
				-->readValue			(; value)
				-->checkValue			(value, range ; result)
				IF			// problem detected
				-->logProblem			
					-c-▶	new	(value ; problemReport)
				ENDIF			
				-->assessReliability			
		ENDDO					

Figure 4-13. A single-thread solution.

Someone creates a thread object and asks it to start. At that point, the thread becomes runnable. When that runnable thread gets a turn to run, the thread object tells its corresponding zone object to run, and so the thread begins winding its way through the scenario.

In Java, it looks like this:

```
public class Zone extends Object implements Runnable {
✂
    // attributes / private / thread
    private Thread mainThread;

    // attributes / private / object connections
    private Vector sensors = new Vector();

    // methods / public / activation
    public void activate() {
        // create the main thread and start it
        this.mainThread = new Thread(this);
        this.mainThread.start(); }

    // methods / public / Runnable implementation
    public void run() {
        for(;;) { // loop forever until thread is stopped
            this.monitor(); } }

    // methods / public / conducting business
    public void monitor() {
        // iterate through the vector of sensors and tell each sensor to
        // readAndCheck
        Enumeration sensorList = this.sensors.elements();
        while (sensorList.hasMoreElements()) {
            // must cast the element to a Sensor
            Sensor aSensor = (Sensor)sensorList.nextElement();
            aSensor.readAndCheckValue(); } }
✂
}
```

Code notes: This is just the snippet for Zone. To kick things off we have an activate method that creates the main thread and tells it to start. The run method has an internal loop that will continue to call monitor until the main thread is stopped. The monitor method iterates through the vector of sensors, telling each one to read and check its value.

A single thread winds its way through each zone and its sensors. For each sensor, the thread reads a sensor, compares the reading with a threshold, logs any detected problems, and assesses sensor reliability.

Just one thread runs through the objects. There is no one to fight with, and nothing to fight over, so no sync's are needed.

This simplest design will work, if the thread can run around fast enough and get everything done on time.

But what if you have hundreds of zones and thousands of sensors? A single thread might still be okay.

You must look at how long it takes to run a single thread through every zone and its sensors and then compare it with the required sampling rate. If the processing time is 10 minutes (a very long time) and the sampling rate is once per hour, then a single-thread design will get the job done.

It's not elegant. It's not high-tech cool, but it is a cost-effective, more easily implemented solution. Come to think of it, that *is* high-tech cool.

4.3.2 Prioritized-Object Threads

What if a single-thread solution is just not fast enough? Then what?

Mindlessly adding threads with the hope of making things run faster is an exercise in futility. Threads add overhead—context switch time, sync and end-sync times—and might actually slow down your app.

Multiple threads will save you time, and make the application appear to run faster, *if and only if* some threads can run at a higher priority than other threads.

One approach is to add threads within higher prioritized objects.

What are the priority objects in this system?

Zone—low

Some sensors—high

Some sensors—medium

So use three prioritized-object threads.

This is a multithreaded solution, with multiple threads running through the same object. Sensor status is the attribute that both threads use.

In a multithreaded design, look for where threads intersect. Here, the threads intersect at the status of a sensor.

Let's use the "zoom in and sync" strategy to move in as close as we can. Rather than sync these large methods—sync readAndCheckValue and sync monitor—let's sync as close as possible to the intersection of these threads, a pair of methods that act as "value gatekeepers," namely, sync getStatus and sync setStatus (Figure 4-14).

In Java, it looks like this:

```
public class Zone extends Object implements Runnable {
✂
    // attributes / private / thread
    private Thread myThread;

    // attributes / private / object connections
    private Vector sensors = new Vector();

    // methods / public / activation
    public void activate(int priority) {
        // create my thread and start it
        this.myThread = new Thread(this);
        this.myThread.setPriority(priority);
        this.myThread.start(); }
```

Threads1To3	Zone	SensorHi	SensorLo	ProblemReport
start	run monitor	checkStatus getStatus run readAndCheckValue readValue checkValue setStatus logProblem assessReliability	checkStatus getStatus run readAndCheckValue readValue checkValue setStatus logProblem assessReliability	new

Name: Prioritized-object threads

Threads1To3	Zone	SensorHi	SensorLo	ProblemReport	Comments:
start					// LOW priority
	- -▶ run				
	DO				// do again and again for each zone
	-->monitor				
		-n-▶ checkStatus			(; status)
		SYNC			
		-->getStatus			(; status)
		ENDSYNC			
		-n- - - -▶	checkStatus		(; status)
			SYNC		
			-->getStatus		(; status)
			ENDSYNC		
	ENDDO				
start					// HIGH priority
	- - - - -▶	run			
		DO			
		-->readAndCheckValue			
		-->readValue			(; value)
		-->checkValue			(value, range ; result)
		SYNC			
		-->setStatus			(; value)
		ENDSYNC			
		IF			// problem detected
		-->logProblem			
		-c- - - -▶		new	(value ; problemReport)
		ENDIF			
		-->assessReliability			
		ENDDO			
start					// MEDIUM priority
	- - - - - - - - -▶		run		
			DO		
			-->readAndCheckValue		
			-->readValue		(; value)
			-->checkValue		(value, range ; result)
			SYNC		
			-->setStatus		
			ENDSYNC		
			IF		// problem detected
			logProblem		
			-c-▶	new	(value ; problemReport)
			ENDIF		
			-->assessReliability		
			ENDDO		

Figure 4-14. A trio of prioritized-*object* threads.

```
    // methods / public / Runnable implementation
    public void run() {
        for(;;) { // loop forever until thread is stopped
            this.monitor();
            try {Thread.sleep(100);} catch(InterruptedException e){}} }

    // methods / public / conducting business
    public void monitor() {
        // iterate through the vector of sensors and tell each sensor to check
        // Status
        Enumeration sensorList = this.sensors.elements();
        while (sensorList.hasMoreElements()) {
            // must cast the element to a Sensor
            Sensor aSensor = (Sensor)SensorList.nextElement();
            String status = aSensor.checkStatus();
            /* evaluate status */ } }
✂
}
```

Code notes: This time, the activate method takes a parameter to set the priority of the thread. Also, because each sensor performs readAndCheckValue on its own thread, we simply ask each sensor for its status.

```
public class Sensor extends Object implements Runnable {
✂
    // attributes / private / thread
    private Thread myThread;

    // methods / public / activation
    public void activate(int priority) {
        // create my thread and start it
        this.myThread = new Thread(this);
        this.myThread.setPriority(priority);
        this.myThread.start(); }

    // methods / public / Runnable implementation
    public void run() {
        for(;;) { // loop forever until thread is stopped
            this.readAndCheckValue();
            try {Thread.sleep(100);} catch(InterruptedException e){}} }

    // methods / public / conducting business
    public String checkStatus() {
        /* code goes here */ }
```

```
    // methods / protected synchronized / conducting business
    protected synchronized String getStatus() { /* code goes here */ }
    protected synchronized void setStatus(String status) {
        /* code goes here */ }

    // methods / protected / conducting business
    protected void readAndCheckValue() {
        /* code goes here
           calls the following methods:
             readValue, checkValue, logProblem, and assessReliability */ }
    protected int readValue() { /* code goes here */ }
    protected int checkValue(int value, Range aRange) { /* code goes here */ }
    protected void logProblem() { /* code goes here */ }
    protected void assessReliability() { /* code goes here */ }
✂
}
```

Code notes: This time, Sensor needs its own activate method and priority parameter, just like Zone. We limited the visibility of most of the major conducting business methods. The only main public method, other than activate and run, is the checkStatus method, which is invoked by a zone. The getStatus and setStatus methods must be synchronized.

That looks just fine. However, there is an added problem that you need to consider whenever you have different priorities for threads with the same basic responsibilities; it's called "starvation."

Starvation occurs when a low-priority thread never gets a turn; this happens when high priority threads always keep the processor busy.

Starvation is not a problem if the amount of processing time is small compared to the total time available.

As processing time approaches total time available, the likelihood of starvation of one or more threads increases. If timely servicing of low-priority threads is not a big deal, then all is well.

In Zoe's case, starvation will cause zones to be starved of their monitoring behavior first, followed by the starvation of both monitoring and accessing behavior of the lower priority sensors. Not a good thing for Zoe or her customers.

If timely servicing of low-priority threads is important, however, then we've got two options to consider:

1. Add a thread manager. A thread manager can tell all high-priority threads to go to sleep for a short period of time, making sure that low-priority threads get executed along the way. It's like adding a socialized government to make sure everyone gets their fair share.
2. Don't use prioritized-object threads; we're merely applying a single-thread solution on a sensor-by-sensor basis; indeed, a single-thread solution would be simpler and faster.

4.3.3 Prioritized-Method Threads

We've tried single threads and prioritized-object threads.

However, if high-priority methods within some objects are still not getting executed in a timely fashion, we can take a look at another prioritization scheme: *give execution priority to those methods.*

Here's how to do it:

Prioritized-Methods Strategy: *Prioritize your methods. Separate out cohesive functions with different priorities. Run higher priority methods in higher priority threads; run lower priority methods in lower priority threads.*

The higher priority thread, now relieved of doing lower priority work, will run in less time. So in places where a single-thread approach fails because it's not fast enough, prioritized-method threads can save the day.

The cost? Some added design complexity is required, but it is well worth it.

What are the method priorities in this system?

Monitor zone—low

Assess sensor reliability—medium

Monitor sensor—high

What if the sampling rate for reading sensors is so fast that at times we just cannot keep up?

The key words here are "at times." After all, if we are always too slow, time-averaging some of the work will be of no help at all.

If we cannot keep up at times, we can spin off lower priority work into a separate thread (or threads), and then let the app catch up on that work after a while.

For sensor monitoring, we could strip it down to "read and save a sample" and then let another thread take care of "checking and logging a problem report, if any."

We'll pursue that design in Chapter 5.

For now, let's stick with three prioritized-method threads: monitor zone, assess sensor reliability, and monitor sensor (Figure 4-15).

This is another multithreaded solution, with multiple threads running through the same object (sensor). Sensor status is the attribute that both threads use.

In Java, it looks like this:

```
public class Sensor extends Object implements Runnable {
✂
    // attributes / private / threads
    private Thread monitorThread;
    private Thread assessingThread;

    // methods / public / activation
    public void activate(int monitoringPriority, int assessingPriority) {
        // create monitoring thread and start it
        this.monitoringThread = new Thread(this);
        this.monitoringThread.setPriority(monitoringPriority);
        this.monitoringThread.start();
```

Thread1To3		Zone		Sensor		ProblemReport
start		run monitor		checkStatus getStatus run readAndCheckValue readValue checkValue setStatus logProblem assessReliability		new

Name:

Prioritized-method thread

Comments:

Thread1To3		Zone		Sensor		ProblemReport	Comments
start							// LOW priority
	c →	run					
		DO					
		-->monitor					
			--→	checkStatus			(; status)
				SYNC			
				-->getStatus			(; status)
				ENDSYNC			
		ENDDO					
start							// HIGH priority
	-----	-----	--→	run			
				DO			
				-->readAndCheckValue			
				-->readValue			(; value)
				-->checkValue			(value, range ; result)
				SYNC			
				-->setStatus			(status ;)
				ENDSYNC			
				IF			// problem detected
				-->logProblem			
					c →	new	(value ; problemReport)
				ENDIF			
				ENDDO			
start							// MEDIUM priority
	-----	-----	--→	run			
				DO			
				-->assessReliability			
				ENDDO			

Figure 4-15. A trio of prioritized-*method* threads.

```
        // create assessing thread and start it
        this.assessingThread = new Thread(this);
        this.assessingThread.setPriority(assessingPriority);
        this.assessingThread.start(); }

    // methods / public / Runnable implementation
    public void run() {
        // if the current thread entering run is the monitoring thread,
        // then read and check until stopped.
        if (Thread.currentThread == this.monitoringThread ) {
            for(;;) { // loop forever until thread is stopped
                this.readAndCheck();
                try {Thread.sleep(100);} catch(InterruptedException e){} } }

        // else if the current thread entering run is the assessing thread,
        // then assess reliability until stopped
        if (Thread.currentThread == this.assessingThread ) {
            for(;;) { // loop forever until thread is stopped
                this.assessReliability();
                try {Thread.sleep(100);} catch(InterruptedException e){} } } }

    // methods / public / conducting business
    public String checkStatus() {
        /* code goes here */ }

    // methods / protected synchronized / conducting business
    protected synchronized String getStatus() { /* code goes here */ }
    protected synchronized void setStatus(String status) {
        /* code goes here */ }

    // methods / protected / conducting business
    protected void readAndCheckValue() {
        /* code goes here
            calls the following methods:
              readValue, checkValue, and logProblem. */ }
    protected int readValue() { /* code goes here */ }
    protected int checkValue(int value, Range aRange) { /* code goes here */ }
    protected void logProblem() { /* code goes here */ }
    protected void assessReliability() { /* code goes here */ }
✂
}
```

Code notes: The Zone remains the same. Sensor's activate method now takes two parameters: one for the monitoring thread priority and one for the assessing thread priority. The run method checks the current thread and performs the appropriate loop. This time, the readAndCheckValue method does not call the assessReliability method because this method has its own thread.

4.3.4 Prioritized-Method Prioritized-Object Threads

We've tried single threads, prioritized-method threads, and prioritized-object threads.

However, if the simpler approaches won't get the job done, if we need maximum prioritization flexibility, then we can prioritize methods *and* objects.

If we have some methods that are more important than others, and if we have some objects that are more important than others, and if processing time is approaching actual time, then this approach is one to consider carefully.

Based on prioritized methods, what threads do we need, and what are the relative priorities?

Monitor sensor, across all sensors—high

Assess sensor reliability, across all sensors—medium

Monitor zone, across all zones—low

Based on prioritized objects, what threads do we need, and what are the relative priorities?

High-priority sensors—high

Low-priority sensors—medium

Zone—low

Merging these lists yields five kinds of threads in this design:

Monitor a high-priority sensor—very high

Monitor a low-priority sensor—high

Assess a high-priority sensor—medium

Assess a low-priority sensor—low

Monitor a zone—very low.

Notice that monitoring *lower* priority sensors is still at a higher level of priority than assessing the reliability of the *higher* priority sensors. In this way, all monitoring runs at a higher level of priority than any assessing.

Hence, the overall thread count for this design works out to

One thread per zone object

Two threads per high-priority or low-priority sensor

That's a lot, it's true. This is an extreme case. The good thing about this design is that it's got room for a lot of fine tuning and tweaking. The bad thing about this design is that it uses lots and lots of threads, which isn't a good thing, unless it must be done to meet system response time requirements for high-priority sensors. Hence, the following strategy:

Thread Count Strategy: *Justify the existence of each thread in your design. If you can reduce the thread count and meet response time requirements, do so.*

Figure 4-16 depicts a scenario view that represents six threads, two zones, two priorities of sensors, two thread priorities within each sensor, and a partridge in a pear tree.

In Java, it looks like this:

Code notes: It's the same source code as in the previous example. When creating sensors, adjust the priority parameters in the activate method so that high-priority sensors have a higher monitoring priority than low-priority sensors. Make sure that the assessing priority for the high-priority sensors is lower than the monitoring priority for the low-priority sensors, or low-priority sensors may not have enough processing time to perform their monitoring. For example:

```
// set monitoring priority to 8 and assessing priority to 3
Sensor aSensorHi = new Sensor();
aSensorHi.activate(8,3);
```

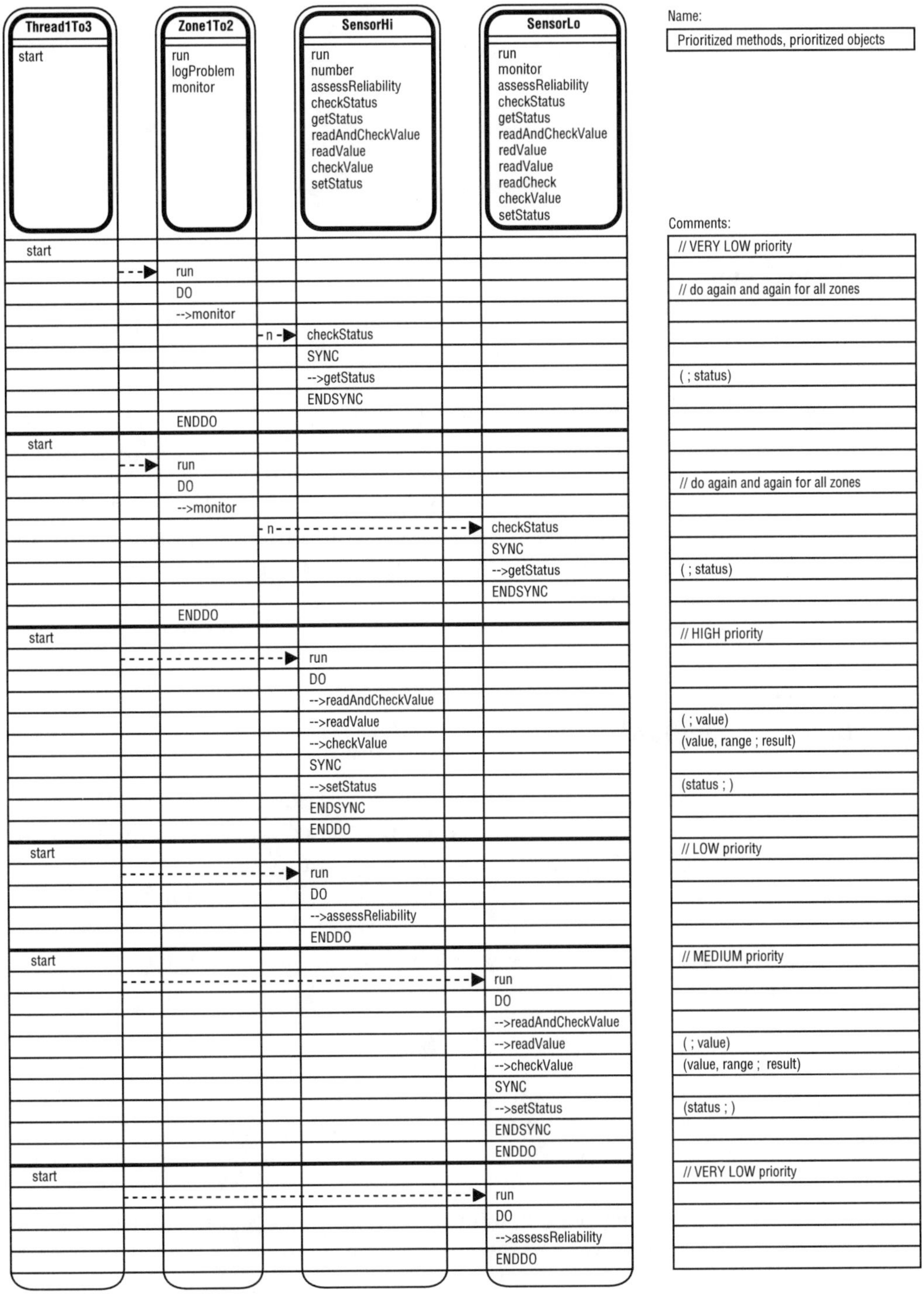

Thread1To3	Zone1To2	SensorHi	SensorLo
start	run logProblem monitor	run number assessReliability checkStatus getStatus readAndCheckValue readValue checkValue setStatus	run monitor assessReliability checkStatus getStatus readAndCheckValue redValue readValue readCheck checkValue setStatus

Name:

Prioritized methods, prioritized objects

Comments:

Thread1To3	Zone1To2	SensorHi	SensorLo	Comments
start				// VERY LOW priority
- - -▶	run			
	DO			// do again and again for all zones
	-->monitor			
	- n -▶	checkStatus		
		SYNC		
		-->getStatus		(; status)
		ENDSYNC		
	ENDDO			
start				
- - -▶	run			
	DO			// do again and again for all zones
	-->monitor			
	- n - - -	- - - - - - - - - - -	- - -▶ checkStatus	
			SYNC	
			-->getStatus	(; status)
			ENDSYNC	
	ENDDO			
start				// HIGH priority
- - - -	- - - - - - - - - -▶	run		
		DO		
		-->readAndCheckValue		
		-->readValue		(; value)
		-->checkValue		(value, range ; result)
		SYNC		
		-->setStatus		(status ;)
		ENDSYNC		
		ENDDO		
start				// LOW priority
- - - -	- - - - - - - - - -▶	run		
		DO		
		-->assessReliability		
		ENDDO		
start				// MEDIUM priority
- - - -	- - - - - - - - - -	- - - - - - - - - - -	- - -▶ run	
			DO	
			-->readAndCheckValue	
			-->readValue	(; value)
			-->checkValue	(value, range ; result)
			SYNC	
			-->setStatus	(status ;)
			ENDSYNC	
			ENDDO	
start				// VERY LOW priority
- - - -	- - - - - - - - - -	- - - - - - - - - - -	- - -▶ run	
			DO	
			-->assessReliability	
			ENDDO	

Figure 4-16. Prioritized methods, prioritized objects, and lots and lots of threads.

```
// set monitoring priority to 7 and assessing priority to 2
Sensor aSensorLo = new Sensor();
aSensorLo.activate(7,2);
```

This approach allows the greatest flexibility and lots of room for fine tuning.

4.3.5 Overall Point

The overall point here is keep it simple.

Use a single-thread design whenever you can.

If you cannot get the job done that way, then you've got to prioritize what you do. Identify priority methods, adding submethods to separate out cohesive functions with different priorities. Give priority to certain objects. Give priority to certain methods. Or give priority to both.

4.4 Interface Adapters

Designing with threads is an advanced design topic. Designing with interface adapters is even more advanced. So, depending on your background in this area, you might opt to jump ahead to the summary at the end of this chapter and tackle this section another day.

Let's explore the wonderful world of interface adapters.

4.4.1 Need

A thread object is rather single minded in what it communicates to another object. A thread object sends a "run" message. That's it.

So what happens if multiple thread objects want to message the same object but yet invoke different methods for each one?

4.4.2 One Approach: Dispatcher

One approach is to add a test and a case statement to the run method (Figure 4-17).

The test statement asks a thread class which thread has just entered. The case statement routes the thread to the method it really needs to be running through.

However, a "case" statement at the beginning of any method implies some pretty lame internal cohesion.

A thread should be able to invoke the method it needs. If multiple threads want to invoke different methods in the same object, however, we need to add an intermediary: an interface adapter.

4.4.3 A Better Approach: Interface Adapters

Why not let each thread invoke the method it really wants to invoke rather than just a "run" method?

But how can we do this, when a thread implements the Runnable interface (run) rather than an application-specific message?

The answer is use an interface adapter (Figure 4-18).

A sender tells an adapter to do something; that adapter translates the method call in one interface to another interface. Hence, the adapter is called an "interface adapter."

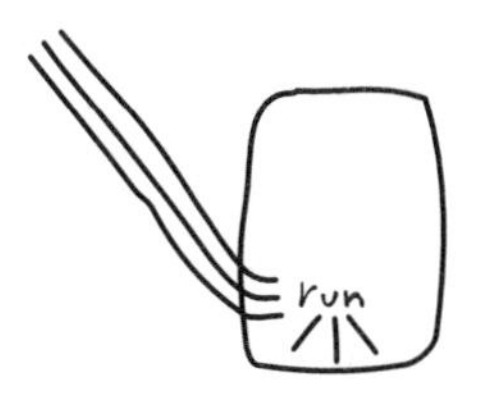

Figure 4-17. Threads wanting to invoke different methods, but they're being forced through one entry point.

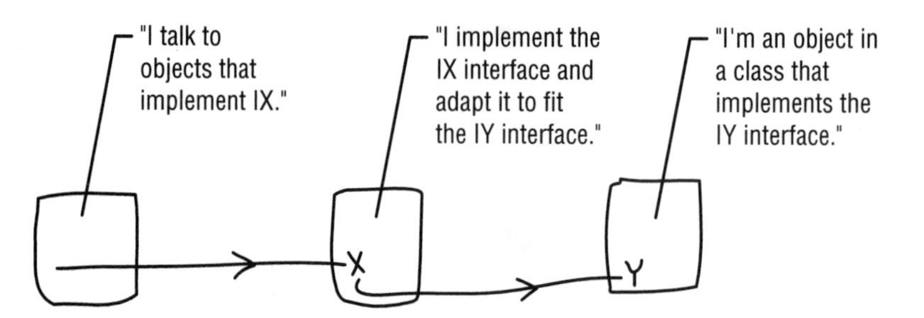

Figure 4-18. An interface adapter adapts interfaces.

4.4.4 What an Interface Adapter Looks Like

Figure 4-19 illustrates an object-model pattern, the interface-adapter pattern.

Note that the interface names in Figure 4-19 are not really interface names at all. They are abstractions of interface names that you might use when applying this object-model pattern in a specific context.

The specific interfaces you choose to use will be different for each kind of interface-adapter class that you define for your application. For Zoe's Zones, we'll use this pattern to model something called, "thread-Runnable-to-IMonitor adapter-sensors." Before we do that,

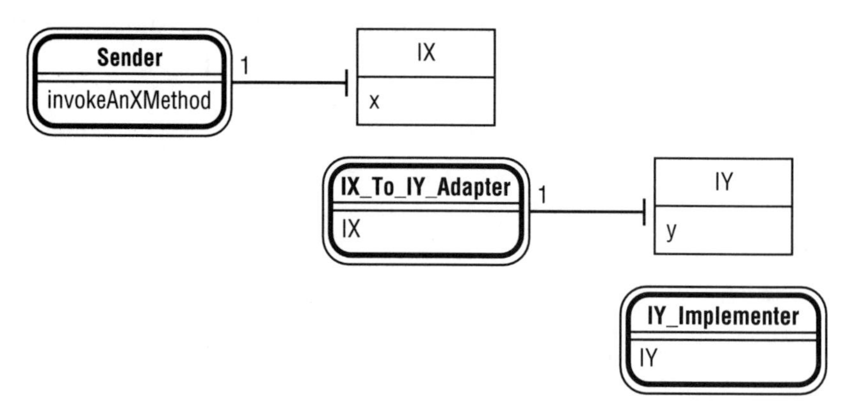

Figure 4-19. The interface-adapter pattern.

however, let's take a look at the scenario view for this pattern, so we can consider its stereotypical interactions.

A receiver

- sends a message to create an interface adapter and it
- sends a message to create a sender (sending an interface adapter as an argument).

Then a sender sends a message to its "IX-to-IY" adapter. And finally, that interface adapter sends a message to its object that implements the "IY" interface.

This is illustrated in Figure 4-20.

In Java, it looks like this:

```
public interface IX {
    void x(); }
public interface IY {
    void y(); }
```

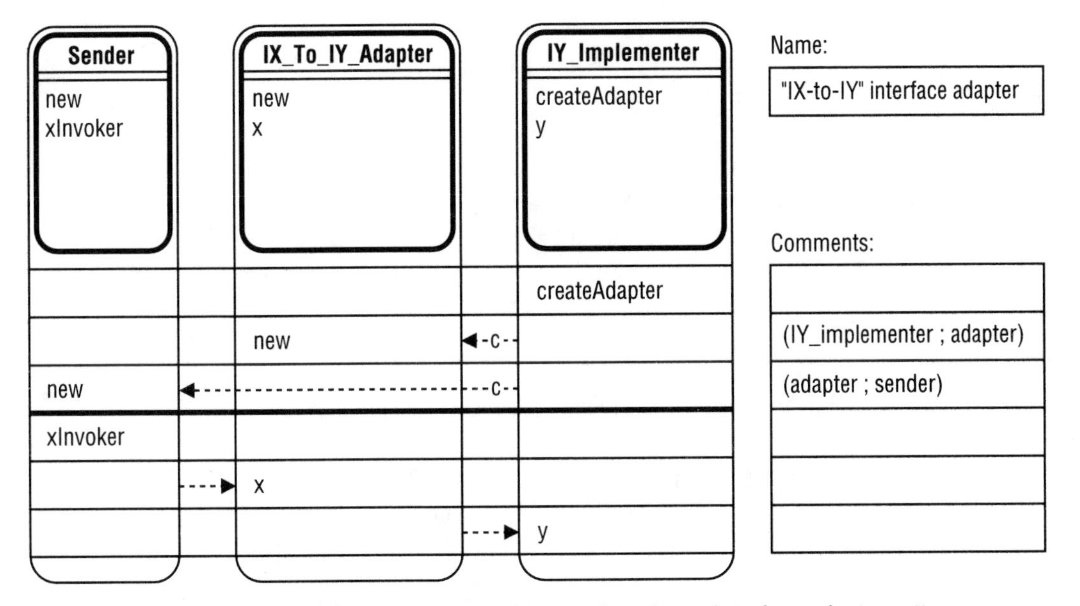

Figure 4-20. Stereotypical interactions for an interface-adapter pattern.

```
public class Sender extends Object {
✂
    // attributes / private / object connection
    private IX myIX;

    // methods / public / conducting business
    public void xInvoker() {
        // send the message x to myIX
        this.myIX.x(); }

    // constructors
    public Sender(IX anIX) {
        // set myIX to anIX
        this.myIX = anIX; }
✂
}

public class IX_to_IY_Adapter extends Object implements IX {
✂
    // attributes / private / object connection
    private IY myIY;

    // methods / public / IX implementation
    public void x () {
        // send the message y to myIY
        this.myIY.y(); }

    // constructors
    public Sender(IY anIY) {
        // set myIY to anIY
        this.myIY = anIY; }
✂
}

public class IY_Implementer extends Object implements IY {
✂
    // attributes / private / object connections
    private IX_to_IY_Adapter myAdapter;
    private Sender mySender;
```

```
    // methods / public / adapter creation
    public void createAdapter () {
        // create an adapter and pass myself as the parameter
        this.myAdapter = new IX_to_IY_Adapter(this);
        // create a sender and pass myAdapter as the parameter
        this.mySender = new Sender(this.myAdapter); }

    // methods / public / IY implementation
    public void y() { /* code goes here */ }
✂
}
```

When should you use interface adapters for threads? Only when you need them. When do you need them? In the context of working with thread objects, you need interface adapters whenever you have multiple thread objects that you would like to invoke different methods in an object. And in a broader context, they are needed whenever you want to adapt a message-send from one object into some other message-send that is suitable for another object.

4.4.5 Interface Adapters for Zoe's Zones

Here is what happens for Zoe's Zones for the "prioritized methods" approach.

We need threads to wind through each of the following:

A zone-monitoring thread

A sensor-monitoring thread

A sensor-assessing thread

4.4.6 A Zone-Monitoring Thread

A zone-monitoring thread needs no interface adapter because there is only one method to service—the "monitor" method. See Figure 4-21 for the scenario view.

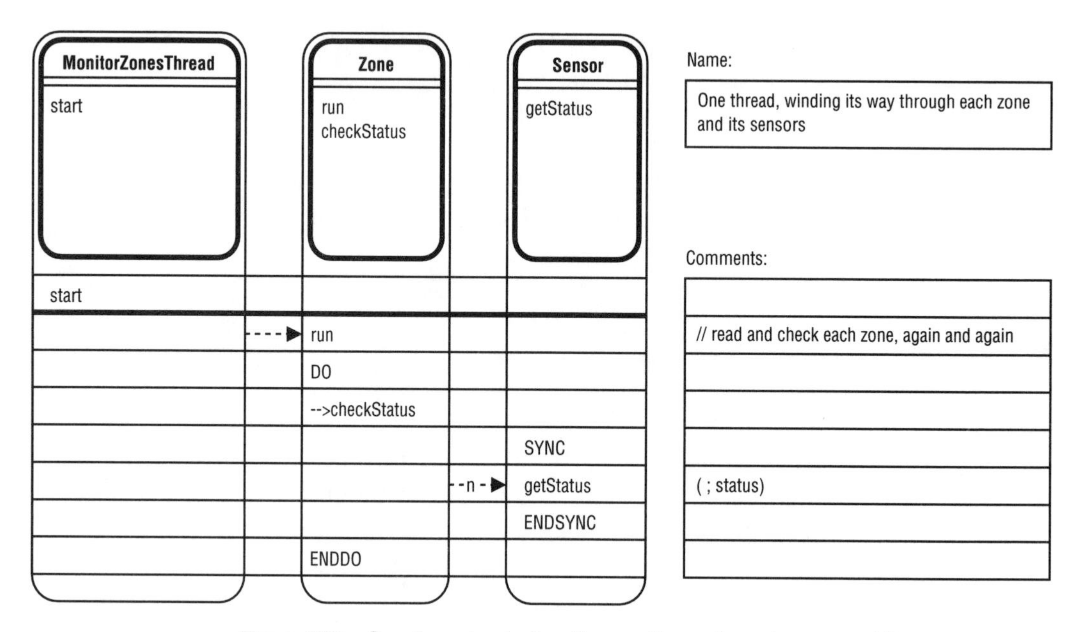

Figure 4-21. One thread, winding its way through each zone and its sensors.

Note that the Zone class implements the Runnable interface, so a thread object can send a zone object a "run" message.

4.4.7 A Sensor-Assessing Thread and a Sensor-Monitoring Thread

Okay. Let's get ready for the next scenario view.

Now we can apply the interface-adapter pattern. Applied in this context, the pattern looks like Figure 4-22.

Hmmm. We need a class that will implement the IMonitor interface. An object in that class will know all of the sensor objects in the application.

Note that normally we could embed this "across the collection" responsibility within the Sensor class itself (making sure that, upon creating a sensor object, we add it to that collection).

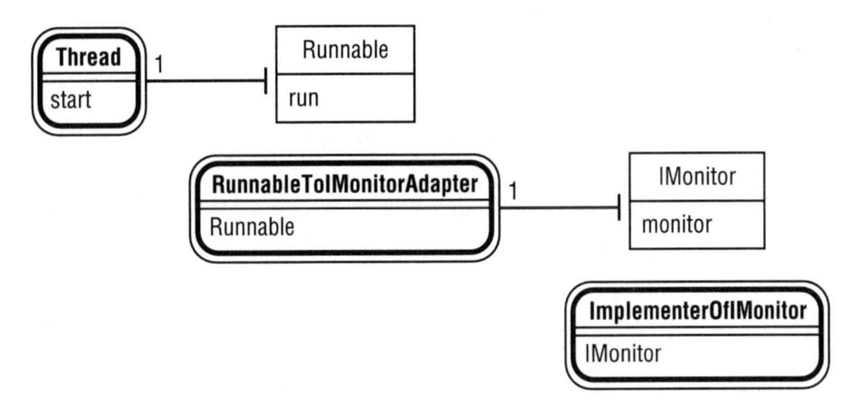

Figure 4-22. Applying the interface-adapter pattern within a specific context.

But here we are dealing with interfaces. And (Java-style) interfaces are intended for object method signatures rather than class method signatures.

The impact in a scenario view is minimal. We just add a "Sensors" column, a class with one object in it, and that object holds a collection of all the sensors in the application.

What other classes do we need here? The RunnableToIMonitorAdapter class implements the simple mapping between "run" and "monitor." The RunnableToIAssessAdapter class implements the simple mapping between "run" and "assess."

For the scenario itself, the following steps are needed just to get things ready to go:

- The "sensors" object sends a message to a RunnableToIMonitorAdapter class to create a "monitor adapter" object (sending itself as a parameter).
- The "sensors" object sends a message to the Thread class to create a thread (sending a "monitor adapter" object as a parameter).
- The "sensors" object sends a message to the RunnableToIAssessAdapter class to create an "assess adapter" object (sending itself as a parameter).

- The "sensors" object sends a message to the Thread class to create another thread (sending an "assess adapter" object).

At this point, we're ready for business:

- The "sensors" object asks its "monitor sensors" thread to start.
- The "monitor sensors" object sends a "run" message to its "Runnable-to-IMonitor" adapter object.
- The "Runnable-to-IMonitor" object sends a "monitor all sensors" message to the "sensors" object.

And:

- The "sensors" object asks its "assess sensors" thread to start.
- The "assess sensors" object sends a "run" message to its "Runnable-to-IAssess adapter" object.
- The "Runnable-to-IAssess" object sends an "assess all sensors" message to the "sensors" object.

Figure 4-23 depicts the scenario view.

In Java, it looks like this:

```
public interface IMonitor {
    void monitor(); }

public interface IAssess {
    void assess(); }

public class RunnableToIMonitorAdapter extends Object implements Runnable
{
✂
    // attributes / private / object connection
    private IMonitor myIMonitor;

    // methods / public / Runnable implementation
    public void run() {
        this.myIMonitor.monitor(); }
```

Name: Using interface adapters

MonitorSensorsThread	AssessSensorsThread	RunnableToIMonitorAdapter	RunnableToIAssessAdapter	Sensor	Comments:
new start	new start	new run	new run	setUpThreadsAndAdapters monitor readAndCheck assess assessReliability	
				setUpThreadsAndAdapters	
		new		c	(sensor ; adapter)
new				c	(adapter ; thread)
			new	c	(sensor ; adapter)
	new			c	(adapter ; thread)
start					
		run			// RUN MONITORING THREAD
				monitor	
				DO	
				-->readAndCheckValue	
				ENDDO	
	start				
			run		// RUN ASSESSING THREAD
				assess	
				DO	
				-->assessReliability	
				ENDDO	

Figure 4-23. Monitoring and assessing threads, with corresponding interface adapters.

```
    // constructors
    public RunnableToIMonitorAdapter(IMonitor anIMonitor) {
        this.myIMonitor = anIMonitor ; }
✂
}

public class RunnableToIAssessAdapter extends Object implements Runnable {
✂
    // attributes / private / object connection
    private IAssess myIAssess;

    // methods / public / Runnable implementation
    public void run() {
        this.myIAssess.assess(); }

    // constructors
    public RunnableToIAssessAdapter(IAssess anIAssess) {
        this.myIAssess = anIAssess ; }
✂
}

public class Sensors extends Object implements IMonitor, IAssess {
✂
    // attributes / private / sensor collection
    private Vector sensorCollection = new Vector();

    // attributes / private / threads
    private Thread monitorThread;
    private Thread assessingThread;

    // attributes / private / interface adapters
    private RunnableToIMonitorAdapter myRunnableToIMonitorAdapter;
    private RunnableToIAssessAdapter myRunnableToIAssessAdapter;

    // methods / public / activation
    public void activate(int monitoringPriority, int assessingPriority) {
        // create the monitoring adapter and pass myself as the
        // parameter
        myRunnableToIMonitorAdapter = new
                RunnableToIMonitorAdapter(this);
```

```
        // create monitoring thread and pass the monitoring adapter as the
        // parameter
        this.monitoringThread = new Thread(myRunnableToIMonitorAdapter);
        this.monitoringThread.setPriority(monitoringPriority);
        this.monitoringThread.start();

        // create the assessing adapter and pass myself as the
        // parameter
        myRunnableToIAssessAdapter = new
                RunnableToIAssessAdapter(this);

        // create monitoring thread and pass the assessing adapter as the
        // parameter
        this.assessingThread = new Thread(myRunnableToIAssessAdapter);
        this.assessingThread.setPriority(assessingPriority);
        this.assessingThread.start(); }

    // methods / public / IMonitor implementation
    public void monitor() {
        for(;;) { // loop forever until thread is stopped
                this.readAndCheckValue();
                try {Thread.sleep(100);}catch(InterruptedException e){} } }

    // methods / public / IAssess implementation
    public void assess() {
        for(;;) { // loop forever until thread is stopped
                this.assessReliability();
                try {Thread.sleep(100);}catch(InterruptedException e){} } }

    // methods / public / conducting business
    public String checkStatus() {
        /* code goes here */ }

    // methods / protected / conducting business
    protected void readAndCheckValue() {
        /* code goes here.
           iterate through my sensor collection and
           ask each sensor to readAndCheckValue. */ }
    protected void assessReliability() {
        /* code goes here.
           iterate through my sensor collection and
           ask each sensor to assessReliability. */ }

✂
}
```

Code notes: The Zone remains the same. Sensors now implements the interfaces for two interface adapters and no longer implements the Runnable interface. The monitoring thread now enters through the IMonitor interface and the assessing thread now enters through the IAssess interface.*

4.5 Summary

In this chapter, you've worked with threads, streams of program execution.

For an application to run, you must have at least one thread.

Why bother with multiple threads?

Most designs must account for multiple streams of program execution; this chapter shows how to do that safely.

Multiple threads let you give the appearance of doing more than one thing at a time. For example, your application can serve multiple clients at the same time.

Threads also give you the clean, simple way to design in the main thing you want your application to do, along with other things that you'd like it to be aware of or check on from time to time.

The strategies you learned and applied in this chapter are

Sync Access to Values Strategy: *When multiple threads compete for values(s) within an object—and you try other thread paths but cannot avoid competition for these values—use sync'd methods to limit access (one thread at a time). For multithreaded objects, sync each method that compares, operates on, gets, or sets internal values.*

---

*Java is strongly typed. All possible message-sends must be established at compile time. You cannot design with dynamic message dispatching (meaning, there is no mechanism like in C++ to create a pointer to a function and then de-reference that pointer [invoke the method it points to], and at any time reassign that pointer and then again de-reference that pointer [invoke the method it points to now]).

Zoom In and Sync Strategy: *Zoom in on exactly what you need to sync, factor it out into a separate method, and sync that method. Why? Sync for as little time as possible so other (potentially higher priority) threads waiting at the start of other sync methods for that object will get to run sooner rather than later.*

Sync Access to Objects Strategy: *When multiple threads compete for entry into each other's sync'd methods, use a gatekeeper to control access one thread at a time, and make sure the objects that the gatekeeper protects have no sync methods.*

Value Gatekeeper Strategy: *Look for a method that increments or decrements a count of a limited resource. Sync that method; give it exclusive access to that count.*

Object Gatekeeper Strategy: *Look for a method that reserves or issues a limited resource, represented by the objects in that collection. Sync that method and give it exclusive access to that collection of objects.*

Four Thread Designs Strategy: *Apply these thread designs, looking for the simplest one that will satisfy your performance requirements. From simplest to most complex, consider: (1) single thread, (2) prioritized-object threads, (3) prioritized-method threads, (4) prioritized-method prioritized-object threads.*

Prioritized-Methods Strategy: *Prioritize your methods. Separate out cohesive functions with different priorities. Run higher priority methods in higher priority threads; run lower priority methods in lower priority threads.*

Thread Count Strategy: *Justify the existence of each thread in your design. If you can reduce the thread count and meet response time requirements, do so.*

Chapter 5

Design with Notification

In this chapter, we explore three major notification mechanisms:

- passive: someone asks me if I've changed;
- timer-based: someone wakes me up; and
- active: an observable notifies its observers.

Passive notification is simple but resource intensive.

Timer-based notification is a useful pattern.

Active notification, with its many variations, is most interesting; it's an essential ingredient for problem–domain object reuse; it's an essential ingredient for designing loosely coupled subsystems. Java's own active notification mechanism (observable-observer) is a step in the right direction, but has some defects. This chapter goes beyond current weaknesses, showing you how to get the job done.

5.1 Passive Notification

Passive notification is the simplest of all notification mechanisms.

Passive notification is also known as polling. One object polls others, asking each one for its current status to see if it has changed in some meaningful way.

Perhaps you have a boss like this—always checking on you, always wondering how you are doing—in three words, a real pain (Figure 5-1).

Figure 5-2 depicts an object model for passive notification.

As shown in the scenario in Figure 5-3, the corresponding object interactions are just what you'd expect.

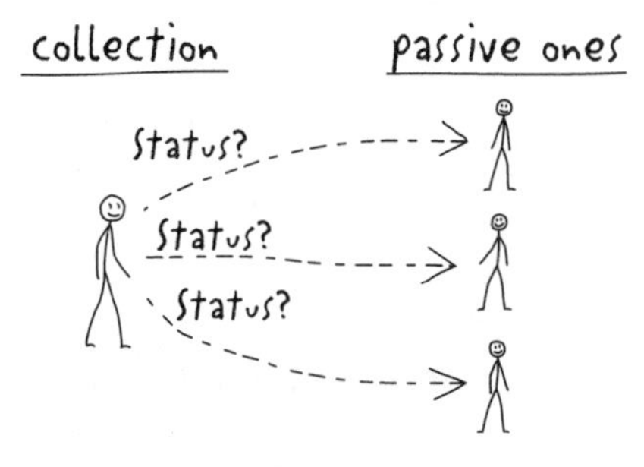

Figure 5-1. Passive notification.

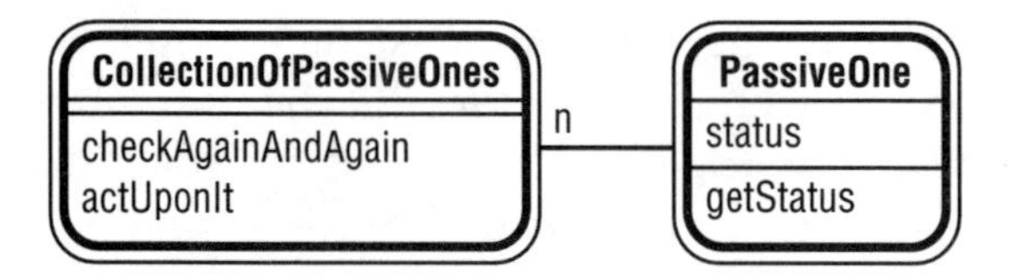

Figure 5-2. An object model for passive notification.

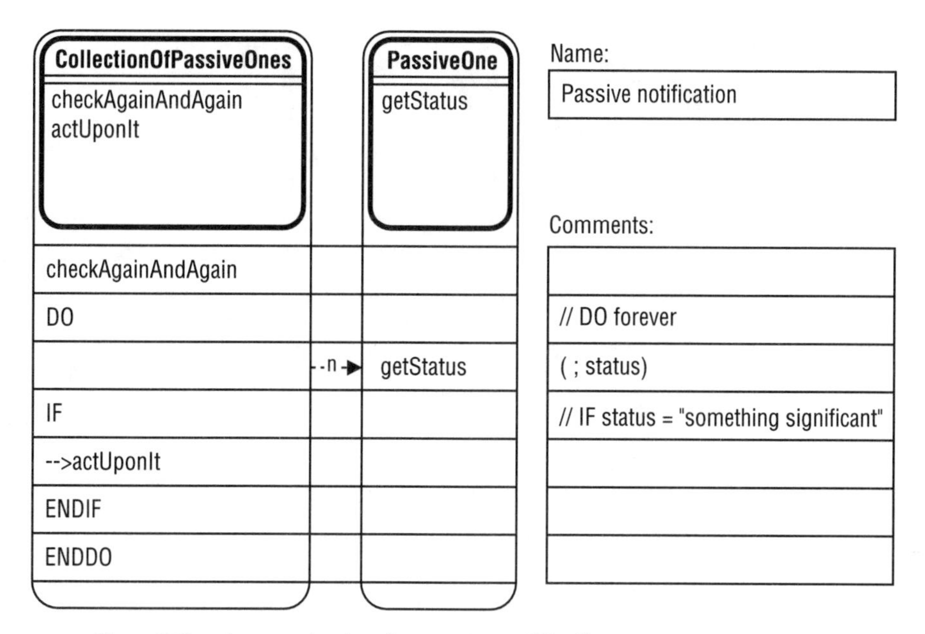

Figure 5-3. A scenario view for passive notification.

Okay, let's apply this notification mechanism to Zoe's Zones (Figures 5-4 and 5-5).

The good news about passive notification is that it is simple.

The bad news is that passive notification is resource intensive in two ways: the loop itself and the number of objects that must be queried. Passive notification consumes resources asking about status even if the status never changes.

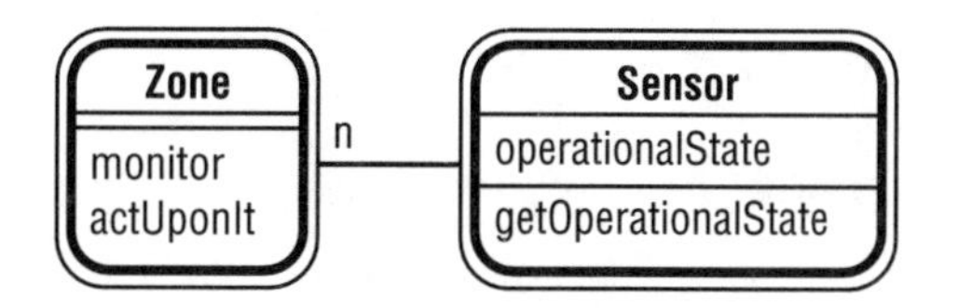

Figure 5-4. Passive notification for Zoe's Zones—object model.

Zone: monitor, actUponIt

Sensor: getOperationalState

Name: Sensors—and passive notification

Zone		Sensor	Comments:
monitor			
DO			
	-n-▶	getOperationalState	(; operationalState)
IF			// IF operationalState = "out of bounds"
-->actUponIt			
ENDIF			
ENDDO			

Figure 5-5. Passive notification for Zoe's Zones—scenario view.

You can take care of the resource-intensive aspect of the loop itself by adding a timer (something we'll explore later in this chapter). However, the response time suffers. And if a problem occurs while you are sleeping, it might go undetected (depending on the problem domain you are working on).

When you have hundreds or thousands of objects to watch over (for example, the hundreds of items that might appear in a list within a UI), passive notification is still too awkward, and too slow.

5.2 Timer-Based Notification

Timer-based notification is another notification mechanism.

The idea behind a timer is simple: put a thread to sleep for a specified period of time, then let it wake up and continue.

5.2.1 Timer-Notification Pattern

The timer will sleep until a specified duration has passed. Figure 5-6 shows the object model.

Note the object-connection interface constraints. This is just another way of showing that an object holds a collection of objects from classes that implement a given interface. For example, as a thread object, "I hold one runnable object, meaning, one object from any class that implements the runnable interface."

Throughout this chapter, we'll need the following strategy:

Holder-Interface Strategy: *Establish a collection; define an interface.*

Figure 5-7 illustrates how that strategy fits in with the timer object model.

Figure 5-8 shows the timer scenario view with a builder object to set up and activate a timer.

In Java, it looks like this:

```
public interface ITime {
    void wakeup(); }
```

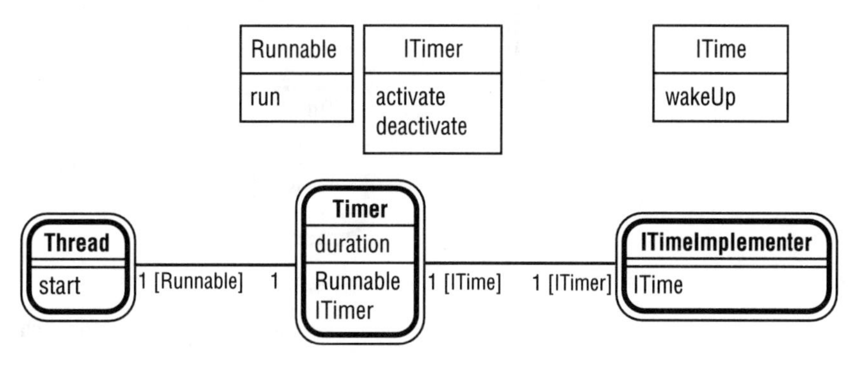

Figure 5-6a. Timer object model.

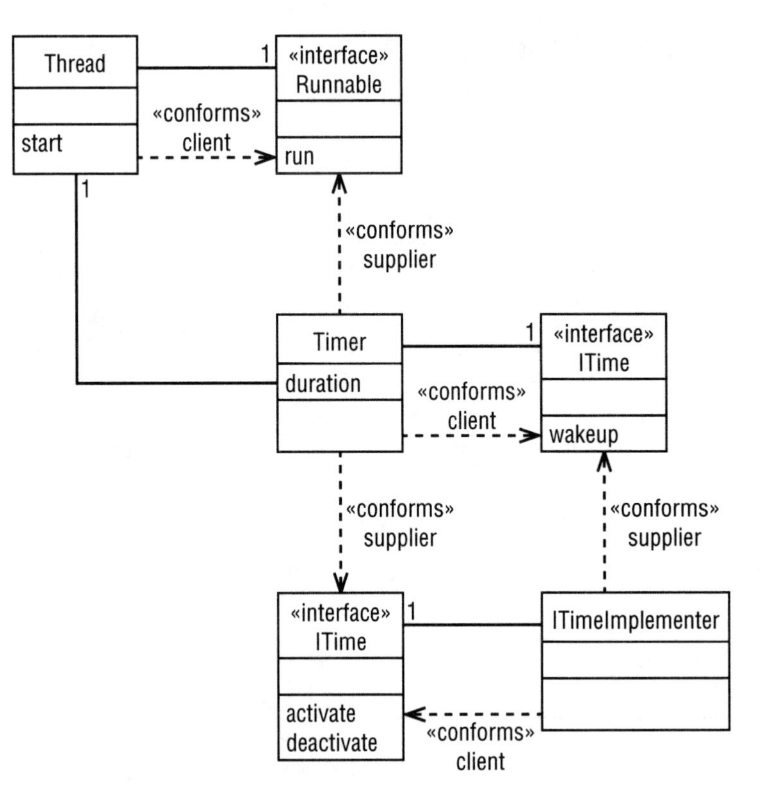

Figure 5-6b. Timer object model (UML notation).

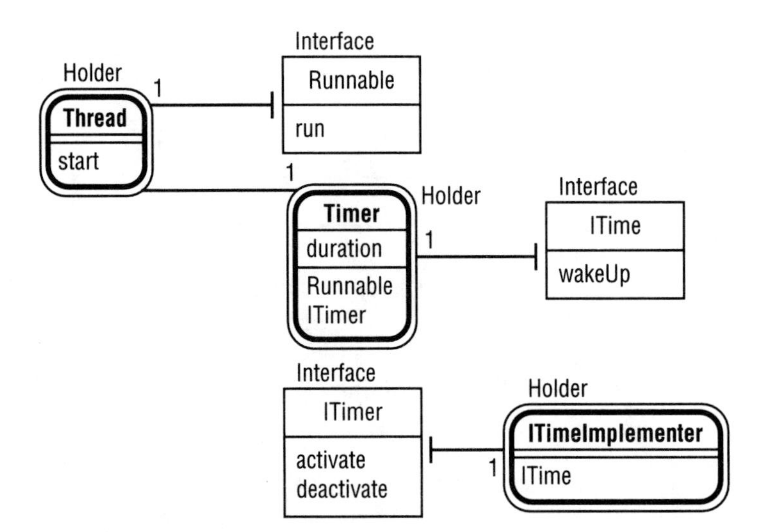

Figure 5-7. Holder-interface, again and again.

ITime Implementer		Timer (ITimer, IRunnable Implementer)		Thread	Comments
setup activateTimer wakeUp deactivateTimer		new activate run deactivate		new start sleep stop	Name: An ITime implementer and its separately-threaded timer
setup					
	--c-->	new			(; timer)
			--c-->	new	(timer ; thread)
activateTimer					
	---->	activate			(duration ;)
			---->	start	
		run	<----		
		DO			// DO until someone stops (kills) this thread
			--c-->	sleep	(duration ;)
wakeUp	<----				
		ENDDO			
deactivateTimer					
	---->	deactivate			
			---->	stop	

Figure 5-8. Timer scenario view.

```
public interface ITimer {
    void activate(long duration);
    void deactivate(); }

public class Timer extends Object implements Runnable, ITimer {
✂
    // attributes / private
    private long duration = 0;      // in milliseconds

    // attributes / private / object connection
    private ITime myITime;
    Thread myThread;
```

```
    // methods / public / Runnable implementation
    public void run() {
        for (;;) { // continue sleep/wake-up cycle until thread is stopped
            try {
              Thread.sleep(this.duration);
            } catch (InterruptedExecution e) {};
            this.myITime.wakeup(); } }
```

Code notes: Sleep is a class method. So we send a message to the Thread class itself, asking it to put this thread to sleep.

```
    // methods / public / ITimer implementation
    public void activate(int aDuration) {
        // remember the duration
        this.duration = aDuration;
        // create and start a thread
        myThread = new Thread(this);
        myThread.start(); }

    public void deactivate() {
        myThread.stop(); }
✂
}
```

Code notes: Make sure to catch the exception that's thrown when putting a thread to sleep, or the compiler will complain.

```
public class ITimeImplementer extends Object implements ITime {
✂
    // attributes / private
    private ITimer myITimer;

    // methods / public / conducting business
    public void setup() {
        this.myITimer = new Timer(); }

    public void activateTimer() {
        this.myITimer.activate(3600000);   /* 1 hr = 3600000 milliseconds */ }

    public void deactivateTimer() {
        this.myITimer.deactivate(); }
```

```
    // methods / public / ITime implementation
    public void wakeUp() {
        /* code goes here */ }
✂
}
```

Code notes: We put the creation of the timer in the setup method and the activation of the timer in the activateTimer method. Alternatively, we could put both of these steps in the constructor of ITimeImplementer if we want to create and start a timer right away.

5.2.2 A Timer for Charlie's Charters

Suppose that once per day we need to generate a list of expiring reservations for each agent.

This requires timer(s) and low-priority thread(s).

We can design this in several ways:

- One thread, beginning with an "agents" object (a collection of all agents). The thread could wind its way from one agent to the next to the next, asking each one to build its own list of expiring reservations.
- One thread, beginning with an "agency" object (a collection of all reservations). The thread could wind its way through the reservations for that agency, building up a list of expiring reservations for each agent.
- One thread per agent, each one beginning with an "agent" object. Each thread could wind its way through the reservations for that agent.

The "one thread per agent" approach has more low-priority threads, but it also points to a simpler overall design. Let's take a closer look.

Figure 5-9 depicts the object model.

Figure 5-10 shows the scenario view.

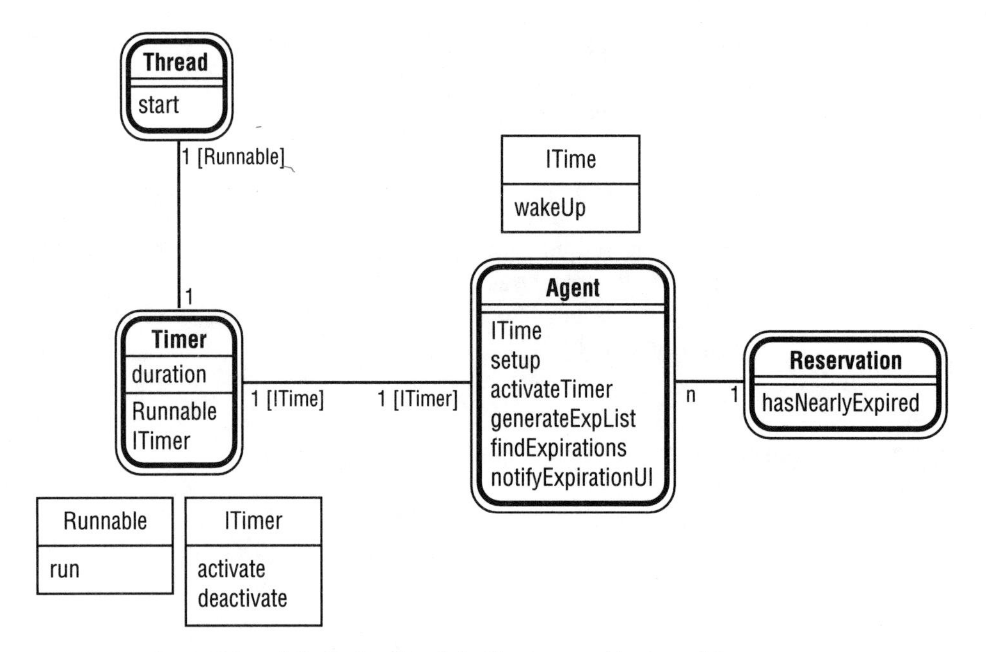

Figure 5-9. A timer for Charlie's Charters—object model.

In Java, it looks like this:

```
public class Agent extends Object implements ITime {

    // private / attributes
    private ITimer myITimer;

    // methods / public / conducting business
    public void setup() {
        this.myITimer = new Timer(); }

    public void activateTimer() {
        this.myITimer.activate(86400000);         /* 24 hr */ }

    public void deactivateTimer() {
        this.myITimer.deactivate(); }

    // methods / public / ITime implementation
    public void wakeUp() {
        /* - generate expiration list
```

Name: An agent and its separately-threaded timer

Agent (ITime Implementer)		Timer (ITimer, Runnable Implementer)		Thread		Reservation	Comments
setup activateTimer generateExpList findExpirations notifyExpirationUI wakeUp deactivateTimer		new activate run deactivate		new start stop sleep		hasNearlyExpired	
setup							
	- - c - ->	new					(; timer)
			- - c - ->	new			(timer ; thread)
activateTimer							
	- - - ->	activate					(duration ;)
			- - - ->	start			
		run	<- - - -				
		DO					// DO until someone stops (kills) this thread
			- - c - ->	sleep			(duration ;)
wakeUp	<- - - -						
-->generateExpList							
-->findExpirations							
	- - n - - -	- - - - - - - -	- - - -	- - - -	- - - ->	hasNearlyExpired	(; hasNearlyExpired)
-->notifyExpirationUI							// This is something for active notification (next up in this chapter).
		ENDDO					
deactivateTimer							
	- - - ->	deactivate					
			- - - ->	stop			

Figure 5-10. A timer for Charlie's Charters—scenario view.

```
        - find expirations
        - notify expiration UI */ }
✂
}
```

Code notes: We set the timer to wake us up every 24 hours. When the agent is told to wake up, it generates a list of expiring reservations and notifies the appropriate UI component.

5.3 Active Notification

Active notification puts the notification responsibility within the object that changes. That object takes action.

Hmmm. Sounds much more like an object-oriented approach: I change; I let others (who have registered interest in me) know that I've changed.

We can summarize active notification in two words: observable-observer.

Let's take a closer look at observable-observer and significant variations on that theme:

- Observer-observable
- A pair of classes (one extreme)
- A pair of interfaces (another extreme)
- Classes and an interface (middle ground, yet shaky ground)
- Should we inherit from Java's Observable class?
- Can we use Java's Observer interface?
- Composition to the rescue (higher ground)
- Charlie's Charters' flight descriptions
- Using a repeater
- Spawning a notification thread

5.3.1 Observable-Observer

Observable-observer is an object-model pattern. It is also known as publisher-subscriber, model-view, and document-view (Figure 5-11).

Here's how it works.

First, someone tells an observable who its observers are:

- Some object (let's call it a builder) asks an observable to add an observer.
- An observable adds that observer to its list of observers.

Then, an observable notifies its observers:

- When an observable object changes itself in a significant way (meaning, in a way that someone else might be interested in), it notifies each of its observers.

Finally, each observer does its thing:

- Each observer gets whatever it needs.
- Each observer takes whatever action it deems appropriate.

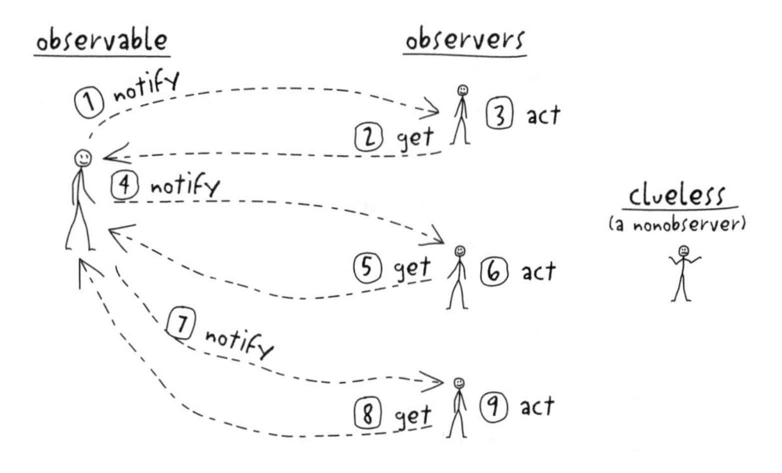

Figure 5-11. An observable and its observers.

Okay, okay, we hear you out there. Are there lots of messages? Compared with passive notification

- Observable-observer *reduces* overall message traffic.
- Observable-observer *reduces* the coupling that an observable has with its observers.

Let's consider the point about reduced coupling.

Observable-observer lets us put together PD and UI objects in such a way that PD objects know very, very little about UI objects. PD objects are not hopelessly attached to UI objects, which is a very good thing. Observable-observer facilitates reuse of PD objects.

In a similar vein, observable-observer lets us put together a subsystem with other, supporting subsystems. A subsystem knows very, very little about the supporting subsystems. That subsystem no longer has a fatal attraction to its supporting subsystems. Observable-observer facilitates reuse of a subsystem (loose coupling); at the same time, it facilitates extensibility as well (easy to add, change, or remove supporting subsystems, as needed).

Okay, then. So how might we model (and ultimately implement) something called observable-observer, classes and inheritance, or composition and interfaces, for example.

Several options are possible.

Balanced Design Strategy: *Design at two extremes and then somewhere in between. Design connotes looking at alternatives and picking a reasonable approach.*

Let's first consider the extremes and then the middle ground.

5.3.2 A Pair of Classes (One Extreme)

One extreme is a pair of classes, with or without inheritance.

Without inheritance, we'd need to design and build both observable and observer into the classes that needed them, each and every time, from scratch (Figure 5-12).

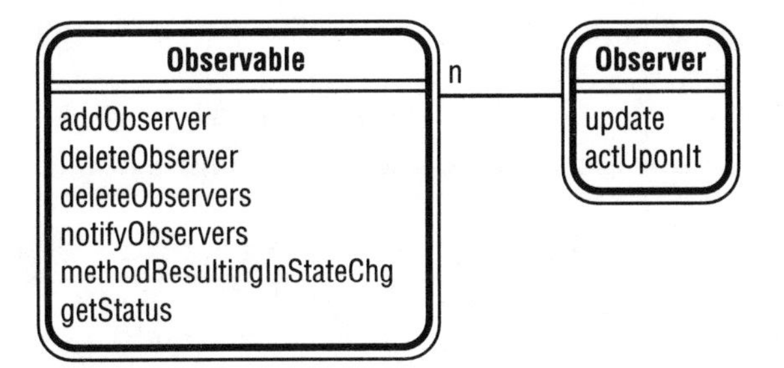

Figure 5-12. A pair of classes.

Sounds like too much work. We can do better than that.

Some methods remain the same:

addObserver—adds an object to a list of observers

deleteObserver—deletes an object from a list of observers

deleteObservers—deletes *all* observers from a list of observers

notifyObservers—sends an "update" message to each observer, letting it know about a change that has taken place

Yet some methods must be customized for a specific observable and its observers:

Observable

- methodResultingInStateChg—do something significant, something worth notifying the observers about
- getStatus—get the value(s) requested by an observer, something it needs to ask, upon notification that what it is watching (the observable) has changed in some way.

Observer

- update—initiate an observer's response to a notification from an observable
- actUponIt—upon notification, this is the action that each observer takes

Some methods remain the same; some methods must be customized.

This sounds like a good opportunity for inheritance, showing what is the same (superclass) and what is different (subclasses).

But is this a good idea (remember Chapter 2, Design with Composition, Rather than Inheritance)? Let's evaluate this, in the pages ahead. For now, though, we're in the midst of considering an extreme: a classes-only approach.

Let's try it out. Figure 5-13 shows an object model.

A SpecializedObservable class needs its own method name for methodResultingInStateChg and getStatus. It also needs its own implementation for those methods.

A SpecializedObserver class needs its own method name for actUponIt, and it needs its own implementation for it.

But what about the update method? It's listed in both Observer and SpecializedObserver. In an object model, seeing a method name appear in a class and a subclass indicates that

- the superclass establishes that the method signature must be implemented by all of its specialization classes, or

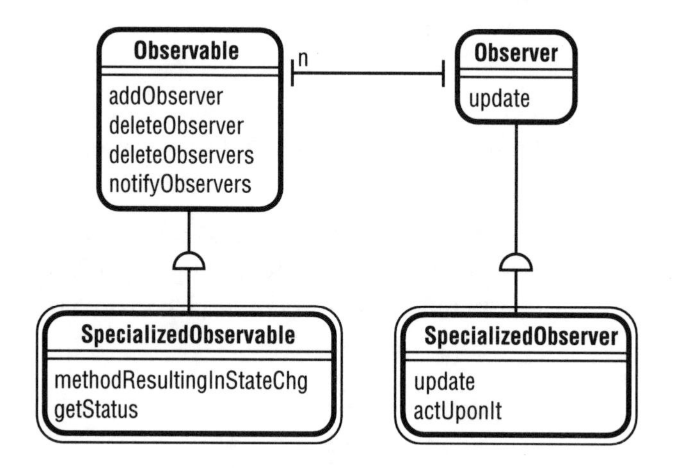

Figure 5-13. A pair of specialized classes.

- the superclass establishes a method signature and some common capability, and now a subclass is extending that common capability.

What about in this case? The Observer class has an update method. There is no implementation behind it; every "update" method is something we must work out for each subclass of Observer. No implementation? That sounds exactly like what an interface is all about: an interface is a list of one or more method signatures—no implementation. Just method signatures, no implementation: that's a good hint that we should be using an interface here.

Extracting Interfaces from a Class Hierarchy Strategy: *When you find that a subclass is inheriting one or more methods that are merely method signatures, use an interface for those method signatures. (That's exactly what an interface is for.)*

Let's also take a look at the corresponding scenario view (Figure 5-14).

Consider the parameters for the update method.

SpecializedObservable		SpecializedObserver	Comments
methodResultingInStateChg getStatus		update actUponIt	Name: Objects from a pair of specialized classes
methodResultingInStateChg			
	---n-->	update	(specializedObservable, chgCode ;)
getStatus	<-----		(; status)
		-->actUponIt	

Figure 5-14. Interactions for objects in a pair of specialized classes.

The first parameter tells the observer object whom it needs to be talking to, and it obviates the need for an observer to keep a list of its observables. So including the first parameter simplifies an observer: there is one less collection to maintain.

The second parameter tells the observer what kind of change has occurred, and it obviates the need for an observer to ask for every status-related attribute in each observable, hoping to find out what has indeed changed. So including the second parameter simplifies an observer's job, reducing the number of object interactions between an observer and each of its observables.

5.3.3 A Pair of Interfaces (Another Extreme)

Let's continue to be extremists, at least for a while longer.

Interfaces are cool. How about a solution made up entirely of interfaces? (Figure 5-15)

But wait a minute. We can't draw something like that—it makes a promise that we can't keep. You see, an interface can't be required to hold a collection of objects.

An interface is simply a collection of method signatures, no more, no less.

Can an interface imply that an implementer might hold some number of other objects?

Yes, with some agreed-upon naming conventions, we could imply attributes (get, set) and object connections (add, remove). Still, we

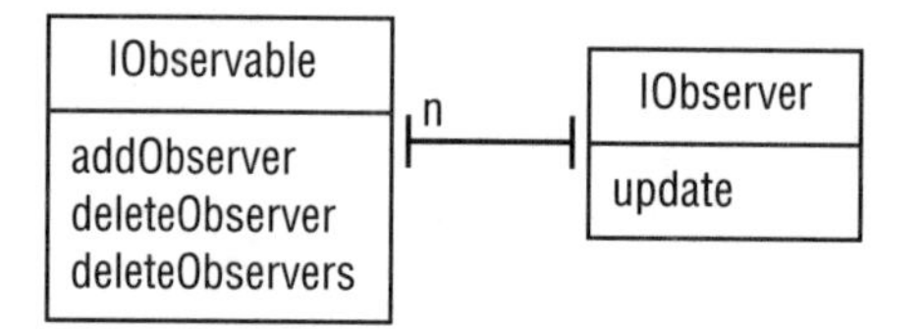

Figure 5-15. An interfaces–only object model.

cannot require an implementer of that interface to build it that way. Remember, an interface is a collection of method signatures—that's all.

Here, we need more than just interfaces; interfaces are not enough, when it comes to building effective object models. We also need classes that implement those interfaces.

5.3.4 Classes and An Interface (Standing on Shaky Ground)

Let's go for the middle ground: inheritance for observables, interfaces for observers.

In fact, Java includes an Observable class and an Observer interface.

In other words, Observable has implementation and interface we can inherit; Observer defines an interface we can implement.

The middle ground looks something like Figure 5-16.

From the model in Figure 5-16, we see that a specialized observable object knows some number of observers (objects in classes that implement the Observer interface, that is). That makes good sense.

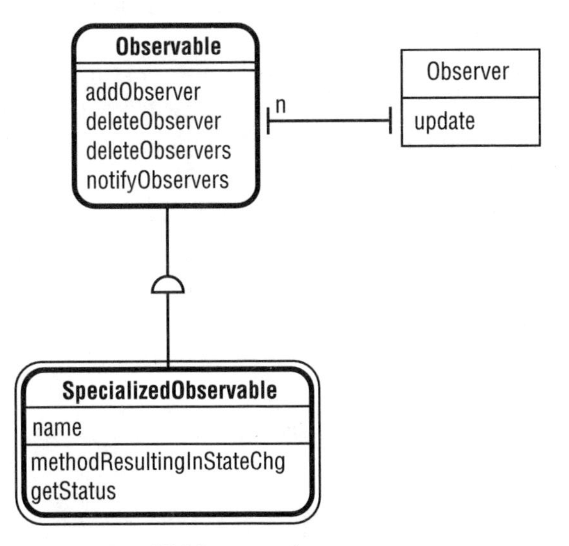

Figure 5-16. Middle ground.

5.3.5 Java's Observable Class?

Is it really such a good idea to inherit from Observable? Is this really the way to go on this?

Let's check it out.

Each time we have a new kind of observable, we must add a new specialized observable class and new classes that implement the corresponding observer interfaces.

For example, suppose we add a specialization of Observable, called Person. If PersonObservable includes name and address, then we would add:

- A specialized observable class (Person)

  with getName and setName methods
- An observer interface for name (IName)
- An observer interface for address (IAddress)

We could reuse the interfaces, as long as the parameter lists for the method signatures are not hardwired back to objects in a specific class (such as PersonObservable, for example).

Yet is Observable, specializing into Person, really a valid use of inheritance? Let's apply the strategy from Chapter 2, Design with Composition Rather than Inheritance.

When to Inherit Strategy: *Inheritance is used to extend attributes and methods, but encapsulation is weak within a class hierarchy, so use of this mechanism is limited. Use it when you can satisfy the following criteria:*

1. *"Is a special kind of," not "is a role played by a"*
2. *Never needs to transmute to be an object in some other class*
3. *Extends rather than overrides or nullifies*

4. *Does not subclass what is merely a utility class*
5. *Within PD: Expresses special kinds of roles, transactions, or devices.*

Person, if made a subclass of Observable, would subclass what is merely a utility class. Not a good idea.

Hence, we really ought to use composition here, rather than inheritance. Why? Composition is easier to change, easier to add to existing classes, and it's easier when it comes to providing several flavors of that functionality (should the need arise).

Should we inherit from Java's Observable class? The answer is no. Java's Observable class is not very useful. An ObservableComponent class would be far better (that's something we'll consider further in the pages ahead).

5.3.6 Java's Observer Interface?

Java has an Observer interface. It looks like this:

```
public interface Observer {
    void update(Observable observed, Object argument); }
```

At this point we'd like to (1) build our own ObservableComponent class, so we can use observable components whenever we want to by using composition (rather than inheritance), and (2) use a corresponding Observer interface.

Can we use Java's Observer interface? Or do we need to define one of our own?

Let's take a closer look at that interface declaration, specifically at the parameter:

```
    Observable observed
```

The designer of this Java interface severely limited its usefulness by specifying that the interface should work with objects in the class

Observable or its subclasses, rather than allowing for objects from Object or its subclasses, such as:

```
Object observed
```

Java's Observer interface assumes that it only needs to work with objects that are in the Observable class or its subclasses. Hmmm. That's not good news; we've already seen that inheriting from Observable is not the way to go.

In fact, we cannot use Java's Observer interface in our design. Why? That interface assumes that it works only with objects in the class Observable or its subclasses. But we need an interface that will work with objects from our own ObservableComponent class.

Can we use Java's Observer interface? No. In fact, its design weakness inspired the following strategy:

Don't Limit Your Interfaces with Needless Assumptions Strategy: *Type your interface parameters as a built-in type (for example: int, float, String, StringBuffer, Object). Let each implementer of that interface test for the specific classes of objects it works with. Reason for use: to increase the likelihood of reuse of each interface.*

How do we overcome this problem? We simply introduce a very similar, but more general interface, called IObserver:

```
public interface IObserver {
    void update(Object observed, Object argument); }
```

5.3.7 Composition and Interfaces (to the Rescue)

Composition and interfaces are an awesome combination!

Actually, we used this "composition and interface" dynamic duo earlier in this book, in Chapter 3, Design with Interfaces, with:

- DateReserveUI—a *composition* of objects it interacts with

- IDateReserve—a corresponding *interface* implemented by the classes corresponding to the objects that DateReserveUI is composed of

We *add in* capability by building the composition and implementing the promised interface. The composition object ends up with some "added-in" capabilities.*

It's now time to apply both ObservableComponent and IObserver.

Figure 5-17 is an informal sketch of this application.

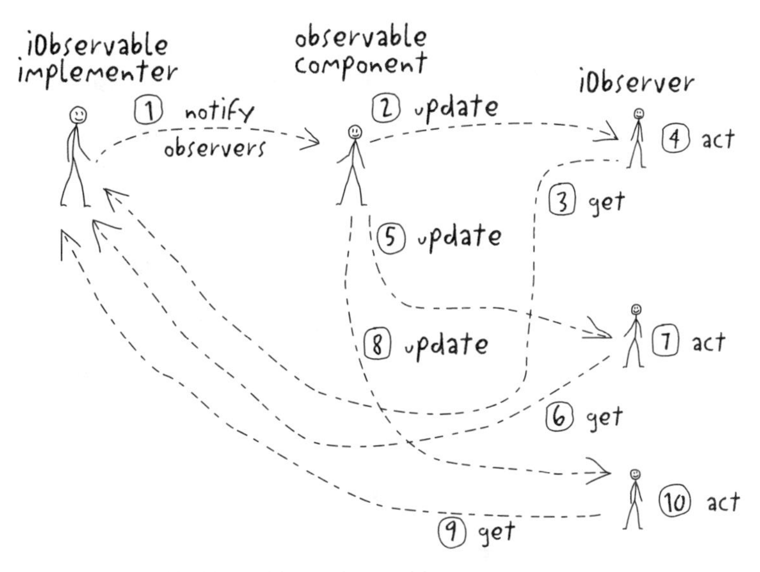

Figure 5-17. Working with an observable component.

*The same design approach may be applied when building C++ apps. You can dedicate part of your class hierarchies to expressing interfaces, namely, C++ classes that consist only of method signatures. On the other hand, when designing C++ apps, you can also "mix in" behaviors from multiple superclasses; however, the ever-decreasing amount of encapsulation within a class hierarchy with multiple-inheritance behavior makes this an unwieldy approach (something to avoid, when possible).

Figure 5-18 illustrates the object model.

A scenario view is depicted next (Figure 5-19). Note that in the scenario view:

- A builder object sets up an observable and its observers.
- A sender object sends a message to an observable, resulting in something of significance happening in the observable.

Here is what happens:

- When an observable has a state change, it sends a message to its own observable component object.
- For each of its observers, that observable component object,

  Sends an update message to an observer.

Then each observer

- Evaluates the change code from that observer;
- Sends messages to get whatever it needs; and
- Acts upon it.

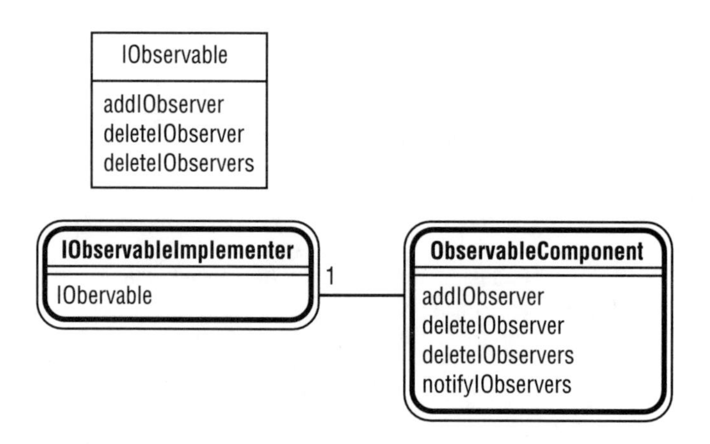

Figure 5-18. Using an observable component.

Builder		Sender		IObservable Implementer		ObservableComponent		IObserver Implementer	Comments
setup		invokeMethodResultingInStateChange		new addIObserver methodResultingInStateChange getStatus		new addIObserver notifyIObservers		new update updateStatus actUponIt	
setup									
	- c - - →			new					(; iObservable)
					- c →	new			(; observableComponent)
	- c - - →							new	(; iObserver)
	- - - →			addIObserver					(iObserver ;)
					- - →	addIObserver			(iObserver ;)
		invokeMethodResultingInStateChange							
			- - →	methodResultingInStateChange					
					- - →	notifyIObservers			(iObservable, chgCode ;)
							- n →	update	(iObservable, chgCode ;)
								IF	// chgCode = "status"
								-->updateStatus	
				getStatus	← - -		- - -		(; status)
								-->actUponIt	
								ENDIF	

Name: Interactions with an observable component

Figure 5-19. Interactions with an observable component.

In Java, it looks like this:

```
public interface IObserver {
    void update(Object theObserved, Object changeCode); }

public interface IObservable {
    void addIObserver(IObserver anIObserver);
    void deleteIObserver(IObserver anIObserver);
    void deleteIObservers(); }

public class ObservableComponent extends Object {
✂
    // attributes / private / object connections
    private Vector myIObservers = new Vector();

    // methods / public / accessors for object connection values
    public void addIObserver(IObserver anIObserver) {
        this.myIObservers.addElement(anIObserver); }

    public void deleteIObserver(IObserver anIObserver) {
        this.myIObservers.removeElement(anIObserver); }

    public void deleteIObservers() {
        this.myIObservers.removeAllElements(); }

    // methods / public / notification
    public void notifyIObservers(Object theObserved, Object changeCode) {
        // iterate through the vector of IObservers and
        // tell each IObserver to update
        Enumeration myIObserversList = this.myIObservers.elements();
        while (myIObserversList.hasMoreElements()) {
            // must cast the element to IObserver
            IObserver anIObserver =
                    (IObserver) myIObserversList.nextElement();
            anIObserver.update(theObserved, changeCode); } }
✂
}

public class IObserverImplementer extends Object implements IObserver {
✂
```

```
    // methods / public / IObserver implementation
    public void update(Object theObserved, Object changeCode) {
        if (changeCode instanceof String) {
            String theChangeCode = (String)changeCode;
            /* if theChangeCode is the one I'm looking for,
               then get the status from theObserved */ } }
✂
}

public class IObservableImplementer extends Object  implements IObservable {
✂
    // attributes / private
    private int state;              // something that represents my state

    // attributes / private / object connections
    private ObservableComponent myObservableComponent =
            new ObservableComponent();

    // methods / public / IObservable implementation
    public void addIObserver(IObserver anIObserver) {
        this.myObservableComponent.addIObserver(anIObserver); }

    public void deleteIObserver(IObserver anIObserver) {
        this.myObservableComponent.deleteObserver(anIObserver); }

    public void deleteIObservers() {
        this.myObservableComponent.deleteIObservers(); }

    // methods / public / resulting in a state change
    public void methodResultingInStateChange(int newState) {
        this.state = newState;
        // instruct my observable component to notify the IObservers
        // pass myself as the observed and "state" as the change code
        this.myObservableComponent.notifyIObservers(this, "state"); }
✂
}
```

Code notes: The Builder in the previous scenario can be just about any object that builds the relationships between an IObservableImplementer object and its IObserverImplementer objects.

5.3.8 PD-to-UI Notification for Charlie's Charters

Let's apply this "observable component–IObserver interface" pattern to Charlie's Charters and its flight descriptions.

When should we message and when should we notify?

Message Inward, Notify Outward Strategy:

> *UI-invoked changes: message inward from UI to PD.*
>
> *PD-invoked changes: notify outward from PD to UI.*

Consider what happens when the state of a flight description changes. For example, if the departureTime changes, any UI observers of that flight description should be notified, so the UI observers can update themselves accordingly.

Applying the "observable component–IObserver interface" pattern, we get Figure 5-20.

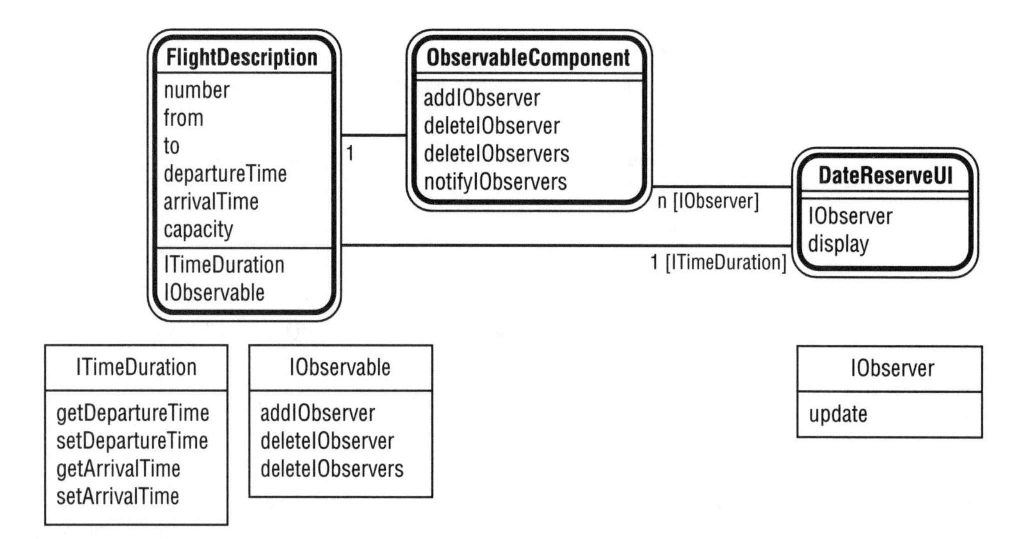

Figure 5-20a. A flight description and its observable component.

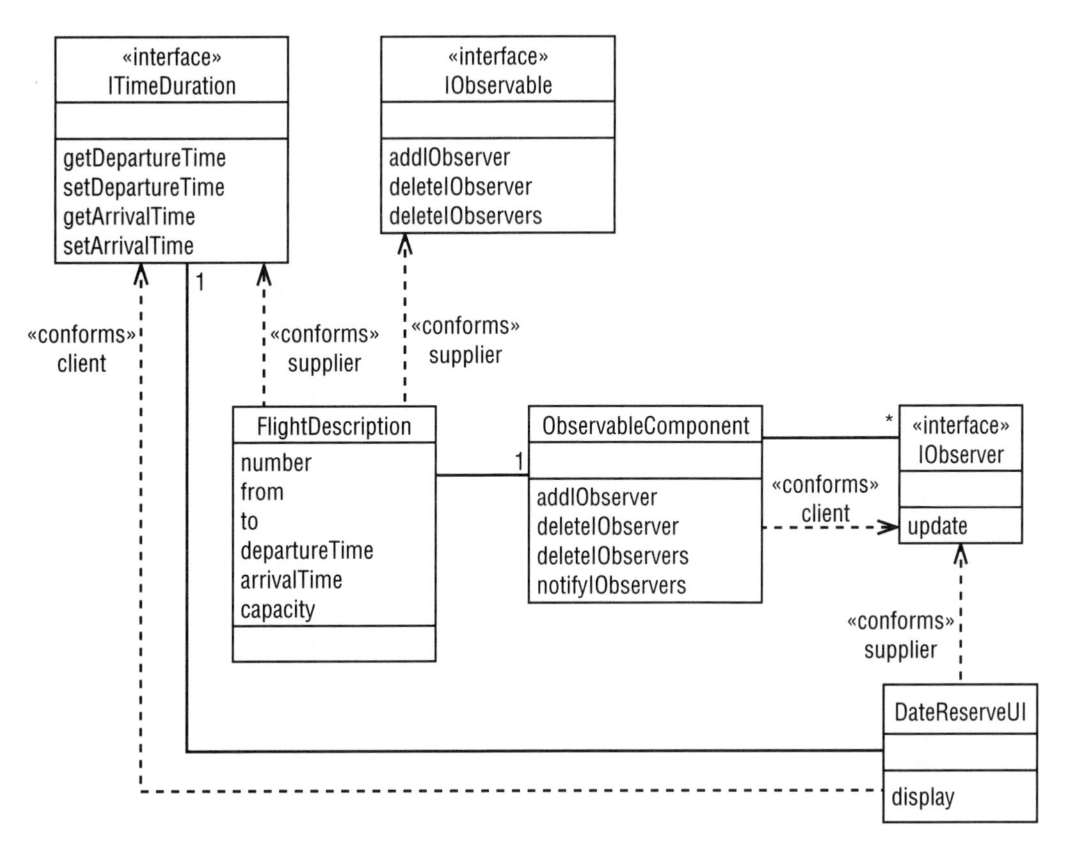

Figure 5-20b. A flight description and its observable component (UML notation).

The flight-description class is application specific. The DateReserveUI is something that can be reused in an analogous (in this case, date reserving) application. And the ObservableComponent class is reused as is (it stays the same, for any application).

A scenario view? It needs a builder object to set things up. It needs a sender object, representing some PD object or a UI object that sends a setFrom message. Then it's ready to roll (Figure 5-21).

In Java, it looks like this:

```
public interface ITimeDuration {
    Date getDepartureTime();
```

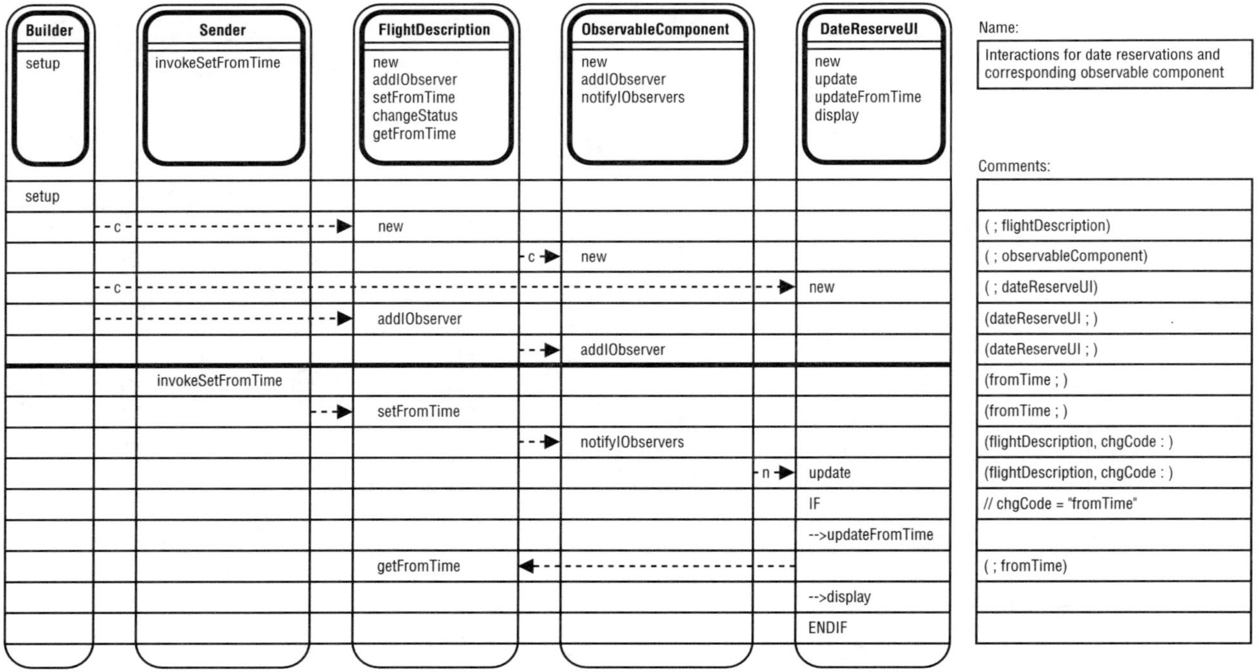

Builder	Sender	FlightDescription	ObservableComponent	DateReserveUI
setup	invokeSetFromTime	new addIObserver setFromTime changeStatus getFromTime	new addIObserver notifyIObservers	new update updateFromTime display

Name: Interactions for date reservations and corresponding observable component

Builder		Sender		FlightDescription		ObservableComponent		DateReserveUI	Comments
setup									
	c			new					(; flightDescription)
					c	new			(; observableComponent)
	c							new	(; dateReserveUI)
				addIObserver					(dateReserveUI ;)
						addIObserver			(dateReserveUI ;)
		invokeSetFromTime							(fromTime ;)
				setFromTime					(fromTime ;)
						notifyIObservers			(flightDescription, chgCode :)
							n	update	(flightDescription, chgCode :)
								IF	// chgCode = "fromTime"
								-->updateFromTime	
				getFromTime					(; fromTime)
								-->display	
								ENDIF	

Figure 5-21. Interactions for a flight description and its observable component.

```
    void setDepartureTime(Date aTime);
    Date getArrivalTime();
    void setArrivalTime(Date aTime); }
```

Code notes: In Java both dates and times are handled in the Date class.

```
public class FlightDescription extends Object implements ITimeDuration {
✂
    // attributes / private
    private Date departureTime;
    private Date arrivalTime;

    // attributes / private / object connections
    private ObservableComponent myObservableComponent =
            new ObservableComponent();

    // methods / public / ITimeDuration implementation
    public Date getDepartureTime() {
        return this.departureTime; }

    public void setDepartureTime(Date aTime) {
        this.departureTime = aTime;
        // tell my observable component to notify the IObservers
        this.myObservableComponent.notifyIObservers(
            this, "departureTime");
    public Date getArrivalTime() {
        return this.arrivalTime; }

    public void setArrivalTime(Date aTime) {
        this.arrivalTime = aTime;
        // tell my observable component to notify the IObservers
        this.myObservableComponent.notifyIObservers(this, "arrivalTime");
✂
}

public class DateReserveUI  implements IObserver {
✂
    // methods / public / IObserver implementation
    public void update(Object theObserved, Object changeCode) {
        // make sure the change code is a string
```

```
        if (changeCode instanceof String) {
            String theChangeCode = (String)changeCode;

            // check to see if the correct change code
            if (theChangeCode.equalsIgnoreCase("departureTime")) {

              // make sure the observed is an ITimeDuration
              if (theObserved instanceof ITimeDuration) {
                    ITimeDuration anITimeDuration =
                            (ITimeDuration)theObserved;

                    // get the new departure time from the iTimeDuration
                    Date newDepartureTime =
                            anITimeDuration.getDepartureTime();
                    /* update the UI with the new departure time */}}}}
✂
}
```

Code notes: We use three nested if statements in the update method. It can be written as three separate if statements that immediately return from the method if a condition is *not* met. We make these types of checks just to be on the safe side.

ObservableComponent is the same code as the previous example.

So, just how important is "observable component-IObserver interface?"

"Observable component-IObserver interface" is *the* notification mechanism for keeping UI objects in sync with corresponding PD objects.

Without it, we'd be stuck with

- UI objects that continuously poll for changes (acceptable only for the simplest of UIs), or
- PD objects that are hardwired to UI objects, prohibiting any meaningful reuse of PD objects—within this application or in subsequent applications.

Yechhh!

Now let's consider a variation on this theme: repeaters.

5.3.9 Observable Component–Repeater Pattern

A repeater takes a message as is, verbatim, and sends it along to potentially some number of objects.

So what is a repeater? A repeater first acts as an observer; then it passes along the news, as an observable (Figure 5-22).

Why use a repeater? If you want to change from one observer to another and yet continue to use the same list of observers, a repeater makes that change much simpler (Figure 5-23).

Here's the strategy:

Repeater Strategy: *Use a repeater when you need to build a standard list of observers, so you can change observables and still use that standard list as is.*

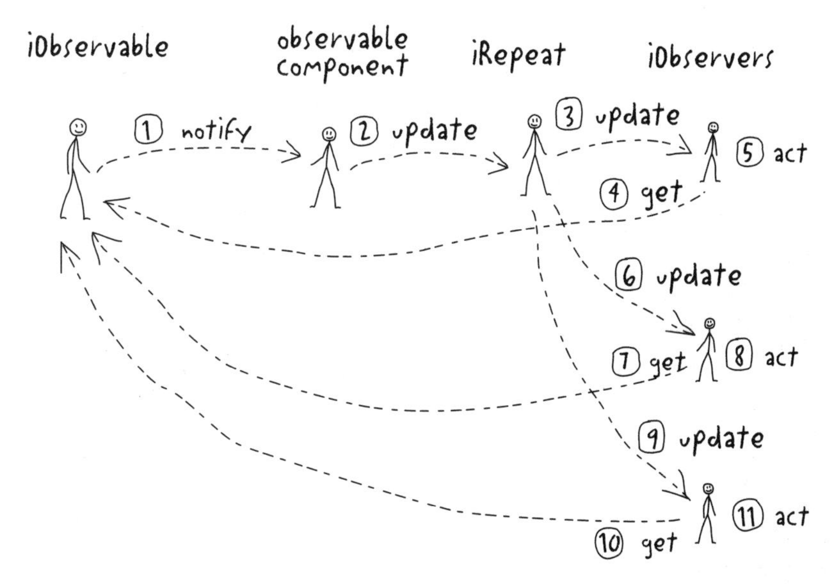

Figure 5-22. A repeater repeats a notification to its own list of observers (single thread).

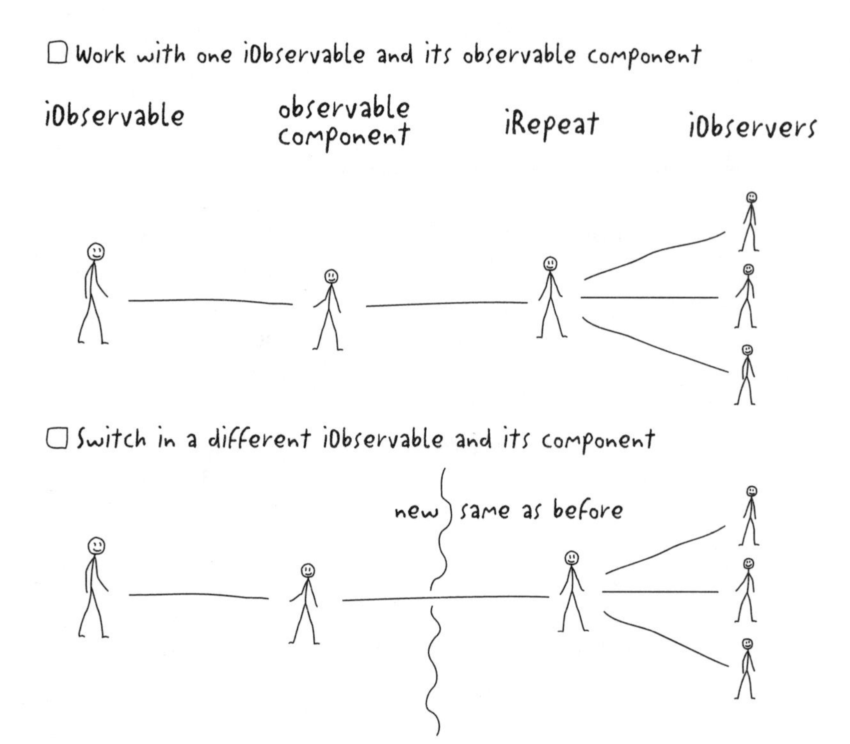

Figure 5-23. The motivation for using a repeater.

We already have an IObservable interface. Now we need an IRepeat interface, a combination of both IObservable and IObserver interfaces. The resulting object model is shown in Figure 5-24.

A scenario view? Well, we'll need two sections:

- Setup

  Add an iRepeat object and an iObserver object to an iObservable object.

- Notification

  An iObservable notifies its iRepeat objects.

  Each iRepeat object notifies its iObserver objects.

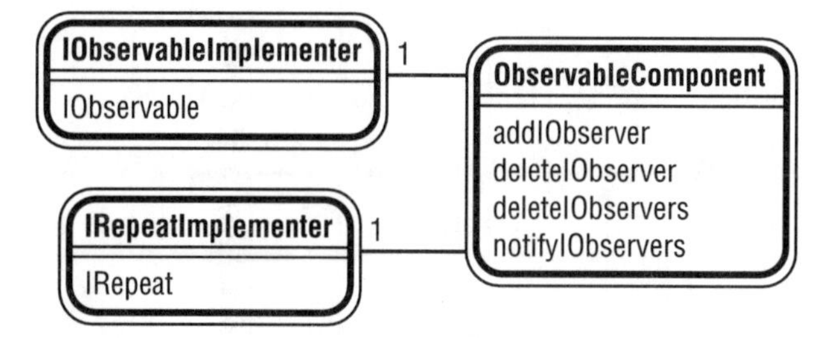

Figure 5-24. A repeater is a combination of both observable and observer.

Each iObserver object gets what it needs from its iObservable.

Each iObserver acts accordingly.

Sometimes it's helpful to begin with a preliminary scenario sketch, before working out dynamics in detail with a scenario view. Figure 5-25 is such a sketch.

Figure 5-26 shows the scenario view itself.

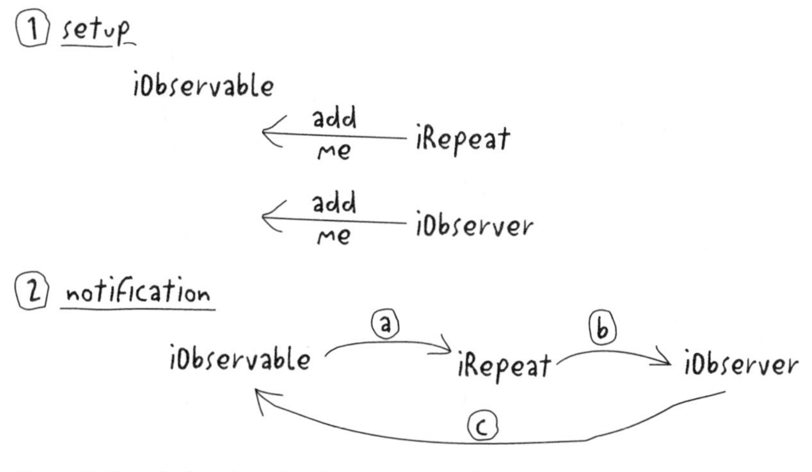

Figure 5-25. A planning sketch for an upcoming scenario view.

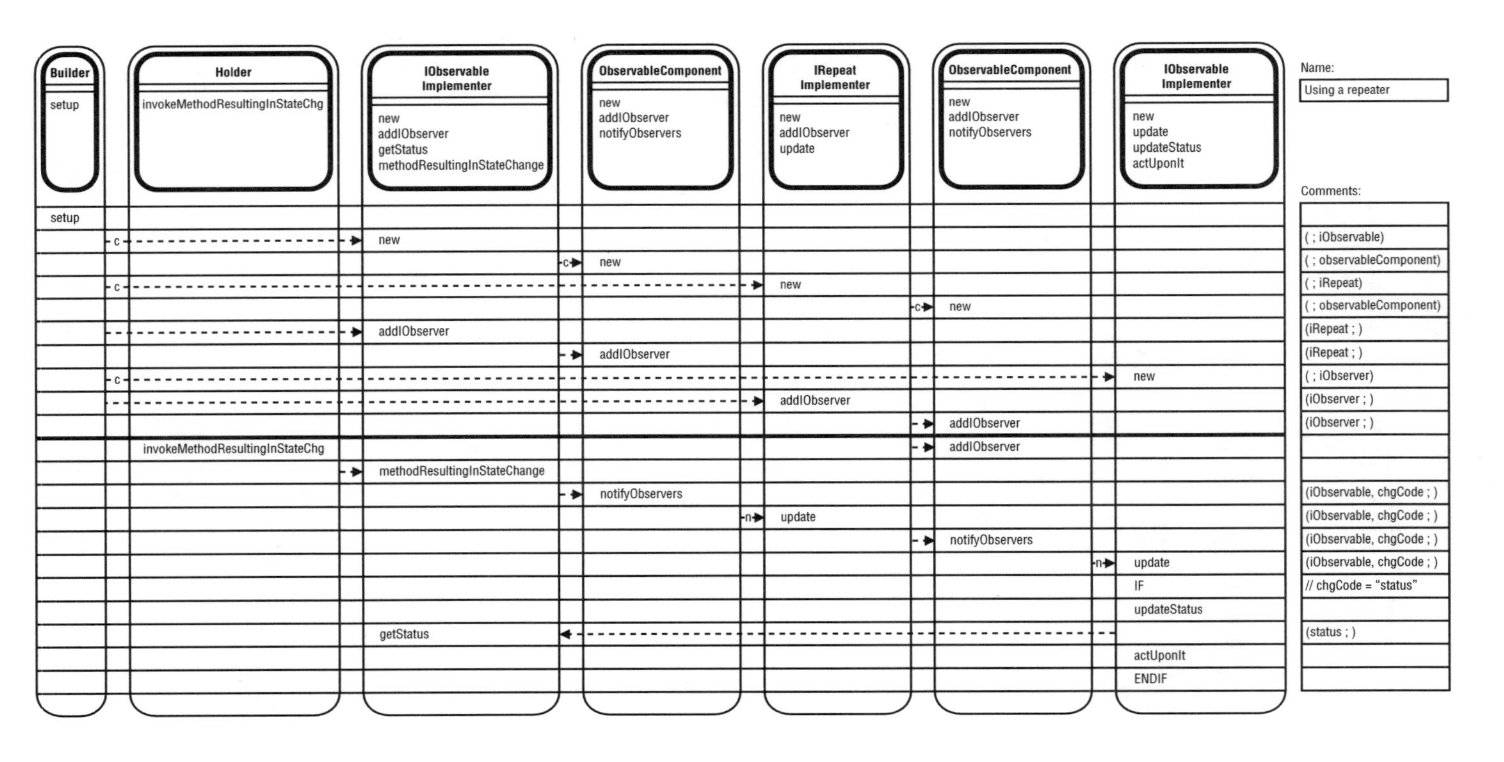

Figure 5-26. Using a repeater.

In Java, it looks like this:

```
public interface IRepeat extends IObservable, IObserver {}

public class IRepeatImplementer extends Object  implements IRepeat {
✂
    // attributes / private / object connections
    private ObservableComponent myObservableComponent =
            new ObservableComponent();

    // methods / public / IRepeat implementation
    public void addIObserver(IObserver anIObserver) {
        this.myObservableComponent.addIObserver(anIObserver); }

    public void deleteIObserver(IObserver anIObserver) {
        this.myObservableComponent.deleteIObserver(anIObserver); }

    public void deleteIObservers() {
        this.myObservableComponent.deleteIObservers(); }

    public void update(Object theObserved, Object changeCode) {
        // my update is to notify my iObservers with these parameters
        this.myObservableComponent.notifyIObservers(
            theObserved, changeCode); }
✂
}
```

Code notes: We could use a generic name for this class like Repeater. An IRepeatImplementer object behaves like a component since it just passes along the update parameters to its own ObservableComponent object.

5.3.10 Threaded-Observable Component

So far, we've been working with a single-thread solution, as shown in Figure 5-27.

However we could run notification on a different thread

- at a lower priority if the thread running through iObservable is more important, or

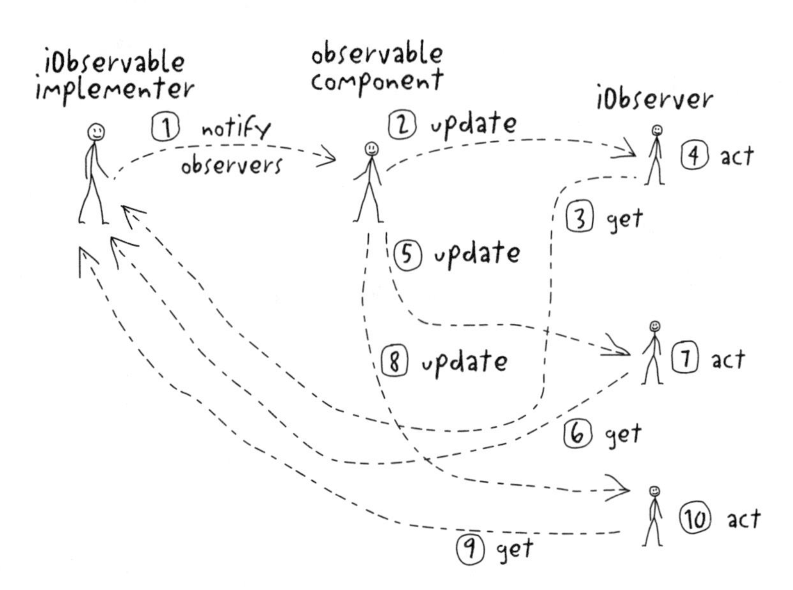

Figure 5-27. Active notification, with a single thread.

- at a higher priority if the thread running through iObservers is more important.

Figure 5-28 shows what this might look like.

The notification thread can run as long as it needs to as long as it has updates to take care of. When no more updates are pending, then an observable component can kill that notification thread.

It's time for an object model—this time with a threaded-observable component (Figure 5-29).

The scenario view in Figure 5-30 includes: (1) setup, (2) an observable thread, and (3) a notification thread. Check it out.

So far, so good. But what happens when a single threaded-observable component receives another notifyIObservers message even before the first one is done?

- The notification thread keeps on running through its lists of iObservers.

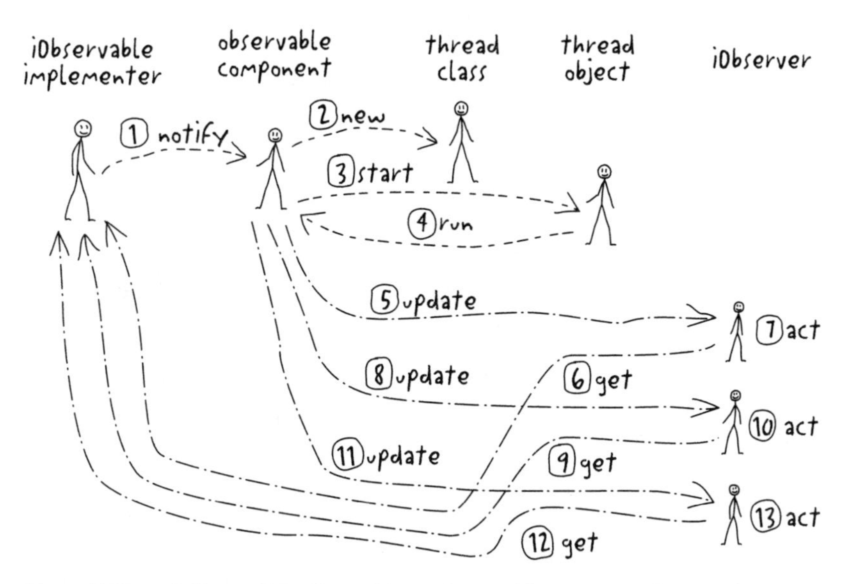

Figure 5-28. Active notification with an observable component spawning a separate notification thread.

- The threaded observable component queues up additional notification requests (meaning, it queues up the change codes that come in).
- The notification thread, once it's made it through its list of iObservers, grabs the next notification request from the queue, and begins another pass through its list of iObservables.
- Eventually, the notification thread comes back and finds that the queue is empty. At that point, the observable component tells the notification thread to stop (die).

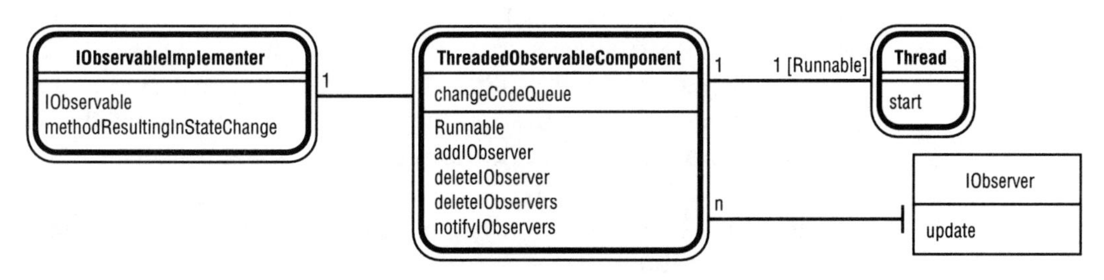

Figure 5-29a. Adding a threaded-observable component.

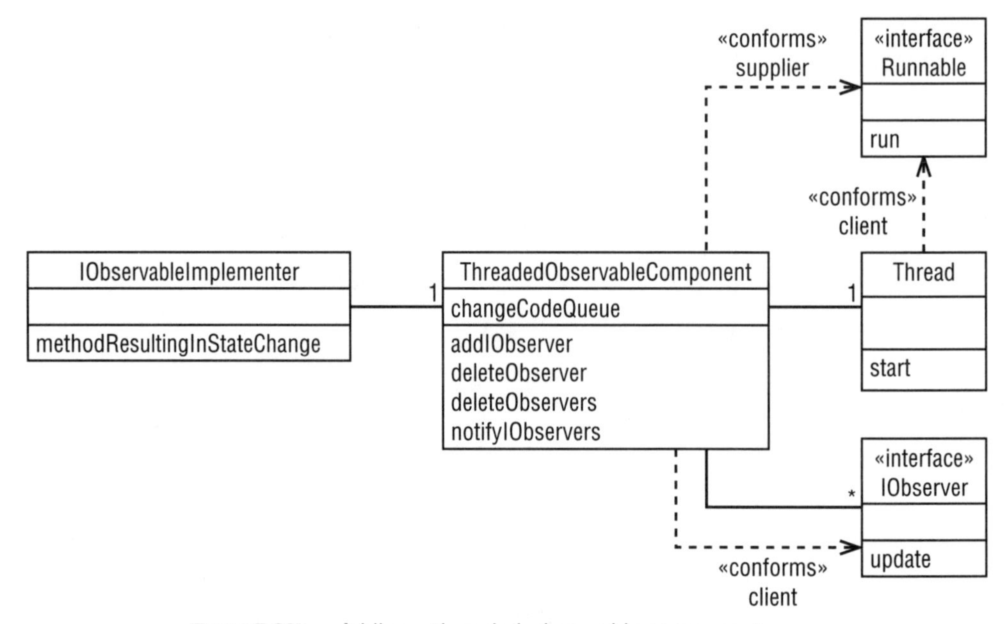

Figure 5-29b. Adding a threaded-observable component.

- Upon arrival of a notifyIObservers message, the whole thing begins anew.

Figure 5-31 offers a more detailed look at a threaded-observable component in an object model.

The details of working with a notification queue are spelled out in the following scenario view shown in Figure 5-32.

Take a closer look at the sync blocks in Figure 5-32. The first sync makes sure that just one notification thread is spawned. The second sync makes sure that the observable thread, which at some point invokes setStatus, is kept from interfering while the notification thread runs through getStatus. The third sync makes sure that we can stop (kill) a notification thread without some other thread getting in and adding a notification request at the same time.

What about the rest of the design? Well, yes, anyone that accesses the status attribute needs to use a sync, to ensure thread-safe access. That about does it.

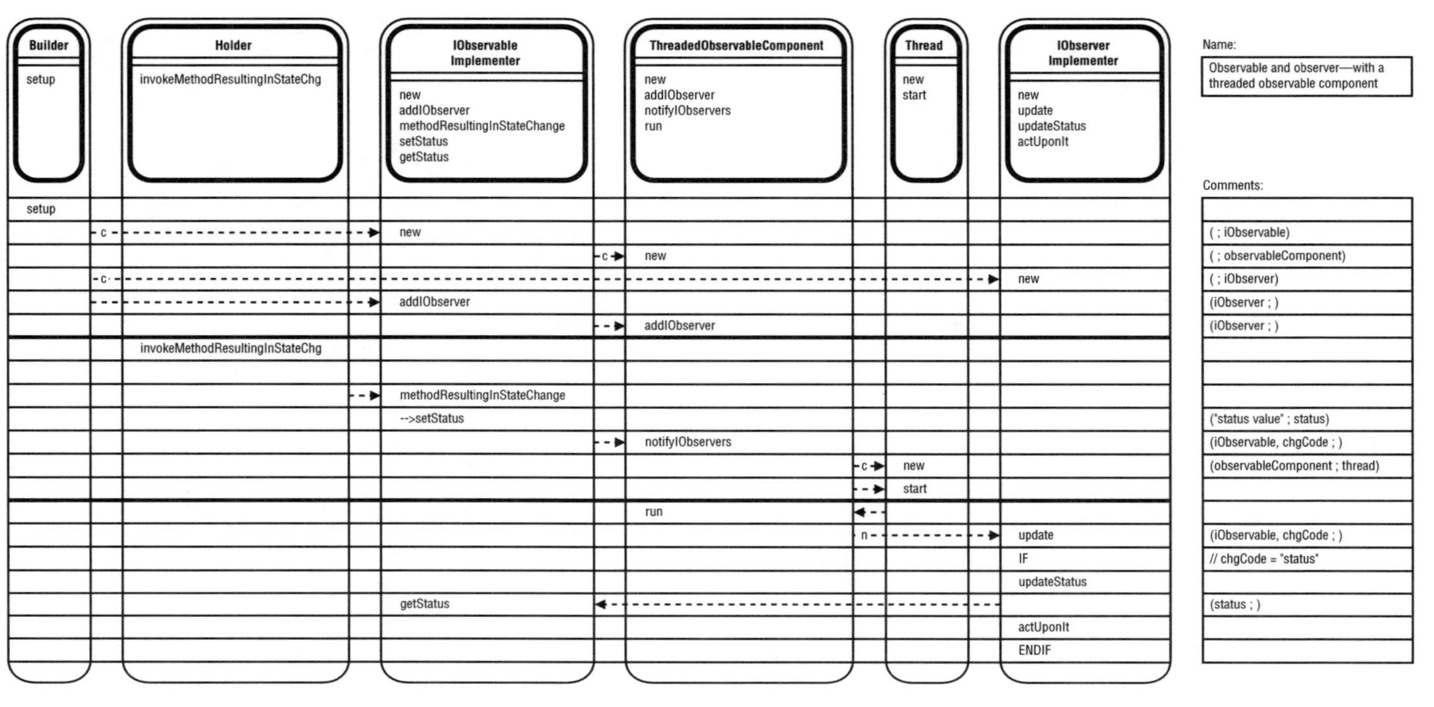

Figure 5-30. A threaded-observable component spawns a separate thread, so it can wind its way through, notifying observers.

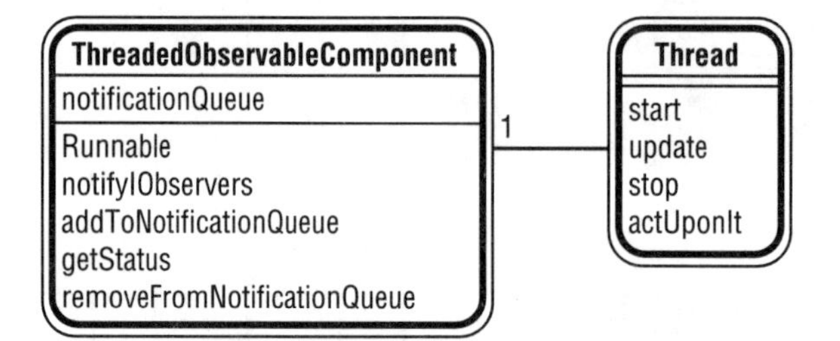

Figure 5-31. A more detailed look at a threaded-observable component.

In Java, it looks like this:

```
public class ThreadedObservableComponent extends Object implements
        Runnable {

    // attributes / private
    private Vector notificationQueue = new Vector();

    // attributes / private / object connections
    private Vector myIObservers = new Vector();
    private Thread notificationThread;

    // methods / public / notification
    public void notifyIObservers(Object theObserved, Object changeCode) {
        this.addToNotificationQueue(theObserved, changeCode); }

    // methods / public / Runnable implementation
    public void run() {
        do { // while the notification queue is not empty
            // get the observed and the change code from the
            // notification queue
            Object theObserved = this.notificationQueue.elementAt(0);
            Object changeCode = this.notificationQuese.elementAt(1);
            // iterate through the vector of IObservers and tell
            // each IObserver to update
            Enumeration myIObserversList = this.myIObservers.elements();
            while (myIObserversList.hasMoreElements()) {
              // must cast the element to IObserver
              IObserver anIObserver = (IObserver)
                      myIObserversList.nextElement();
              anIObserver.update(theObserved, changeCode); } }
        while (this.removeFromNotificationQueue()); }
```

Name:

Detailed interaction with a threaded-observable component

ThreadedObservable Implementer	ThreadedObservableComponent	Thread	IObserver Implementer	Comments:
notify getStatus	notifyObservers addToNotificationQueue run removeFromNotificationQueue addToQueue	new start stop actUponIt	update	
notify				
	---> notifyObservers			(observedOne, changeCode ;)
	SYNC			
	-->addToNotificationQueue			(observedOne, changeCode ;)
	IF			// IF queue is empty
		-c-> new		(; thread)
		---> start		
	ENDIF			
	ENDSYNC			
	run <---			
	DO			// DO until queue is empty
		-n--->	update	(observedOne, changeCode ;)
			IF	// IF chgCode = "This condition"
SYNC				
getStatus <---			---	(; status)
ENDSYNC				
			ENDIF	
	SYNC			
	-->removeFromNotificationQueue			
	IF			// IF queue is empty
		---> stop		// Kill the thread.
	ENDIF			
	ENDSYNC			
	ENDDO			

Figure 5-32. Detailed interactions for a threaded-observable component.

```
    // methods / protected / synchronized
    protected synchronized
        void addToNotificationQueue(Object theObserved,
                    Object changeCode) {
            this.notificationQueue.addElement(theObserved);
            this.notificationQueue.addElement(changeCode);
            if (this.notificationQueue.size() == 2) {
                    // the queue was empty so create an start a thread
                    this.notificationThread = new Thread(this);
                    this.notificationThread.start(); } }

    protected synchronized
        boolean removeFromNotificationQueue() {
            // remove first two elements from the notification queue
            this.notificationQueue.removeElementAt(0);
            this.notificationQueue.removeElementAt(0);
            if (this.notificationQueue.size() == 0) {
              // the queue is empty so kill the thread and return false
              this.notificationThread.stop();
              return false; }
            return true; /* queue is not empty so return true */ }
✂
}
```

Code notes: There are many ways to implement the notification queue. We decided to use a vector so that we can add new notifications to the end of the queue and can remove old notifications from the beginning of the queue.

5.3.11 Active Notification: Conclusion

Observable-observer is a vital means of active notification. In a nutshell:

1. Stay away from Java's Observable class and Observer interface. The former encourages an inappropriate use of inheritance (too susceptible to change over time). The latter is hardwired to work only with observable objects (needlessly limiting).

2. Apply the "observable component–IObserver" pattern.
3. Add a repeater when you need to keep changing the observable that a list of observers works with.
4. Add a multithreaded observable component when you need to run notification on a separate thread.

5.4 Summary

In this chapter, you've worked with notification and how it lets other objects know that something significant has happened.

Passive notification is simple but resource intensive. Timer-based notification is a useful pattern. Active notification is most interesting; it's an essential ingredient for problem-domain object reuse; it's an essential ingredient for designing loosely coupled subsystems.

Together, we explored three major notification mechanisms:

- Passive: someone asks me if I've changed
- Timer-based: someone wakes me up
- Active: an observable notifies its observers (there are many variations on this theme)

The strategies you learned and applied in this chapter are:

Holder-Interface Strategy: *Establish a collection; define an interface.*

Balanced Design Strategy: *Design at two extremes and then somewhere in between. Design connotes looking at alternatives and picking a reasonable approach.*

Extracting Interfaces from a Class Hierarchy Strategy: *When you find that a subclass is inheriting one or more methods that are merely method signatures, use an interface for those method signatures. (That's exactly what an interface is for.)*

Don't Limit Your Interfaces with Needless Assumptions Strategy: *Type your interface parameters as a built-in type (for example: int, float, String, StringBuffer, Object). Let each implementer of that interface test for the specific classes of objects it works with. Reason for use: to increase the likelihood of reuse of each interface.*

Message Inward, Notify Outward Strategy:

UI-invoked changes: message inward from UI to PD.

PD-invoked changes: notify outward from PD to UI.

Repeater Strategy: *Use a repeater when you need to build a standard list of observers, so you can change observables and still use that standard list as is.*

Have *fun* with Java!

Appendix A

Design Strategies

1. Design by Example

Identify Purpose Strategy: *State the purpose of the system in 25 words or less.*

Identify Features Strategy: *List the features for setting up and conducting the business and assessing business results.*

Select Classes Strategy: *Feature by feature, look for: role-player, role, transaction (moment or interval), place, container, or catalog-like description. For real-time systems, also look for data acquisition and control devices.*

UI Content Strategy: *Feature by feature, establish content: selections, lists, entry fields, display fields, actions, assessments.*

High-Value Scenarios Strategy: *Build scenario views that will exercise each "conducting business" and "assessing results" feature.*

Action Sentence Strategy: *Describe the action in a complete sentence. Put the action in the object (person, place, or thing) that has the "what I know" and "who I know" to get the job done.*

Build an Object Model Strategy:

Start with scenario classes and methods.

Add attributes—content for methods.

Add attributes—content for the UI.

Add object connections—message paths for methods.

Add object connections—look-up paths for the UI.

2. Design with Composition, Rather than Inheritance

Composition Strategy: *Use Composition to extend responsibilities by delegating work to other objects.*

When to Inherit Strategy: *Inheritance is used to extend attributes and methods; but encapsulation is weak within a class hierarchy, so use of this mechanism is limited. Use it when you can satisfy the following criteria:*

1. *"Is a special kind of," not "is a role played by a"*
2. *Never needs to transmute to be an object in some other class*
3. *Extends rather than overrides or nullifies superclass*
4. *Does not subclass what is merely a utility class (useful functionality you'd like to reuse)*
5. *Within PD: expresses special kinds of roles, transactions, or devices*

3. Design with Interfaces

Challenge Each Object Connection Strategy: *Is this connection hardwired only to objects in that class (simpler), or is this a connection to* *any object that implements a certain interface (more flexible, extensible, pluggable)?*

Challenge Each Message-Send Strategy: *Is this message-send hardwired only to objects in that class (simpler), or is this a message-send to any object that implements a certain interface (more flexible, extensible, pluggable)?*

Factor Out Repeaters Strategy: *Factor out method signatures that repeat within your object model. Resolve synonyms into a single signature. Generalize overly specific names into a single signature. Reasons for use: to explicitly capture the common, reusable behavior and to bring a higher level of abstraction into the model.*

Factor Out to a Proxy Strategy: *Factor out method signatures into a proxy, an object with a solo connection to some other object. Reason for use: to simplify the proxy within an object model and its scenario views.*

Factor Out for Analogous Apps Strategy: *Factor out method signatures that could be applicable in analogous apps. Reason for use: to increase likelihood of using and reusing off-the-shelf classes.*

Factor Out for Future Expansion Strategy: *Factor out method signatures now, so objects from different classes can be graciously accommodated in the future. Reason for use: to embrace change flexibility.*

4. Design with Threads

Sync Access to Values Strategy: *When multiple threads compete for values(s) within an object—and you try other thread paths but cannot avoid competition for these values—use sync'd methods to limit access (one thread at a time). For multithreaded objects, sync each method that compares, operates on, gets, or sets internal values.*

Zoom In and Sync Strategy: *Zoom in on exactly what you need to sync, factor it out into a separate method, and sync that method. Why? Sync for as little time as possible so other (potentially* *higher priority) threads waiting at the start of other sync methods for that object will get to run sooner rather than later.*

Sync Access to Objects Strategy: *When multiple threads compete for entry into each other's sync'd methods, use a gatekeeper to control access one thread at a time, and make sure the objects that the gatekeeper protects have no sync methods.*

Value Gatekeeper Strategy: *Look for a method that increments or decrements a count of a limited resource. Sync that method; give it exclusive access to that count.*

Object Gatekeeper Strategy: *Look for a method that reserves or issues a limited resource, represented by the objects in that collection. Sync that method and give it exclusive access to that collection of objects.*

Four Thread Designs Strategy: *Apply these thread designs, looking for the simplest one that will satisfy your performance requirements. From simplest to most complex, consider: (1) single thread, (2) prioritized-object threads, (3) prioritized-method threads, (4) prioritized-method prioritized-object threads.*

Prioritized-Methods Strategy: *Prioritize your methods. Separate out cohesive functions with different priorities. Run higher priority methods in higher priority threads; run lower priority methods in lower priority threads.*

Thread Count Strategy: *Justify the existence of each thread in your design. If you can reduce the thread count and meet response time requirements, do so.*

5. Design with Notification

Holder-Interface Strategy: *Establish a collection; define an interface.*

Balanced Design Strategy: *Design at two extremes and then somewhere in between. Design connotes looking at alternatives and picking a reasonable approach.*

Extracting Interfaces from a Class Hierarchy Strategy: *When you find that a subclass is inheriting one or more methods that are merely method signatures, use an interface for those method signatures. (That's exactly what an interface is for.)*

Don't Limit Your Interfaces with Needless Assumptions Strategy: *Type your interface parameters as a built-in type (for example: int, float, String, StringBuffer, Object). Let each implementer of that interface test for the specific classes of objects it works with. Reason for use: to increase the likelihood of reuse of each interface.*

Message Inward, Notify Outward Strategy:

UI-invoked changes: message inward from UI to PD.

PD-invoked changes: notify outward from PD to UI.

Repeater Strategy: *Use a repeater when you need to build a standard list of observers, so you can change observables and still use that standard list as is.*

Appendix B

Notation Summary

Here is a convenient notation summary, featuring Coad notation, plus a subset of Unified Modeling Language (UML):

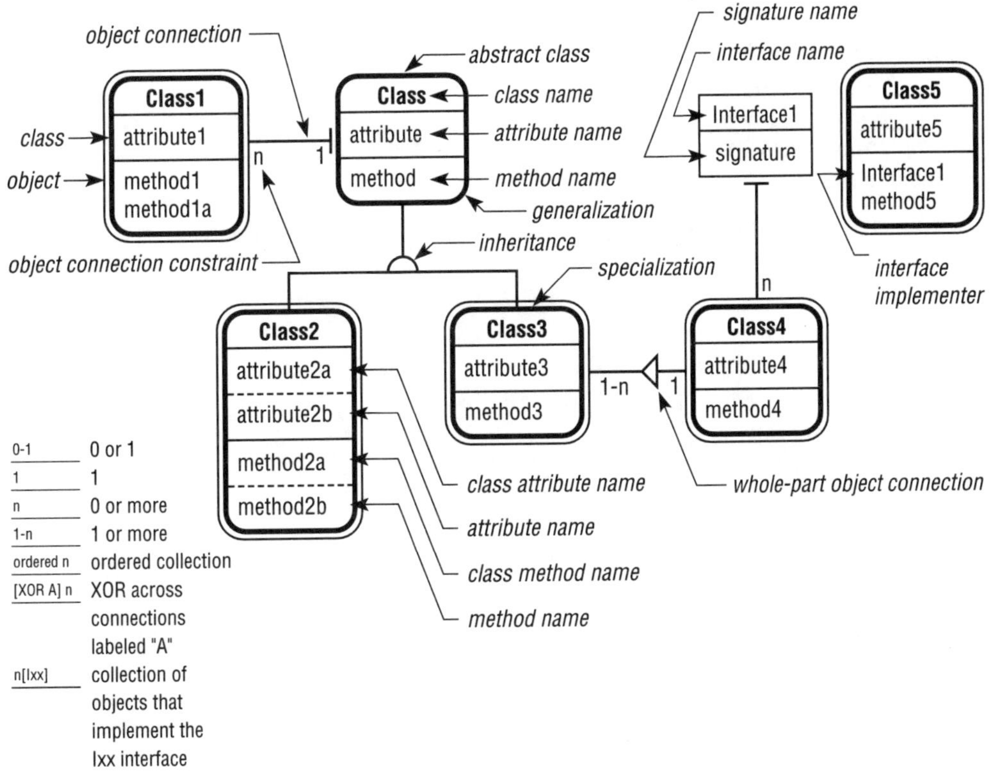

Figure B-1. Coad object model notation.

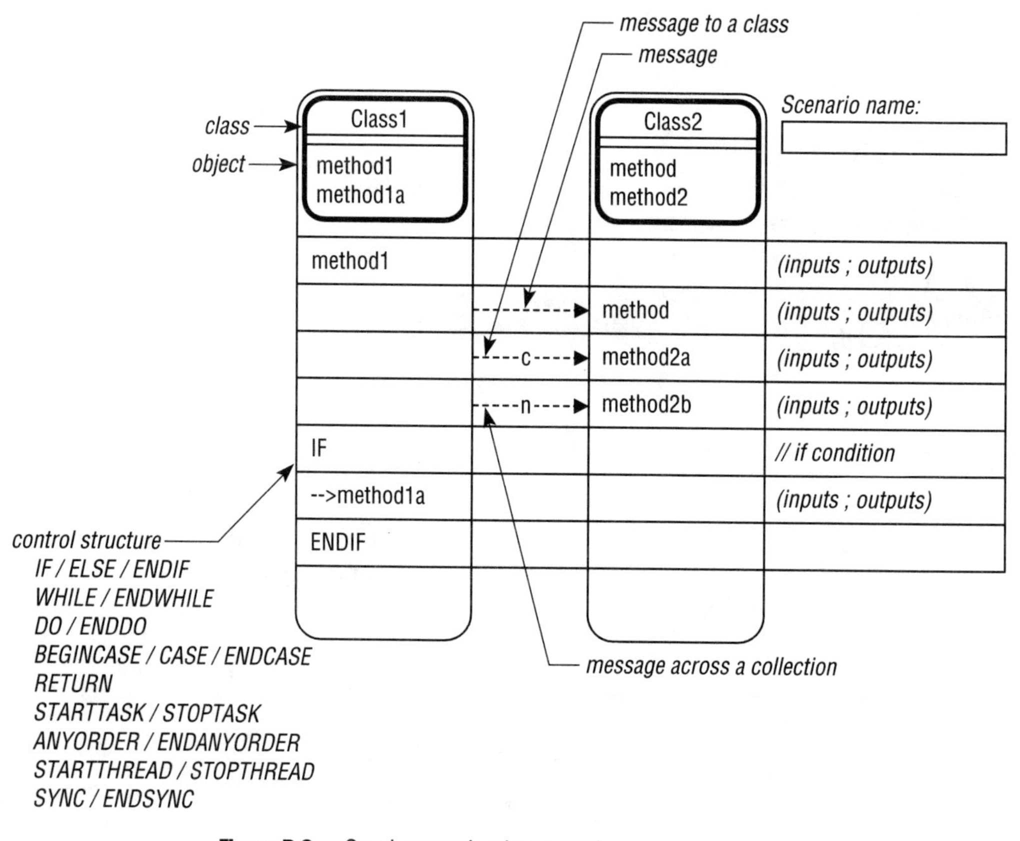

Figure B-2. Coad scenario view notation.

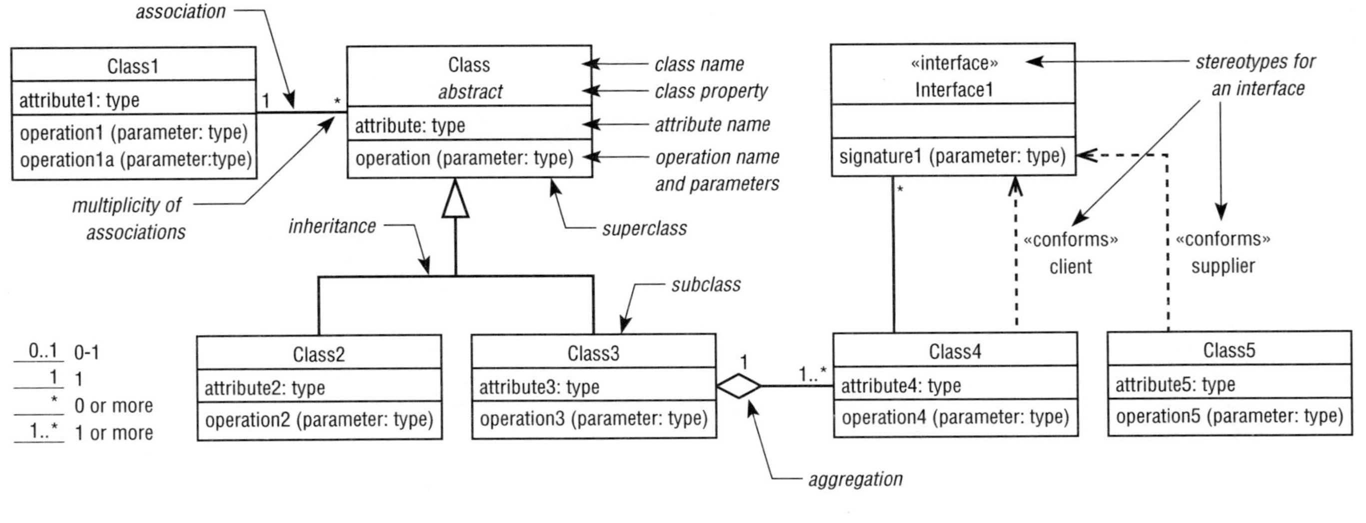

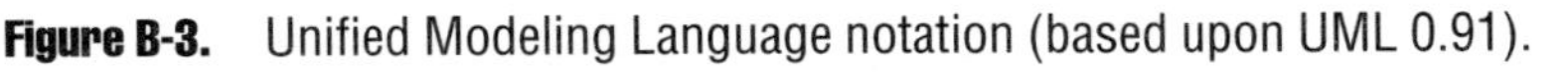

Figure B-3. Unified Modeling Language notation (based upon UML 0.91).

Appendix C

Java Visibility

The Java programming language includes public, protected, default, and private visibility.

Figure C-1 presents a concise summary.

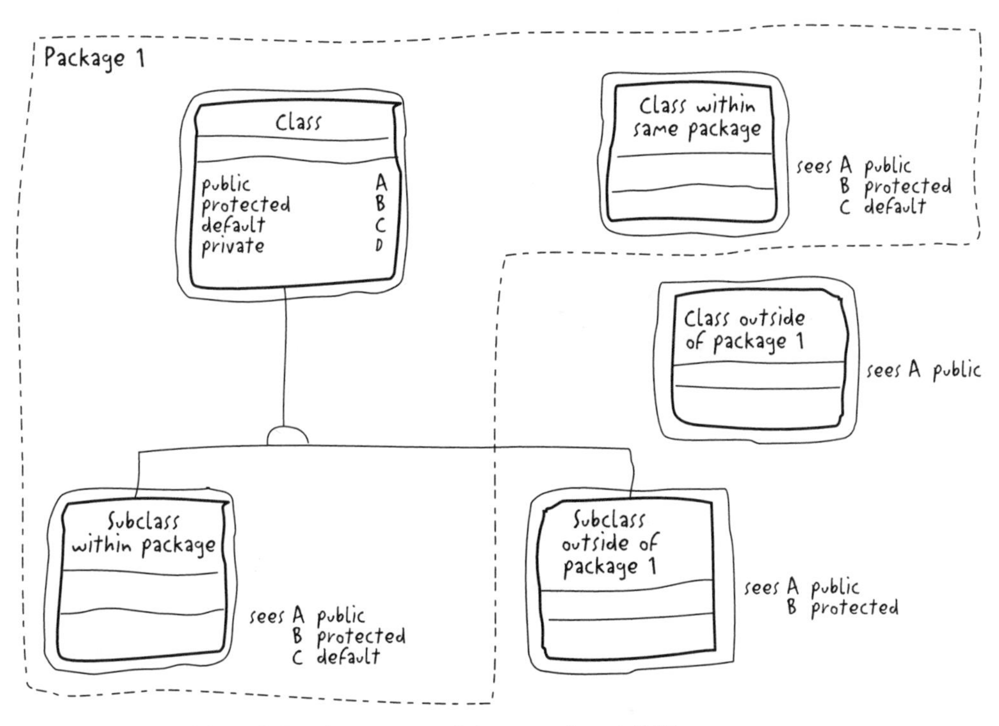

Figure C-1. A summary of Java scoping visibility.

Bibliography

[CoadLetter] Coad, Peter, *The Coad Letter.* http://www.oi.com/coad-letter

The Coad Letter is a technical newsletter. It features new advances in building object models. Delivered exclusively by e-mail. Free.

[Coad97] Coad, Peter, with David North and Mark Mayfield, *Object Models: Strategies, Patterns and Applications,* 2nd ed. Englewood Cliffs, N.J.: Prentice Hall, 1997.

This teaches how to build better object models (3 business apps, 2 real-time apps; 177 strategies, 31 patterns; key results in Coad, OMT, and UML notations).

Cornell, Gary and Horstmann, Cay, *Core Java,* Englewood Cliffs, N.J.: Prentice Hall, 1996.

This programming book has a good blend of illustrations and source code. It also includes quite a bit of material on threads.

Flanagan, David, *Java in a Nutshell,* Sebastopol, CA: O'Reilly & Associates, 1996.

This programming book is source-code intensive. There are few illustrations although it includes lots of well-commented Java code.

Index

LICENSE AGREEMENT AND LIMITED WARRANTY

READ THE FOLLOWING TERMS AND CONDITIONS CAREFULLY BEFORE OPENING THIS SOFTWARE PACKAGE. THIS LEGAL DOCUMENT IS AN AGREEMENT BETWEEN YOU AND PRENTICE-HALL, INC. (THE "COMPANY"). BY OPENING THIS SEALED SOFTWARE PACKAGE, YOU ARE AGREEING TO BE BOUND BY THESE TERMS AND CONDITIONS. IF YOU DO NOT AGREE WITH THESE TERMS AND CONDITIONS, DO NOT OPEN THE SOFTWARE PACKAGE. PROMPTLY RETURN THE UNOPENED SOFTWARE PACKAGE AND ALL ACCOMPANYING ITEMS TO THE PLACE YOU OBTAINED THEM FOR A FULL REFUND OF ANY SUMS YOU HAVE PAID.

1. GRANT OF LICENSE: In consideration of your payment of the license fee, which is part of the price you paid for this product, and your agreement to abide by the terms and conditions of this Agreement, the Company grants to you a nonexclusive right to use and display the copy of the enclosed software program (hereinafter the "SOFTWARE") on a single computer (i.e., with a single CPU) at a single location so long as you comply with the terms of this Agreement. The Company reserves all rights not expressly granted to you under this Agreement.

2. OWNERSHIP OF SOFTWARE: You own only the magnetic or physical media (the enclosed disks) on which the SOFTWARE is recorded or fixed, but the Company retains all the rights, title, and ownership to the SOFTWARE recorded on the original disk copy(ies) and all subsequent copies of the SOFTWARE, regardless of the form or media on which the original or other copies may exist. This license is not a sale of the original SOFTWARE or any copy to you.

3. COPY RESTRICTIONS: This SOFTWARE and the accompanying printed materials and user manual (the "Documentation") are the subject of copyright. You may not copy the Documentation or the SOFTWARE, except that you may make a single copy of the SOFTWARE for backup or archival purposes only. You may be held legally responsible for any copying or copyright infringement which is caused or encouraged by your failure to abide by the terms of this restriction.

4. USE RESTRICTIONS: You may not network the SOFTWARE or otherwise use it on more than one computer or computer terminal at the same time. You may physically transfer the SOFTWARE from one computer to another provided that the SOFTWARE is used on only one computer at a time. You may not distribute copies of the SOFTWARE or Documentation to others. You may not reverse engineer, disassemble, decompile, modify, adapt, translate, or create derivative works based on the SOFTWARE or the Documentation without the prior written consent of the Company.

5. TRANSFER RESTRICTIONS: The enclosed SOFTWARE is licensed only to you and may not be transferred to any one else without the prior written consent of the Company. Any unauthorized transfer of the SOFTWARE shall result in the immediate termination of this Agreement.

6. TERMINATION: This license is effective until terminated. This license will terminate automatically without notice from the Company and become null and void if you fail to comply with any provisions or limitations of this license. Upon termination, you shall destroy the Documentation and all copies of the SOFTWARE. All provisions of this Agreement as to warranties, limitation of liability, remedies or damages, and our ownership rights shall survive termination.

7. MISCELLANEOUS: This Agreement shall be construed in accordance with the laws of the United States of America and the State of New York and shall benefit the Company, its affiliates, and assignees.

8. LIMITED WARRANTY AND DISCLAIMER OF WARRANTY: The Company warrants that the SOFTWARE, when properly used in accordance with the Documentation, will operate in substantial conformity with the description of the SOFTWARE set forth in the Documentation. The Company does not

warrant that the SOFTWARE will meet your requirements or that the operation of the SOFTWARE will be uninterrupted or error-free. The Company warrants that the media on which the SOFTWARE is delivered shall be free from defects in materials and workmanship under normal use for a period of thirty (30) days from the date of your purchase. Your only remedy and the Company's only obligation under these limited warranties is, at the Company's option, return of the warranted item for a refund of any amounts paid by you or replacement of the item. Any replacement of SOFTWARE or media under the warranties shall not extend the original warranty period. The limited warranty set forth above shall not apply to any SOFTWARE which the Company determines in good faith has been subject to misuse, neglect, improper installation, repair, alteration, or damage by you. EXCEPT FOR THE EXPRESSED WARRANTIES SET FORTH ABOVE, THE COMPANY DISCLAIMS ALL WARRANTIES, EXPRESS OR IMPLIED, INCLUDING WITHOUT LIMITATION, THE IMPLIED WARRANTIES OF MERCHANTABILITY AND FITNESS FOR A PARTICULAR PURPOSE. EXCEPT FOR THE EXPRESS WARRANTY SET FORTH ABOVE, THE COMPANY DOES NOT WARRANT, GUARANTEE, OR MAKE ANY REPRESENTATION REGARDING THE USE OR THE RESULTS OF THE USE OF THE SOFTWARE IN TERMS OF ITS CORRECTNESS, ACCURACY, RELIABILITY, CURRENTNESS, OR OTHERWISE.

IN NO EVENT, SHALL THE COMPANY OR ITS EMPLOYEES, AGENTS, SUPPLIERS, OR CONTRACTORS BE LIABLE FOR ANY INCIDENTAL, INDIRECT, SPECIAL, OR CONSEQUENTIAL DAMAGES ARISING OUT OF OR IN CONNECTION WITH THE LICENSE GRANTED UNDER THIS AGREEMENT, OR FOR LOSS OF USE, LOSS OF DATA, LOSS OF INCOME OR PROFIT, OR OTHER LOSSES, SUSTAINED AS A RESULT OF INJURY TO ANY PERSON, OR LOSS OF OR DAMAGE TO PROPERTY, OR CLAIMS OF THIRD PARTIES, EVEN IF THE COMPANY OR AN AUTHORIZED REPRESENTATIVE OF THE COMPANY HAS BEEN ADVISED OF THE POSSIBILITY OF SUCH DAMAGES. IN NO EVENT SHALL LIABILITY OF THE COMPANY FOR DAMAGES WITH RESPECT TO THE SOFTWARE EXCEED THE AMOUNTS ACTUALLY PAID BY YOU, IF ANY, FOR THE SOFTWARE.

SOME JURISDICTIONS DO NOT ALLOW THE LIMITATION OF IMPLIED WARRANTIES OR LIABILITY FOR INCIDENTAL, INDIRECT, SPECIAL, OR CONSEQUENTIAL DAMAGES, SO THE ABOVE LIMITATIONS MAY NOT ALWAYS APPLY. THE WARRANTIES IN THIS AGREEMENT GIVE YOU SPECIFIC LEGAL RIGHTS AND YOU MAY ALSO HAVE OTHER RIGHTS WHICH VARY IN ACCORDANCE WITH LOCAL LAW.

ACKNOWLEDGMENT

YOU ACKNOWLEDGE THAT YOU HAVE READ THIS AGREEMENT, UNDERSTAND IT, AND AGREE TO BE BOUND BY ITS TERMS AND CONDITIONS. YOU ALSO AGREE THAT THIS AGREEMENT IS THE COMPLETE AND EXCLUSIVE STATEMENT OF THE AGREEMENT BETWEEN YOU AND THE COMPANY AND SUPERSEDES ALL PROPOSALS OR PRIOR AGREEMENTS, ORAL, OR WRITTEN, AND ANY OTHER COMMUNICATIONS BETWEEN YOU AND THE COMPANY OR ANY REPRESENTATIVE OF THE COMPANY RELATING TO THE SUBJECT MATTER OF THIS AGREEMENT.

Should you have any questions concerning this Agreement or if you wish to contact the Company for any reason, please contact in writing at the address below.

Robin Short
Prentice Hall PTR
One Lake Street
Upper Saddle River, New Jersey 07458